Education and Sustainability: Responding to the Global Challenge

IUCN – The World Conservation Union

Founded in 1948, IUCN – The World Conservation Union brings together States, government agencies and a diverse range of non-governmental organizations in a unique world partnership: over 980 members in all, spread across some 140 countries.

As a Union, IUCN seeks to influence, encourage and assist societies throughout the world to conserve the integrity and diversity of nature and to ensure that any use of natural resources is equitable and ecologically sustainable. A central secretariat coordinates the IUCN Programme and serves the Union membership, representing their views on the world stage and providing them with the strategies, services, scientific knowledge and technical support they need to achieve their goals. Through its six Commissions, IUCN draws together over 10,000 expert volunteers in project teams and action groups, focusing in particular on species and biodiversity conservation and the management of habitats and natural resources. The Union has helped many countries to prepare National Conservation Strategies, and demonstrates the application of its knowledge through the field projects it supervises. Operations are increasingly decentralized and are carried forward by an expanding network of regional and country offices, located principally in developing countries.

IUCN builds on the strengths of its members, networks and partners to enhance their capacity and to support global alliances to safeguard natural resources at local, regional and global levels.

IUCN Commission on Education and Communication – CEC

The Commission on Education and Communication is one of IUCN's six Commissions. CEC is a global network of voluntary, active and professional experts in environmental communication and education, who work in NGO, mass media, government and international organizations, professional networks and academic institutions.

In their own work CEC members encourage people to take responsibility in their personal and social behaviour for biodiversity, sustainable development and equity in the costs and benefits from the use of natural resources.

CEC specialists are experts in learning processes. They know how to manage participation essential to engaging stakeholders in planning and working towards a sustainable future. CEC members know how to connect conservation interests to different people's perception. CEC members know how to manage knowledge, networks and stimulate action.

CEC advocates the importance of integrating communication and education in environmental projects, programmes and environmental convention implementation.

CEC promotes more strategic use of communication as a policy tool and builds capacity to better plan and use education and communication for IUCN's mission.

CEC advises IUCN on how to plan and manage communication programmes, knowledge and learning.

CEC undertakes training programmes in communication for IUCN members, gathers and analyses lessons from practice and shares these amongst IUCN constituents.

Education and Sustainability: Responding to the Global Challenge

Editors: Daniella Tilbury, Robert B. Stevenson, John Fien,
     Danie Schreuder

IUCN Commission on Education and Communication (CEC)
IUCN – The World Conservation Union 2002

The designation of geographical entities in this book, and the presentation of the material, do not imply the expression of any opinion whatsoever on the part of IUCN or other participating organizations concerning the legal status of any country, territory, or area, or of its authorities, or concerning the delimitation of its frontiers or boundaries.

The views expressed in this publication do not necessarily reflect those of IUCN or other participating organizations.

Published by: IUCN, Gland, Switzerland and Cambridge, UK

IUCN
The World Conservation Union

Copyright: © 2002 International Union for Conservation of Nature and Natural Resources

Reproduction of this publication for educational or other non-commercial purposes is authorized without prior written permission from the copyright holder provided the source is fully acknowledged.

Reproduction of this publication for resale or other commercial purposes is prohibited without prior written permission of the copyright holder.

Citation: Tilbury, D., Stevenson, R.B., Fien, J., Schreuder, D., (eds.) *Education and Sustainability: Responding to the Global Challenge*, Commission on Education and Communication, IUCN, Gland, Switzerland and Cambridge, UK. xii + 206 pp.

ISBN: 2-8317-0623-8

Cover photo: The Earth at night gives an indication of the areas of high energy use and by inference some of the major producers of CO_2 emissions affecting climate. This map is made up of a composite of hundreds of pictures made by the orbiting DMSP satellites.
Credit: Image by Craig Mayhew and Robert Simmon, NASA GSFC, based on DMSP data courtesy Christopher Elvidge, NOAA National Geophysical Data Center
http://heasarc.gsfc.nasa.gov/docs/heasarc/missions/dmsp.html.

Layout by: ROSSEELS Printing Company, Belgium

Produced by: Wendy Goldstein, IUCN

Printed by: ROSSEELS Printing Company, Belgium

Available from: IUCN Publications Services Unit
219c Huntingdon Road, Cambridge CB3 ODL, United Kingdom
Tel: +44 1223 277894, Fax: +44 1223 277175
E-mail: info@books.iucn.org
http://www.iucn.org
A catalogue of IUCN publications is also available

The text of this book is printed on Cyclus Offset, 80gsm, chlorine-free paper.

Contents

Foreword

The World Summit on Sustainable Development, Johannesburg, August 2002, will be an occasion for tens of thousands from all walks of life to gather and confirm commitments to continue to work for sustainable development. An essential part of those commitments must be in public education, awareness, capacity building and communication.

In 1992 the government of Brazil hosted the United Nations Conference on Environment and Development, UNCED in Rio de Janeiro where governments agreed to a blueprint for action for the world – in a non- binding document – *Agenda 21*. The *Rio Principles* were also agreed to guide us on the path to sustainable development. Three Conventions were signed and have since become ratified by the requisite number of national governments, and more, to make them international law – the *Convention on Biological Diversity, The United Nations Framework on Climate Change*, UNFCC, and the *Convention on Desertification*.

I was involved with the Brazilian government's preparations for the Rio Conference as I am and will be involved with Brazil's preparations for the World Summit. In that ten-year period my path has become linked more and more closely with IUCN. At first IUCN's impact was indirect, stemming from IUCN giving the term "sustainable development" currency in 1980 with *The World Conservation Strategy*. IUCN gave stimulus to natural resource strategic planning and engaging stakeholders in the process, including governments working with NGOs. IUCN also initiated and gave guidance on the drafting of the *Convention on Biological Diversity*.

The organiser of the parallel UNCED NGO Forum in Rio, Yolanda Kakabadse, is now the President of IUCN, and leader of the IUCN Council of which I became a member in October, 2000 as Chair of the IUCN Commission on Education and Communication, CEC.

Although I did not know the IUCN Commission on Education and Communication in 1992, the previous Chair, Frits Hesselink, was at the NGO Forum with members of the Commission. CEC was activating workshops in the NGO Forum on national strategic approaches to education for sustainable development. Meanwhile I had set up a display on the Amazonian Indians sustainable development projects at the Rio Paço Imperial.

My path soon became meshed with CEC. In 1995 I was invited to join a South American IUCN CEC meeting held in Quito in co-operation with UNESCO and UNEP to discuss strategies for sustainable development education and communication. This meeting was part of the stimulus that CEC was undertaking at regional level to review and reflect on progress of Agenda 21, chapter 36, first in Europe (1993) with UNESCO and 1996 in Asia, with UNESCO and UNEP.

Subsequent to the Quito meeting, I became involved in CEC and later Regional CEC Chair and active in advocating for Education for Sustainable Development in the Americas regional fora. CEC with partners developed a manual *"Ambiente y Desarrollo Sostenible"* to integrate environment and gender in development work.

Agenda 21, Chapter 36, is about Education, Awareness and Training and UNESCO is Task Manager of its implementation. As well, the need for awareness, education, capacity building and training are mentioned in most other chapters of Agenda 21, revealing its importance as an instrument to achieve the objectives of all other

components. In fact the "educational" instrument is the second most frequently used word after "governments" in Agenda 21. Yet, in 1996 the Secretary General's status report on Chapter 36 to the Commission on Sustainable Development, stated that education was likely to be the "forgotten priority of Rio".

CEC took up the slogan and the cause with increased vigour. CEC saw that the Commission on Sustainable Development, CSD, charged with monitoring and stimulating Agenda 21, and governments needed some impetus for Chapter 36. CEC prepared an advocacy position with CEC members and by using Commission members and IUCN Government Members brought the ideas to the CSD meeting in 1996. The result was the adoption of a work plan as described in chapter 2 of this book.

The main lines of the CEC suggestions in 1996 were:

1. An international strategic alliance amongst UNESCO, UNEP, World Bank, UNICEF, WHO, UNDP and international NGOs like WWF and IUCN and others is formed;

2. The alliance develops and implements a work programme with specified performance criteria;

3. The work programme acts to improve the integration of communication instruments and education in the policy cycle of national plans for sustainability and biodiversity;

   • Supports the development and implementation of national action plans for communication and education for sustainable development engaging a bottom up approach among a broad range of groups described in Agenda 21.

   • Builds capacity to plan, develop and implement education and communication programmes;

   • Acts to increase funding to support communication and education in support of sustainable development. Education loans, it was proposed, should support sustainable development principles.

   • Shapes a new international framework for education for sustainable development, which states the objectives, concepts, skills and values. This framework should be based on the integration of social (well being, justice, cultural) economic, and ecological factors. New methodologies and approaches would be incorporated consistent with enabling people to participate in shaping a sustainable future.

At the IUCN Congress in 1996 in Montreal, Canada, CEC and UNESCO convened a meeting of some of those organisations it saw should be part of a strategic alliance to catalyse education for sustainable development. They included the then UNEP Executive Director, Elisabeth Dowdeswell, then UNESCO Director, Gustavo López Ospina, the then IUCN Director General, David McDowell and IUCN President to be Yolanda Kakabadse, participants from the World Bank, UNDP, IUCN Members and CEC members.

However, in the report on progress towards sustainability in the decade since the United Nations Conference on Environment and Development in Rio de Janeiro, 1992, United Nations Secretary-General Kofi Annan (2001) noted that

"Progress towards the goals established at Rio has been slower than anticipated and in some respects conditions are worse than they were ten years ago."

He went on to say that Agenda 21 "still serves as 'powerful and long-term vision', and remains as valid today as it was at Rio". CEC looks forward to the Summit to identify the blockages, and plan strategies to address the areas where achievable goals can be set and met. Education for sustainability will be a strategic tool in the global partnership that results. We need to recognise that we do not have the solutions for environmental and social problems. We all need to learn along the path to sustainable development and particularly how to manage in new ways in a participatory process.

With this in mind I hope that the stories in this book are a help and inspiration to people working in education for sustainable development.

Denise Hamú
Chair Commission on Education and Communication

Preface

Around the world, many people in community groups, in government agencies, and in schools, colleges and universities are using educational processes to help build a degree of sustainability into their lives and those of their neighbours. It is from this group that we asked people to write the case studies for this book. As we witnessed, heard or read about their experiences, we realized that these educators should have the opportunity to share their efforts and learning experiences – to tell their stories.

More and more people are rediscovering the value of story telling as a means of articulating and communicating knowledge constructed from critically reflecting on one's experiences. Story telling has a long tradition in education and, along with art, dance, demonstration and ceremony, was a key way in which indigenous or traditional knowledge was communicated across generations. Very few original nations had any means of communicating knowledge other than through telling stories. Such knowledge was chiefly environmental knowledge; it was knowledge for everyday and inter-generational survival.

Two examples from South Africa demonstrate the wisdom of indigenous knowledge. The first concerns the Nguni story about the Hamerkop bird (uthekwane – the lightning bird). Children are taught that if one kills this bird, or steals its eggs, their homes will be struck by lightning. Hamerkop birds eat frogs, and so do snakes. If the birds are not there to catch the frogs, snakes will be attracted to the watering holes. They hold great danger for the people. Somebody must have made this scientific discovery through experience and observation, and this knowledge has been articulated through this wonderful story for many generations. Another story that Nguni children learn is that they should never urinate in water, because if they do, they will undergo an instant sex change. This story serves to prevent the spreading of water-borne disease, such as bilharzia, which kills thousands of people in Africa each year. There are, of course, many other examples of how story telling has been used through the ages to articulate and disseminate indigenous knowledge or the traditions of a culture and the lessons learned from observations of nature.

The current revival of interest in story telling and indigenous knowledge is not, however, unproblematic. As Le Roux (1999, p. 17) notes, sometimes it represents "romanticism and nostalgia" and an idealistic "return to a lost Eden which was probably never an Eden at all". These concerns need to be taken seriously, and are reflected in the strategies being developed for integrating indigenous perspectives and story telling strategies into the school curriculum (e.g., see Fien, Heck and Ferreira, 1997).

Increasingly, we are being urged by scientists, educationists and social researchers to tell our stories of research, of science, of discovering new knowledge, of how we have learned to know and understand. These calls can be seen within the framework of post-modern thinking and the rediscovering of alternative ways of learning and knowing. Western societies are accustomed to the traditions of modernist research and knowledge generation, which usually involve reporting in research journals in such ways that the wisdom often gets lost in complex academic writing. Only a privileged few can share in these stories.

Story telling provides a productive and authentic way for communities to communicate their experiences and knowledge. As we find ourselves in an age that is becoming increasingly post-modern, it is not surprising that we are revisiting traditional or 'pre-modern' ways of codifying and sharing knowledge.

This book presents stories told by some of the many people around the world who are searching and struggling for ways of shaping their educational programmes or activities to the challenges of sustainable development. However, the stories are not just narratives – although chapter authors have provided rich descriptions of their educational efforts. Writing the stories, and reflecting on the tensions, issues and problems they encountered also provided the authors with opportunities to learn from their experiences. As Gough (1997) has suggested, we can learn much from reflecting on the way our personal and professional stories are permeated with our histories and hopes and how our interpretations of these stories influence our thoughts actions.

Reading the stories of others also is a good way to learn about ourselves. The stories of others can serve as mirrors into which we can see our own contexts, hopes, plans and experiences reflected. The situations in a story will not be the same as ours, but identifying the similarities and differences can help us contextualize the stories and take from them the lessons that can enrich our own ways of developing educational responses to the challenges of sustainable development.

This book is essentially an anthology of stories from different parts of the world that document ways in which the international educational community is responding to the challenge of creating a sustainable world.

Two chapters in this first section contextualize the stories by providing an overview of the concept of sustainability and highlight the international scope of formal and non-formal educational efforts to promote sustainable development.

The main body of the book is devoted to 15 stories, organized on a regional basis, to illustrate how the challenge of educating for sustainability is being taken up in culturally different settings around the world. This section contains reports of educational initiatives in schools and universities (including teacher education) as well as in projects organized by local community groups, national parks, national governments, and international development assistance agencies. The examples range from stories of community theatre in the south-west Pacific, ecotourism in Nepal and community development in Ontario to those of 'sustainability for real' in Wales, resource development in South Africa and national education planning in Latin America. The final chapter provides an overview of these different stories and analyses the issues that emerge from them by way of providing themes for future reflection, debate and action.

We invite you to use these stories to reflect not only on your own stories that you have to tell, but also on those that you have dreamed but have yet to unfold. We hope they inspire you to educate others in responding locally to the global challenge of creating more sustainable ways of living on this earth.

The Editors

References

Fien, J., D. Heck and J. Ferreira, J. (eds.) (1997). *Learning for a Sustainable Environment: A Professional Development Guide for Teacher Educators*. UNESCO Asia-Pacific Programme of Educational Innovation for Development, Bangkok. Chapter 4 (Storytelling) and Chapter 5 (Indigenous Knowledge).

Gough, A. (1997). *Education and the Environment: policy, trends and the problems of marginalisation*. Australian Council for Educational Research: Melbourne.

Le Roux, K. (1997). "Towards sustainable conversation: Developing environmental education processes" in *Southern African Journal of Environmental Education*, 17:47-52.

Chapter 1

The global challenge of sustainability

John Fien and Daniella Tilbury

> Our vision is a world in which there are many opportunities to learn about
> sustainable development. A world where a skilled population makes informed
> decisions in their home, community and working lives and in their leisure
> activities. A world where people understand and take responsibility for the impact
> they have on the quality of life of other people, locally and globally.
> (Sustainable Development Education Panel 1999, p.11)

Understanding sustainable development

Following the Brundtland Report of the World Commission on Environment and
Development, the 1992 Earth Summit in Rio de Janeiro accelerated the process of
awakening the world to the urgency of sustainable development and secured the
beginnings of a process of international cooperation on development and
environmental issues. Among the historical documents signed at Rio was *Agenda 21*
through which countries committed themselves to promoting sustainability through
a great variety of means, including education.

However, the issues underlying sustainable development are complex and they
cannot be encapsulated within the diplomatic language and compromises of an
agreement from an international conference. Perhaps, the most obvious area of
complexity is the increasing divergence between the "natural environment and
economic development" agenda of the primarily rich economically developed
countries of the North and the "social and economic development" agenda shared by
the poorer nations of the South. Many countries of the South, desperate to improve
the standard of living of their citizens through social and economic development,
used the Earth Summit to bring the world's attention to the stark choices they face
between industrialization, with its environmental hazards, and environmental
protection, which is costly to their economies and limits the scope of development.
They also pointed to the excessive impacts on global resources by the mass-
consumption lifestyle of many people in the North and the way that this undermines
global sustainability. This predicament was not a new one since it was the World
Commission on Environment and Development (1987) which first drew
international attention to this issue in its report, *Our Common Future* (the
Brundtland Report), and highlighted how social and economic factors are a
contributory (and often major) cause of environmental problems. However, the
realization at Rio that existing development trends leave increasing numbers of
people poor and vulnerable served to redefine and clarify the links between
environment and development concerns.

Those present at the Earth Summit saw the need to tie the achievement of
environmental sustainability with overcoming the interdependent problems of
poverty, illiteracy and militarism. Elizabeth Dowdeswell, an Executive Director of
the United Nations Environment Programme (UNEP), highlighted the new vision of
sustainability which emerged from the Earth Summit:

> The Earth Summit at Rio de Janeiro saw the essential indivisibility of
> environment, peace and development. It also recognized that global independence
> could no longer be conceived only in economic terms. Alongside, there was the
> calculus of military parity. They were related to the instability spawned by
> widespread poverty, squalor, hunger, disease, illiteracy. They were connected to
> the degradation of the environment. They were enmeshed with inequity and
> injustice.
>
> (Dowdeswell 1995, 2)

Recognizing that no nation could resolve these issues on their own, those attending
the Summit signed agreements on international cooperation for tackling
development and environment concerns such as "the perpetuation of disparities
between and within nations, a worsening of poverty, hunger, ill health and illiteracy
and a continuing deterioration of the ecosystem on which we depend for our well-
being". Most significantly, Agenda 21, of the Earth Summit called for "a global
partnership for sustainable development" (UNESCO 1992, Preamble).

Questions arise regarding the nature of this global partnership, particularly, when the
term "sustainable development" itself is socially and culturally contested. It is open
to widely different interpretations and takes on different meanings not only between
cultures but also between different interest groups within societies. Many of these
differences revolve around questions such as: Over what time period are we talking
sustainability? The human life span? This generation and the next? Or are we
concerned with sustainability on ecological time-scales? And what kind of
development do we want to sustain: social, cultural, political, spiritual and/or
economic? (And are these separable)? What changes are required to achieve
sustainability and how are they to be achieved? What are the implications for
economic growth? Are there limits to economic growth in a sustainable society and,
if so, what are they? Implicit within these questions are differing definitions and
assumptions of "sustainability" and these, in turn, reflect both a variety of contesting
ideologies and an ongoing political debate about the nature of sustainable futures.

The term "sustainable development" was first given currency by the *World
Conservation Strategy* (IUCN, UNEP, WWF 1980) and later reinforced by the
Brundtland Report (World Commission on Environment and Development 1987).
However, it is an evolving concept. The World Conservation Strategy primarily
sought to protect essential ecological processes, life-support systems and genetic
diversity through the sustainable utilization of natural resources. The Strategy linked
poverty, development and environment by drawing attention to the dilemmas facing
rural people in developing countries who are sometimes compelled to over-utilize
natural resources in order to free themselves from starvation and poverty. It gave
increased prominence to the root social, political and economic causes of the
environmental crisis. These ideas were to inform the development of the framework
for the recommendations in the Brundtland Report.

Now, as a direct influence of the Brundtland Report and Agenda 21, the concept of
sustainable development informs many local, national and international policies,
programmes and strategies related to environmental and development concerns. This
reflects a growing acceptance of what is now commonly referred to as "development
that meets the needs of the present without compromising the ability of future
generations to meet their own needs" - a definition initially offered by the
Brundtland Report in 1987. This definition, although widely accepted, is also highly
ambiguous, as we have seen. Perhaps, this definition was chosen precisely because it
was ambiguous and thus, accessible to a wide range of interest groups in society.
While Pezzey (1989) argues that this 'fuzziness' has proven useful in arriving at

consensus for sustainable development, unfortunately it also obscures the political and philosophical issues that remain in tension. Smyth (1995) records how this ambiguity has

> "provoked objections from the policy makers in both industrialised and developing countries who suspect that it represents a 'green' attempt to get away from development, or that it disguises what is to be sustained, namely a 'northern' affluent lifestyle."
>
> (Smyth 1995, p.11)

It is possible, to find many definitions of sustainable development in the literature. The existence of different interpretations of sustainability can result in "paralysis by analysis" and in delays in key changes essential for a more sustainable society. In terms of educational policy and practice, at least one educational philosopher has argued that he would not want his children educated for sustainable development because of this (Jickling 1992). Such paralysis extends to a fear that discussions sponsored by UNESCO about ways of reorienting education towards sustainable development represent a "one-dimensional vision" in which "declaration displaces critical discourse" and which is to be imposed on the international community (Jickling 1999). Despite such views, several critical issues that have implications for educational practice have emerged from debates over the meanings of sustainability in recent years.

First, interpretations of sustainability are value-laden. All definitions – whatever their source – serve particular social and economic interests and need to be critically assessed. Most of these definitions could be categorized into two groups: those that prioritize "sustainable economic growth" and those that give preference to "sustainable human development". The "sustainable economic growth" group (which includes the Brundtland Report, itself) is reformist in that it does not support the transformation of current social or economic systems. In this approach, the natural environment is conceived in a utilitarian way with conservation treated as one of a range of policy options. Great emphasis is placed on the role of technological and economic tools in shifting individual, group and industry activities towards a more sustainable path of economic development. By contrast, the sustainable human development view (perhaps typified by *Beyond the Limits: Global Collapse or a Sustainable Future* by Meadows, Meadows and Randers, 1992) demands radical departures from the current system. Sustainable human development provokes a fundamental challenge to established interests, primarily because it focuses upon issues of social equity and ecological limits, and, thereby, questions world views and development models that are predicated on assumptions of unlimited economic growth. David Orr summarizes the differences between these two approaches in this way:

> The primary differences between the two [groups] have to do with assumptions about future growth, the scale of economic activity, the balance between top-down and grassroots activism, the kinds of technology and the relationship between communities and larger political and economic structures... the former approach reinforces a tendency toward a global technocracy and a continuation along the present path of development, albeit more efficiently. The other view requires a rejuvenation of civic culture and the rise of an ecologically literate competent citizenry who understand global issues.
>
> (Orr 1992, p.1)

A second key point to emerge from recent debates is the realisation that polarised points of view about sustainability miss at least one essential point: the concept of sustainable development requires change and compromise from entrenched positions. Sustainable development is, in the words of David Yencken, a Patron of

the Australian Conservation Foundation, "an inspired way in which a bridge can be built between two conflicting paradigms, between the paradigm that has underlain past Western approaches to the environment and an emerging new environmental paradigm" (Yencken 1994, p. 221). From this perspective, those that argue that sustainable development is too ambiguous a concept upon which to base public (and educational) policy have missed the importance of sustainable development as a way of transcending conflicting worldviews. Indeed, their bi-polar, either-or way of thinking in absolutes could be seen as symptomatic of the reductionist way of thinking of the Western scientific worldview that is one of the root causes of social and ecological decline.

Those that question the value of the concept of sustainable development as a metaphor or heuristic for a social ideal tend to be thinking about sustainable development as a 'product'. Seeing sustainable development as some sort of end-state, Jickling (1992) for example, argues that it is not wise to see sustainable development as a focus of education because visions of an ideal, sustainable future are influenced by history and culture and any educational programmes would, by definition, therefore have to be indoctrination for that kind of future (Jickling 1992). Unfortunately, this argument ignores the wide range of democratic pedagogies that have been discussed in the environmental education literature for over twenty years (e.g. Huckle 1980, 1983a, 1983b, 1986, 1988, 1990,1991; Fien 1993a, 1997, 1998). In addition, this sort of 'input' (i.e. some sort of educational programme) – 'product' (i.e. sustainable development) way of thinking, and the uni-linear view of social change it implies, is inconsistent with the holistic, ecological worldview that looks more to process than product, and recognises the interconnectedness and interdependence of all aspects of human and non-human nature and the systemic view of change associated with this. The lack of wisdom in polarised views of sustainable development was well summarised by UNESCO when it stated that:

> . . . we cannot sacrifice people to save elephants, but neither can we - at least for very long - save people by sacrificing the elephants. Indeed, this is a false dichotomy that must be rejected. We must imagine a new and sustainable relationship between humanity and its habitat: one that places humanity at centre stage, but does not neglect that what is happening in the "wings" may turn the drama of everyday life into a Greek tragedy in which we see a terrible fate approaching, but can muster up neither the collective will nor common means to escape it. (UNESCO 1997, p. 15)

A holistic or systemic view of sustainable development sees it as a process of change guided by a number of values or principles. This process view of sustainable development is embedded, for example, in *Caring for the Earth*, a strategic plan for a sustainable future prepared by a consortium of the world's leading environmental organisations, IUCN – The World Conservation Union, the United Nations Environment Programme (UNEP) and the World Wide Fund for Nature (WWF) in 1991. *Caring for the Earth* focused on the process of 'living sustainably', defining it as:

> ... a kind of development that provides real improvements in the quality of human life and at the same time conserves the vitality and diversity of the Earth. The goal is development that meets these needs in a sustainable way....
>
> Living sustainably depends on a duty to seek harmony with other people and with nature. The guiding rules are that people must share with each other and care for the Earth. Humanity must take no more from nature than nature can replenish. This in turn means adopting lifestyles and development paths that respect and work within nature's limits. It can be done without rejecting the many benefits that modern technology has brought, provided that technology also works within those limits. (IUCN, UNEP and WWF 1991, p. 8)

Such principles were embedded within a credo which *Caring for the Earth called* "a new world ethic of sustainability" based upon two interdependent sets of principles – one related to our responsibility to care for nature (or ecological sustainability) and another related to our responsibility to care for each other (social justice), with four principles in each group:

People and nature: ecological sustainability

Interdependence: People are a part of nature and depend utterly on her. We should respect nature at all times, for nature is life. To respect nature means to approach nature with humility, care and compassion; to be frugal and efficient in resource use; to be guided by the best available knowledge, both traditional and scientific; and to help shape and support public policies that promote sustainability.

Biodiversity: Every life form warrants respect and preservation independently of its worth to people. We should preserve the complexity of ecosystems to ensure the survival of all species, and the safeguarding of their habitats.

Living lightly on the earth: We should take responsibility for their impact on nature. We should maintain ecological processes, the variety of life, renewable resources, and the ecosystems that support them. We should use natural resources and the environment carefully and sustainably, and cooperate to restore degraded ecosystems.

Interspecies equity: We should treat all creatures decently, and protect them from cruelty and avoidable suffering.

People and people: social justice

Basic human needs: The needs of all individuals and societies should be met, within the constraints imposed by the biosphere; and all should have equal opportunity for improving their lot.

Inter-generational equity: Each generation should leave to the future a world that is at least as diverse and productive as the one it inherited. To this end, non-renewable resources should be used sparingly, renewable resources should be used sustainably, and waste should be minimized. The benefits of development should not be consumed now while leaving the costs to the future.

Human rights: All persons should have the fundamental freedoms of conscience and religion, expression, peaceful assembly, and association.

Participation: All persons and communities should be empowered to exercise responsibility for their own lives and for life on earth. Thus everyone must have full access to education, political enfranchisement and sustaining livelihoods, and be able to participate effectively in the decisions that most affect them.

(Adapted from IUCN, UNEP and WWF 1990, p.22; Fien 1997, p.4)

Sustainable community development

Chris Maser (1996) argues that such a process view of sustainable development is flexible and open to community definition, as people seek to interpret such principles in the light of local circumstances and interests. Nevertheless, principles such as those in the IUCN-WWF-UNEP ethic for living sustainably do reflect a "grand narrative for world-wide change". However, this does not mean that principles such as these eight, or any other holistic approach to sustainability, are an undemocratic imposition on global society. The democratic bases of the forms of critical pedagogy that underlie education for sustainability provide committed but professionally ethical approaches for teaching an ethic of care and responsibility for other people and societies and for non-human nature (Fien 1997, 1998).

Global and national ideals in any walk of life represent abstractions that often go beyond the experience and influence of most of us, as individuals, and in our families and neighbourhoods, as we go about our daily lives. This is what ideals and principles are. There is a risk that ideals such as the IUCN-WWF-UNEP ethic for living sustainably could quickly result in despair as we come to increasingly understand our accumulated human impact on the natural world and on other people. The powerful analytical tool of "ecological footprint" can help us calculate and envisage the scale of the task ahead:

> Humanity's Ecological Footprint is as much as 30 percent larger than nature can sustain in the long run. In other words, present consumption exceeds natural income by 30 percent and is therefore partially dependent on capital (wealth) depletion. The lavish partying by the wealthy few today means a hefty bill for everyone tomorrow.
>
> (Wackernagel and Rees 1996, p. 90)

But what does this really mean? What can I do about it? Thinking about the scale of the task can lead to either of two types of decisions – either to despair, or to the realization that sustainability must be worked out by communities in their local areas and can only be built from the bottom up. Yes, governments and international agencies can hold conferences, issue reports and create structures that encourage individuals, communities and companies to change, and these are important in setting broad goals and catalysing action. However, we can only effectively change the things we have most time to work on and, for most of us, this is ourselves and our local communities. It brings to mind the catchphrase, "think globally; act locally" and adds the plea "and live sustainably." Maser (1996) quotes Wendell Berry's advice on this point: "That will-of-the-wisp of the large-scale solution to the large-scale problem, so dear to governments and universities and corporations, serves mostly to distract people from the same, private problems that they may in fact have the power to solve". Therefore, he argues that "Sustainable development must be implemented where people are able to learn, feel, and be empowered to act – at the local level" (p. 166).

Sustainable community development is a process of local empowerment that enhances the ability of people to control their own lives and the conditions under which they live. This involves learning and action to ensure that as many people as possible participate in making decisions about the issues and problems that need addressing and work collaboratively to implement them. Sustainable community development means taking action to ensure that poverty is addressed by actions that both redistribute wealth appropriately and generate productive and stable employment, specifically in industries that operate "in harmony both with the productive capacity and integrity of the environment over time and with human dignity and sense of well-being" (Maser 1996, p. 171). This view of education for sustainable development is subsumed in the UNESCO Background Paper, *Environment and Society: Education and Public Awareness for Sustainability* (UNESCO-EPD 1997) and is not too distinctly different from Sauve's notion of "education for the development of responsible societies" (1999, pp. 28-30).

All the case studies in this book use educational activities as part of the process of sustainable community development. The case studies illustrate the important role of education in motivating and empowering people to participate in local changes towards more sustainable lifestyles and living conditions.

Achieving sustainability: the role of education

It was a quarter of a century ago, that education was described by Schumacher (1973, p. 64) as the "greatest resource" for achieving a just and ecological society. Since then, a series of major international reports have emphasized the critical role education can play in the search for sustainable living. The Brundtland Report, (WCED 1987) argued that teachers had "a crucial role to play in helping to bring about the extensive social changes" (p. xiv) necessary for sustainable development. The 1980 World Conservation Strategy was more explicit about the role of education in bringing about such changes. It argued that:

> A new ethic, embracing plants and animals as well as people is required for human societies to live in harmony with the natural world on which they depend for survival and well-being. The long-term task of environmental education is to foster or reinforce attitudes and behaviours compatible with this new ethic.
>
> (IUCN, UNEP & WWF 1980, sect. 13)

This message was reiterated by *Caring for the Earth* which identified education's vital role in ensuring that people learn, accept and live by the principle of living sustainably.

> Sustainable living must be the new pattern for all levels: individuals, communities, nations and the world. To adopt the new pattern will require a significant change in the attitudes and practices of many people. We will need to ensure that education programs reflect the importance of an ethic for living sustainably.
>
> (IUCN, UNEP & WWF 1991 p. 5)

Agenda 21, the internationally agreed report of the Earth Summit, committed countries to promoting environmental sustainability through education. Chapter 36 on "Promoting education, public awareness and training" was one of the few aspects of *Agenda 21* that did not provoke contention at the Earth Summit. Countries from both North and South agreed that education was critical for promoting sustainable development and increasing the capacity of the people to address environment and development issues (UNESCO-UNEP 1996).

This view was reiterated in the Discussion Paper for the Thessalonikki Conference on Environment and Society: Education and Public Awareness for Sustainability, which stated that:

> It is widely agreed that education is the most effective means that society possess for confronting the challenges of the future. Education, to be certain, is not the whole answer to every problem. But education, in its broadest sense, must be a vital part of all efforts to imagine and create new relations among people and to foster greater respect for the needs of the environment.
>
> (UNESCO 1998, p. 15)

In May 1996, the Commission on Sustainable Development (CSD) (set up by the UN to monitor the follow-up of decisions taken at the Earth Summit) met for its Fourth Session in New York. The noteworthy feature of this session was that Chapter 36 of *Agenda 21* was considered for the first time since 1992. The CSD Session concluded that:

> In order to change unsustainable production and consumption patterns and lifestyles, it (is) essential to give great emphasis to the role of education for sustainable development, including environmental economics as well as environmental awareness.
>
> (UNESCO-UNEP 1996, pp.2-3)

It referred to education for sustainability as "a lifelong process, that needs to be understood as part of a broad new vision of education", (p. 2).

The CSD met again in May 1998 and reiterated that "a fundamental prerequisite for sustainable development is an adequately financed and effective educational system at all levels, that is relevant to the implementation of all chapters of Agenda 21", (p. 7). At this meeting, the CSD also stressed the need to recognize non-formal and informal modes of teaching and learning (e.g., within the family and community) as vital to bringing about changes towards sustainable development. It saw the need for a broader, participatory approach for education for sustainability which took into account "local needs and values".

This comprehensive view of education for sustainability has also been gaining ground at the international and national policy level for some time. For example, the British Government Panel on Sustainable Development (1995) argued that:

> Clearly environmental education far transcends the boundaries of formal educationà The business, commercial and professional communities and the voluntary sector have vital roles in continuing environmental education and training. Sustainable development involves society as a whole.
>
> (BGPSD 1995, p. 6)

These international conference documents have led to regional action plans and national policies taking on board the new vocabulary of education for sustainability and acknowledging the need to educate and mobilize all sectors of society in the task of living sustainability. They not only reflect a growing recognition of the vital role education needs to play in the attainment of sustainability but also serve to define the components of a new educational approach. However, it is highly likely that one's favourite view of sustainable development or philosophy of education may not be represented in these documents. Indeed, it is likely that the views expressed will be a compromise. This is the nature of international reports that seek to accommodate all views but find it impossible to transcend ethnic, linguistic, gender and other hegemonies (Gough 1999). It is also the nature of national and provincial policies that are developed within particular local frames of power and social interest. Therefore, they need to be read contextually and strategically as well as textually (Singh 1995, 1998; Fien 2000) as catalysts for local innovation, educational reform and resistance to unsustainable development processes.

Educational Responses to Sustainability

Although the concept of "sustainability" first emerged in the early 1980s, it was not until the early 1990s, that the term began to form part of the vocabulary of education. IUCN – The World Conservation Union refers to "education for sustainable living", while others have used terms such as "education for sustainability" (National Forum on Partnerships Supporting Education about the Environment, USA 1996), "education for sustainable development" (UNESCO-UNEP 1996), and "education for a sustainable future" (UNESCO-EPD 1997). Some contributors to this book also use terms such as "environmental education for sustainability" or simply "environmental education" or "development education" to refer to their particular educational responses to the challenge of sustainability.

There have been several attempts to define the characteristics of an educational response to sustainability and also much discussion as to how this might differ from conventional approaches to environmental education (e.g., see: Sterling/EDET

Group 1992; Fien 1993a/b; Tilbury 1995, 1997; Huckle and Sterling 1996). The British Environment and Development Education and Training Group's report entitled *Good Earth-Keeping: Education, Training and Awareness for a Sustainable Future* defines the nature of education for sustainability as follows:

> We believe that education for sustainability is a process, which is relevant to all people and that, like sustainable development itself, it is a process rather than a fixed goal. It may precede – and it will always accompany – the building of relationships between individuals, groups and their environment. All people, we believe, are capable of being educators and learners in pursuit of sustainability. (Sterling/EDET Group 1992, p. 2)

In its report, the EDET Group affirmed the validity of the different approaches to environmental education in achieving sustainable development. Tilbury (1995) and Fien (1997) argue that education for sustainability must differ significantly from much of the nature study work carried out under the environmental education banner. Education with the objective of achieving sustainability varies from previous approaches to environmental education in that it focuses sharply on developing closer links among environmental quality, human equality, human rights and peace and their underlying political threads. Issues such as food security, poverty, sustainable tourism, urban quality, women, fair trade, green consumerism, ecological public health and waste management as well as those of climatic change, deforestation, land degradation, desertification, depletion of natural resources and loss of biodiversity are primary concerns for both environmental and development education. Matters of environmental quality and human development are central to education for sustainability, for as Julian Agyeman (1999) argues, we cannot have environmental quality without human equality.

These concerns differ substantially from those of litter, nature study and the planting of trees in the school grounds and other apolitical and aesthetic work that has often been the focus of much school-level environmental education in the past. Studies of the geophysical and biophysical world are a necessary – but not sufficient – prerequisite for learning to live sustainably. The concrete links between social justice and ecological sustainability, identified at the Earth Summit undermine the primacy of what some have termed the ecological foundations of environmental education and suggest a broadening and deepening of the concepts of environment and environmental education. Education about bio-diversity (and other nature-based themes) now needs to be immersed in concepts of human rights, equity and democracy which are the core issues of sustainability (Fien 1998).

Others such as Huckle (1996) point to how education for sustainability invites us to question the assumptions of dominant discourses in education, particularly those objectives, content and teaching methods which favour initiating people into the concepts and skills needed for finding scientific and technological solutions to environmental problems without addressing their root social political and economic causes. This approach is guided by a techno-centric rationality and behaviourist goals of reductionist Western science (Greenall Gough 1993) which often ignores the issues of justice and ecological sustainability. Indeed, eco-feminists, such as Carolyn Merchant (1980) and Vandana Shiva (1989), have identified western science and its patriarchal assumptions and attitudes to nature, women and development as a major cause of environmental exploitation and the increasing marginalization of many of the world's people.

Fien (1995) emphasizes this critique of the assumptions upon which education has developed and the consequent call by Vandana Shiva (1989) for a new

environmental science based upon indigenous ways of knowing, the relationship between ecology and everyday life and a vision of science as a servant of social and ecological change. Fien concludes that, viewed from this perspective, education for sustainability would embrace alternative epistemologies, and would value diverse ways of knowing, identify with the people and communities it purports to serve and respect community-based approaches to social change. This new outlook would extend the focus of education (and environmental education) from schools into the community. Education would no longer be interpreted solely as an academic subject for schools but as a participatory process which would involve all areas of civil society, including businesses and public services.

Such forms of education have the power to guide people in reflection and action on different interpretations of sustainable development (Huckle 1996). This process of critical enquiry, encourages people to explore the complexity and implications of sustainability as well as the economic, political, social, cultural, technological and environmental forces that foster or impede sustainable development. This entails involving people in questions about the ownership of common property resources, issues of international and intergenerational equity, investigations into regional and national ecological footprints and, most importantly, engagement in debates about qualitative versus quantitative growth.

Although the literature has began to identify the components of this new educational focus, the complexity and evolving character of the sustainable development debate suggests that education for sustainability needs to be continually re-conceptualized, and reflected upon, in response to local, national and global change. This needs to occur in a context where educators constantly and critically appraise theories, rationales and their practice. The stories in this book are a part of this reflection on how education can respond to the challenge of sustainability.

References

Agyeman, J. (1999). "Local Sustainability: Quality and Equality". Invited address at the Australian Association for Environmental Education (AAEE) Conference, *Southern Crossings: Pointers for Change*, 14-18 January 1999, University of New South Wales.

British Government Panel on Sustainable Development (1995). *First Report*. HMSO: London

Commission on Sustainable Development (1998). *Transfer of Environmentally Sound Technology, Capacity-building, Education and Public Awareness, and Science for Sustainable Development*. Report of the Sixth Session 20 April to 1 May 1998 CSD.

Dowdeswell, E. (1995). "Editorial" in *Our Planet*, 7(2):2.

European Commission (1995). "Fifth Action Plan for the Environment" in *Official Journal of the European Communities*, Resolution 95/C 345/87.

Fien, J. (1993a). *Environmental Education: A Pathway to Sustainability*. Deakin University Press: Geelong.

Fien, J. (1993b). *Education for the Environment Critical Curriculum Theorising And Environmental Education*. Deakin University Press: Geelong.

Fien, J. (1995). *Teaching for a Sustainable World*. UNESCO-UNEP: Brisbane.

Fien, J. (1997). "Undermining Myths in Environmental Education". Keynote Paper presented at the *Annual Conference Australian Association for Environmental Education*. (January). Hobart, Australia.

Fien, J. (1998). *"Environmental education for a new century"*. In D. Hicks and R.Slaughter (eds.), Futures Education - World Yearbook of Education 1998. London: Kogan Page.

Fien, J. (2000). "Education for the environment - a critique: a response" in *Environmental Education Research, 6(2):* 179-192.

Greenall Gough, A. (1993). *Founders of Environmental Education*. Deakin University Press: Geelong.

Huckle, J. (1980). "Values and the teaching of geography: towards a curriculum rationale" in *Geographical Education,* 3(4): 533-544.

Huckle, J. (1983a). "Environmental education". In J. Huckle (ed.), *Geographical Education: Reflection and Action*. Oxford University Press: Oxford.

Huckle, J. (1983b). "The politics of school geography". In J. Huckle (ed.), *Geographical Education: Reflection and Action*. Oxford University Press: Oxford.

Huckle, J. (1986). "Ten red questions to ask green teachers" in *Green Teacher, 1* (3):11-15.

Huckle, J. (1988). *What We Consume*. Global Environmental Education Programme - Teachers Handbook. World Wide Fund for Nature (UK) and Richmond Publishing: Godalming, Surrey.

Huckle, J. (1990). *Environment and Democracy*. Global Environmental Education Programme - Unit 10. World Wide Fund for Nature (UK) and Richmond Publishing. Godalming, Surrey.

Huckle, J. (1991). "Education for sustainability: assessing pathways to the future, *Australian Journal of Environmental Education,* 7: 49-69.

Huckle, J. (1996). "Realising sustainability in changing times" in J. Huckle and S. Sterling (eds.) *Education for Sustainability*. Earthstar Publications: London.

Huckle, J. and S. Sterling (eds.) (1996). *Education for Sustainability*. Earthstar Publications: London.

IUCN, UNEP, WWF (1980). *World Conservation Strategy: Living Resource Conservation for Sustainable Development*. IUCN: Gland, Switzerland.

IUCN, UNEP, WWF (1991). *Caring for the Earth: A Strategy for Sustainable Living*. IUCN, UNEP, WWF: Gland, Switzerland.

Jickling, B. (1992). "Why I Don't Want My Children To Be Educated For Sustainable Development" in *Journal of Environmental Education,* 23(4):5-8.

Jickling, B. (1999). "Editorial" in *Canadian Journal of Environmental Education,* 4: 5-8.

Maser, C. (1996). *Resolving Environmental Conflict: Towards Sustainable Community Development*. St Lucie Press: Defray Beach, Florida.

Meadows, D., D. Meadows, J. Randers (1992). *Beyond the Limits: Global Collapse or a Sustainable Future*. Earthstar Publications: London.

Merchant, C. (1980). *The Death of Nature: women, ecology and the scientific revolution*. Harper and Row: San Francisco.

National Forum on Partnerships Supporting Education about the Environment (1996). *Education for Sustainability: An Agenda for Action*. US Government Printing Office: Washington, D.C.

National Environmental Education Advisory Council (1996). *Report Assessing Environmental Education in the United States and the Implementation of the National Environmental Education.*

Orr, D. (1992). *Ecological Literacy: Education and the Transition to a Post-modern World*. State University of New York Press: Albany.

Pezzey, J. (1989). *Definitions of Sustainability*. CEED: London.

Redclift, M. and T. Benton (1995). *Social Theory and the Global Environment*. Routledge: London.

Schumacher, F. (1973). *Small is Beautiful: Economics as if People Really Mattered*. Abacus: London.

Shiva, V. (1989). *Staying Alive - women, ecology and development*. Zed Books: London.

Smyth, J. (1995). "Environment and education: a view of a changing scene" in *Environmental Education Research*, 1(1):3-20.

Sterling, S./EDET Group (1992). *Good Earth-Keeping: Education Training and Awareness for a Sustainable Future*. Environment Development Education and Training Group UNEP-UK: London.

Sustainable Development Education Panel (1999). *First Annual Report 1998*. Department of Environment, Transport and Regions: London.

Tilbury, D. (1995). "Environmental education for sustainability: Defining the new focus of environmental education in the 1990s" in *Environmental Education Research*, 1(2):195-212.

Tilbury, D. (1997). "Environmental education and development education: teaching geography for a sustainable world". In D. Tilbury and M. Williams (eds.), *Teaching Geography*. Routledge: London.

Tilbury, D. (1999). "Sustaining Curriculum Policy and Development in Environmental Education: A European action research project" in *Journal of the European Environment*, 9(1):1-11.

UNESCO (1992). *United Nations Conference on Environment and Development: Agenda 21*. UNESCO: Switzerland.

UNESCO-UNEP (1996). "Education for sustainable development", in *Connect* XXI (2) June.

UNESCO (1997). *Educating for a Sustainable Future: A Transdisciplinary Vision for Concerted Action*. Report of the International Conference on Environment and Society: Education and Public Awareness for Sustainability, Thessalonikki: Greece.

Wackernagel, M. and W. Rees (1996). *Our Ecological Footprint: Reducing Human Impact on the Earth*. New Society Publishers: Gabriola Islanda BC.

World Commission on Environment and Development (WCED) (1987). *Our Common Future*. Oxford University Press.

Yencken, D. (1994). "Values, knowledge and action", in L. Grove, D. Evans and D. Yenchen (eds.). *Restoring the Land: Environmental Values, Knowledge and Action*, pp. 217-236. Melbourne University Press: Melbourne, Australia.

Chapter 2

Education for sustainable development: an international perspective

Charles Hopkins and Rosalyn McKeown

Introduction

Education is an essential tool for achieving sustainability. People around the world recognize that current economic development trends are not sustainable and that public awareness, education and training are key to moving society toward sustainability. Beyond that there is little agreement. People argue about the term sustainable development and whether or not it is attainable. They have different visions of what sustainable societies will look like or be. These same people wonder why educators have not developed education for sustainability programmes. Yet, with little agreement about sustainability itself, it is no mystery why education for sustainability (EfS) has experienced difficulty moving forward.

It is curious to note that while we have difficulty envisioning a sustainable world, we have no difficulty detailing what is unsustainable in our societies. We can rapidly create a laundry list of problems – inefficient use of energy, lack of water conservation, pollution, abuses of human rights, overuse of personal transportation, consumerism, etc. However, we should not chide ourselves because we do not have a clear definition of sustainability; many truly great concepts of the human world, such as democracy and justice, are hard to define and have multiple expressions in cultures around the world.

A further discussion around education for sustainable development is what to call it. In this paper, we use two terms synonymously – education for sustainable development (ESD) and education for sustainability (EfS). We use the phrase education for sustainable development (ESD) because it is the terminology used most often at the international level and within UN documents. Another important distinction is the difference between education about sustainable development and education for sustainable development. The first focuses on an awareness and different interpretations. The second is the use of education as a means to encourage sustainability. Locally or nationally the effort may be described or named in many ways.

We cannot expect the formal education system, which in reality touches children for a fraction of their lives, to teach people everything about living, working, and governing in a manner that will achieve sustainability for their community and nation. Fortunately, formal education alone does not carry the responsibility for ESD. The non-formal education sector (e.g., nature centres, non-governmental organizations, public health educators, and agricultural extension agents) and the informal education sector (e.g., local television, newspaper and radio) must work in tandem with the formal education sector to educate people in all generations and walks of life. In addition, education for sustainability is a lifetime endeavour. In an ideal world, these three sectors would divide the enormous task of ESD for the entire population by identifying target audiences as well as themes of sustainability. They would then work creatively within their mutually agreed-upon realms. This

division of effort would reach a broader spectrum of people and prevent redundant efforts.

The purposes of this chapter are to: (a) provide some historical background information about ESD from an international perspective; (b) explain the roles of basic education, the reorientation of existing education to address sustainable development, and public understanding and training in ESD; (c) provide a suggested framework for conceptualizing ESD; and (d) identify some critical next steps in implementing ESD. This paper is written from an international ESD policy perspective, but which represents only one viable perspective.

Origins of ESD

Unlike most education movements, the inception of ESD was not created by the education community. One major outside thrust for ESD came from international political and economic forums (e.g., United Nations, OECD, OAS). In many countries, the concepts and content of ESD are developed by ministries, such as environment and health, and then given to educators to deliver. This outside conceptual development, independent of educators, is seen as a problem both by international education bodies such as UNESCO and by educators themselves.

ESD was crystallized when world leaders agreed that the concept of sustainable development should be actively pursued as a global goal. From the time sustainable development was endorsed in the UN General Assembly in 1987, the parallel concept of education supporting sustainable development was being explored. From 1987 to 1992, the concept of sustainable development matured as committees discussed, negotiated, and wrote the 40 chapters of *Agenda 21*. The initial thoughts concerning ESD were captured in Chapter 36 of *Agenda 21*, "Promoting Education, Public Awareness, and Training" (UNESCO 1992).

It is important to realize that ESD is an evolving concept that has grown and developed in the years since the Earth Summit in Rio de Janeiro in 1992. A series of major UN conferences helped to further develop the concept of sustainable development. The conferences, which dealt with core aspects of sustainability, included the World Conference on Human Rights (Vienna, 1993), the International Conference on Population and Development (Cairo, 1994), the World Summit for Social Development (Copenhagen, 1995), the Fourth World Conference on Women (Beijing, 1995), and the Second World Conference on Human Settlements (Istanbul, 1996). Each major UN Conference also added to the conceptual framework of ESD. Each conference:

- stressed the need for social and human development along with economic development and environmental concern;
- called for the advancement and empowerment of women;
- demanded basic social services for all;
- recognized the critical importance of sustainable livelihoods;
- cited the necessity of broad enabling environments for social and economic development;
- sought to sustain the environment and natural resources on which all people depend;
- underlined the importance of human rights; and
- identified the role of education as critical to achieving sustainability goals.

All of these major UN conferences recognized the importance of education and advanced the evolution of ESD from an international perspective.

In 1992, when the UN appointed "Task Manager"[1] roles for the implementation of *Agenda 21* to various agencies and organizations within the UN system, UNESCO was named to lead the education effort. It is important to note that UNESCO's role is not to implement ESD within nations *per se*, but rather to be a partner in furthering ESD. To this end, the nation members of the UN Commission on Sustainable Development (CSD)[2] have approved a major programme of work to be undertaken by various bodies. Even though UNESCO is task manager for ESD within the UN system, the implementation of the CSD work Programme for ESD is the responsibility of each nation that signed *Agenda 21*.

The table on the next page is a brief summary of that work programme.

Chapter 36 of *Agenda 21*: a starting point

> Education, including formal education, public awareness and training should be recognized as a process by which human beings and societies can reach their fullest potential. Education is critical for promoting sustainable development and improving the capacity of the people to address environment and development issues.
>
> *(Agenda 21*, Chapter 36, p. 3)

Agenda 21 is divided into forty chapters; each chapter focuses on an issue central to sustainability. Chapter 36, "Promoting Education, Public Awareness and Training", is dedicated to the specific issue of education. Like all chapters in *Agenda 21*, an international committee of experts drafted Chapter 36. The chapter was reviewed and revised by national governments as part of the five-year preparatory period that led to the adoption of *Agenda 21* at Rio in 1992. Chapter 36 identifies three major thrusts to begin the work of ESD: improving basic education; reorienting existing education to address sustainable development, and developing public understanding, awareness, and training. It should also be noted that the role of education is not isolated to Chapter 36 but is mentioned in all the other chapters of *Agenda 21*. *Agenda 21* provides a key starting point for planning and implementing ESD.

Improving basic education: the first priority

The first priority of ESD as outlined in Chapter 36 was the promotion of basic education. An educated citizenry is necessary to carry out informed and sustainable development. Nations with high illiteracy rates and unskilled work forces have fewer development options. These nations are largely forced to buy energy and manufactured goods on the international market with hard currency. To acquire hard currency, these countries need to trade, and usually this means exploiting natural resources or converting lands from self-sufficient family-based farming to cash-crop agriculture. An educated work force is key to moving beyond extractive and agricultural economies.

The relationship between education and sustainable development is complex. Generally, research shows that basic education is key to a nation's ability to develop and achieve sustainability targets. Education can improve agricultural productivity, enhance the status of women, reduce population rates, enhance environmental

WORK PROGRAMME OF THE CSD:
EDUCATION, PUBLIC AWARENESS AND TRAINING FOR SUSTAINABILITY*

Priority areas for action	Tasks	Key Actors cited by the CSD
A. Clarify and communicate the concept and key messages of education for sustainable development	A.1 Implement chapter 36 and the CSD work programme as part of integrated follow-up to major UN conferences and conventions	UNESCO, other UN bodies, Governments, major groups
	A.2 Continue to clarify and communicate concept and key messages, with emphasis on regional and national levels	UNESCO
B. Review national education policies and reorient formal educational systems	B.1 Develop policies and strategies for reorienting formal education towards sustainable development	Governments at all levels
	B.2 Include sustainable development objectives in curricula	Governments at all levels
	B.3 Develop guidelines for the reorientation of teacher training	UNESCO
	B.4 Reorient teacher training	Governments
	B.5 Introduce an interdisciplinary approach in teaching and research	Institutions of higher education
	B.6 Give due consideration to how the reform of higher education may support sustainable development	Participants at the conference (October 1998); UNESCO
C. Incorporate education into national strategies and action plans for sustainable development	C.1 Make education and public awareness significant components in regional, national and local strategies and action plans for sustainable development	Governments
	C.2 Complete the survey of existing regional and national strategies and action plans	UNESCO, with UNDP, UN-DESA
	C.3 Integrate education at levels into national and local strategies	Governments at all levels
	C.4 Integrate the aspect of gender balance and empowerment of women into national education strategies	Governments
D. Educate to promote sustainable consumption and production patterns in all countries	D.1 Raise awareness of relation to sustainability of current patterns of consumption and production; use educational tools and consumer feedback for policy-making; develop and promote social instruments; continue to work on indicators	UN-DESA, UNESCO, UNEP, OECD
	D.2 Collect best practices in media and advertising	World Business Council for Sustainable Development, International Chamber of Commerce, trade unions, civil society
	D.3 Report to the Commission at its seventh session on progress made	Secretary-General of the United Nations
E. Promote investments in education	E.1 Consider current levels of financing in education from the perspective of sustainable development	UNDP, World Bank, other international financing institutions
F. Identify and share innovative practices	F.1 Continue work on international electronic registry	UNESCO
	F.2 Develop and strengthen international and regional alliances, associations, networks among educational and training institutions and professional bodies	Not specified
	F.3 Strengthen networks and partnerships	Governments
	F.4 Recognize and use traditional knowledge	Not specified
G. Raise public awareness	G.1 Develop capacities for raising public awareness and access to information	Governments
	G.2 Undertake information campaigns	Governments at all levels, media, advertising agencies
	G.3 Take into account relevant international conventions	Governments

* Summary of decision of the 6th Session of the UN Commission on Sustainable Development (New York, April 1998) to adopt an expanded version of the work programme in chapter 36 of Agenda 21 initiated at its 4th Session in 1996. Prepared by UNESCO as Task Manager for chapter 36.

protection, and generally raise the standard of living. But the relationship is not linear. For example, four to six years of education is the minimum threshold for increasing agricultural productivity (Foster et al. 1994; Phillips 1994; Jamison and Lau 1983). Literacy and numeracy allow farmers to adapt to new methods, cope with risk, and to respond to market signals. Another profound change occurs when women reach the same level of education as men. An average of six to eight years of public education for women is required before the birth rate drops and infant health and children's education improve. Nine to twelve years of education is required before industrial productivity increases nationally. Finally, for a nation to shift to an information or knowledge-based economy – fuelled less on imported technology and more on local innovation and creativity – a subtle combination of higher education, research, and life-long learning must exist (UNESCO-ACEID, 1997).

In many countries, the current level of basic education is too low, severely hindering national plans for a sustainable future. In Latin America and the Caribbean, the average time spent in public education is six years with students often failing two or more of these years. In parts of Asia, especially Bangladesh, Pakistan and India, many children only attend school for an average of five years. A complicating factor in this region is that many girls receive fewer than two years of poor-quality schooling. In parts of Africa, the average attendance in public education is under three months. Unfortunately, the lowest quality of education is often found in the poorest regions or communities. The impact of little and/or poor-quality education severely limits the options available to a nation for developing its short- and long-term sustainability plans. This recognition of the need for quality basic education sets ESD apart from other educational movements such as environmental education, population education.

Reorienting existing education: the second priority

Chapter 36 also emphasized reorienting existing education towards sustainable development. While it is evident that it is difficult to teach environmental literacy without basic literacy, it is equally evident that simply increasing basic literacy, as it is currently taught in most countries, will not support a sustainable society. In fact, the most educated nations have the highest per capita rates of consumption and currently leave the deepest ecological footprints. The figures from the *UNESCO Statistical Yearbook and World Education Report* show tremendous disparity in national averages of years of education. For example, in the USA more than 80% of the population has some post-secondary education. We also know that per capita energy use and waste generation in the USA are nearly the highest in the world. More education has not led to sustainability. Simply educating the citizenry to higher levels is not sufficient to attain sustainable societies.

The term "reorienting education" has become a powerful descriptor that helps administrators and educators at every level to understand the changes required for ESD. An appropriately reoriented basic education includes more principles, skills, perspectives, and values related to sustainability than are currently included in most education systems. Hence, it is not only a question of quantity of education, but also one of appropriateness and relevance. ESD encompasses a vision that integrates environment, economy and society. Reorienting education is also seen as developing an education that involves learning the knowledge, skills, perspectives, and values that will guide and motivate people to lead sustainable livelihoods, to participate in a democratic society, and to live in a sustainable manner.

Public understanding, awareness, and training: The third priority

Training was also stressed in Chapter 36. It was recognized that the world needs a literate yet environmentally aware citizenry and work force to help guide nations to implement their national sustainability plans. All sectors – including business, industry, universities, governments, NGOs, and community organizations – were encouraged to train their leaders in environmental management and to provide training to their workers.

The need for a transdisciplinary approach

The effort to reorient basic education to address economic education, environmental education, and the wide range of social education initiatives (e.g., human rights, anti-racist, peace, and gender issues) needs to be approached with a concerted and integrated effort. To move forward, leaders and individuals from traditional disciplines need to develop ESD in a trans-disciplinary manner. These leaders and skilled professionals should work collaboratively with other sectors including various ministries and NGOs to develop activities ranging from policy to community-based projects. However, each discipline involved in ESD should continue to develop its own discipline and subject areas, each with its own perspectives, strengths and skills. The strength of ESD will come through diverse disciplinary contributions woven together to accomplish a shared vision of sustainability. Furthermore, we need to recognize that no one discipline or group of people can implement ESD alone. ESD takes a concerted effort from many disciplines and sectors of the education community. Fortunately, much of the knowledge, skills and values currently used by educators provide a sound starting point.

What is ESD?

Although sustainable development and hence ESD are difficult to envision, we must create frameworks for initial ESD efforts so others can understand and teach it. In our minds, ESD is a combination of existing and yet to be identified guiding principles, knowledge, skills, perspectives, and values that are organized around sustainability concepts and issues. We recognize that this is one of many possible frameworks or ways to organize ESD. Each community should identify relevant principles to include in their ESD programmes.

Knowledge and skills for ESD

Sustainable development encompasses the interaction between environment, economics, and society. As a result, we need a knowledge base from the natural-sciences, social-sciences, and humanities to understand the principles of sustainable development, how they can be implemented, the values involved, and the ramifications of their implementation. Therefore, a knowledge base from the traditional disciplines supports ESD. The challenge for communities in the process of reorienting curricula is to select knowledge that supports sustainability goals. In addition, the communities need to question topics that have been taught for years but are no longer relevant. This paring of the curriculum will prevent overburdening teachers and pupils with an ever-growing curriculum.

To be successful, ESD, like all good education, must blend knowledge and skills. ESD must provide practical skills that will enable people to continue learning after they leave school, secure sustainable livelihoods, and live sustainable lives. These skills will differ with community conditions. The following partial list of skills will help initiate discussions about the types of skills students will need as adults in those communities. Note that these skills, while totally consistent with good basic education, also fall into one or more of the three realms of sustainable development:

- the ability to communicate effectively both orally and in writing;
- the ability to think about systems (both natural and social systems);
- the ability to think in time – to forecast, to think ahead, and to plan;
- the ability to think critically about value issues;
- the ability to comprehend quantity, quality, and value;
- the capacity to move from awareness to knowledge to action;
- the ability to work cooperatively with other people;
- the capacity to use various processes – knowing, inquiring, acting, judging, imagining, connecting, valuing, questioning and choosing; and
- the capacity to develop an aesthetic response to the environment.[3]

In addition, pupils will need to learn specific skills that will help them manage and interact with their local environment, economy and society. Regarding the environment, such skills may include:

- learning to prepare materials for recycling;
- learning to harvest wild plants without jeopardizing future natural regeneration and production;
- learning to grow low-water-need crops; and
- learning to protect local water sources from contamination.

Perspectives and values

ESD must include more than knowledge and skills; education does not stop at literacy and numeracy. If society is to address sustainability it must also address worldviews, values, perspectives and aspirations. An international perspective of sustainability also carries with it values and perspectives that are reflected in literature and documents from the aforementioned UN conferences held in the 90s. These perspectives include such underlying assumptions as:

- a healthy environment is essential for sustainable development;
- sustainability is a global goal for the betterment of both humanity and the planet;
- sustainability should be achieved through democratic processes;
- sustainability depends on peace, justice, and equity;
- the individual has basic human rights;
- no nation or people should prosper through the explicit impoverishment of another nation;
- diversity, both biological and cultural, is intrinsically valuable;
- development is to be human-centred (i.e., for the betterment of humanity as a whole as opposed to empowerment of a few); and
- intergenerational respect and responsibility will safeguard the rights of future generations.

These are a few of the many values and perspectives that underpin the concept of sustainability. How these broad perspectives and values become reflected in ESD should be developed at the local level. Currently, some values and perspectives are overtly taught within education systems while others are learned from the culture around us.

From time to time however, communities and nations must examine and challenge the values and perspectives underlying ESD and either reaffirm or alter them. Questioning values and perspectives will maintain the evolutionary nature of sustainability and ensure its continuous contribution to the betterment of society.

ESD: issues based

Along with the reorientation of the knowledge, skills, perspectives and values of basic education, ESD must also help society address the major issues that threaten the sustainability of the planet and humans. Issues can be categorized many ways. For this paper, the three main categories are: issues identified in the Rio process and addressed in *Agenda 21*; issues identified for which no agreeable course of action was adopted at Rio; and issues that have evolved since Rio.

Many key issues regarding sustainability were identified by the Brundtland Commission and were incorporated into *Agenda 21* and the Earth Summit process. The 40 issues found in the 40 chapters of *Agenda 21* are the core of ESD and should be reflected in any programme related to reorienting education for sustainability. These 40 issues are organized in four sections within *Agenda 21* (see United Nations Department of Public Information 1997, pp. 265-269).

Section 1: social and economic dimensions
International cooperation, combating poverty, changing consumption patterns, population and sustainability, protecting and promoting human health, sustainable human settlements, decision-making for sustainable development.

Section 2: conservation & management of resources
Protecting the atmosphere, managing land sustainably, combating deforestation, desertification and drought, sustainable mountain development, sustainable agriculture and rural development, conservation of biological diversity, management of biotechnology, protecting and managing the oceans, protecting and managing freshwater, safer use of toxic chemicals, managing hazardous wastes, managing solid waste and sewage, managing radioactive wastes.

Section 3: strengthening the role of major groups
Women in sustainable development, children and youth, indigenous people, partnerships with NGOs, local authorities, workers and trade unions, business and industry, scientists and technologists, strengthening the role of farmers.

Section 4: means of implementation
Financing sustainable development, technology transfer, science for sustainable development, education, awareness and training, creating capacity for sustainable development, organizing for sustainable development, international law, and information for decision-making.

The Rio process also led to the signing of conventions and a statement of principles that shape a framework for ameliorating some pressing global issues: The Statement

on Forests, The Convention on Climate Change, The Convention on Biological Diversity and The Convention on Desertification. Each of these agreements makes recommendations for education, public awareness, and training and relates to issues-based ESD.

While *Agenda 21* clearly laid out many critical issues that governments agreed to address, the Brundtland Commission identified additional issues. These issues were discussed initially, but no formal international agreement or plan of action could be reached. Nevertheless, these additional issues are pertinent to ESD and should be included when relevant and appropriate. These issues include war and militarism, governance, discrimination and nationalism, renewable energy sources, multinationals, refugees, nuclear disarmament, human rights, and media/worldviews.

Important issues (e.g., Multilateral Agreement on Investment) continue to emerge and enhance the concept of sustainability. Such issues should be included in ESD when appropriate in order to identify innovative solutions and develop the global political will to resolve the problems.

Communities creating ESD curricula cannot or need not teach all of the above issues. The quantity of study would be overwhelming. Instead, communities should select a few locally relevant issues from each of the three realms – environment, economics, and society. The issues selected should be exemplary of the guiding principles of sustainability.

Initiating locally appropriate ESD

Going from the holistic and broad concepts of ESD to locally relevant curriculum is a difficult process. Curriculum designers must make many decisions based on assumptions about the future and critiques of the prevalent culture. The process of selecting which knowledge, skills, perspectives, values, and issues (from each of the three realms) to include in the curriculum will invoke many opinions and discussions. Just as no single worldview, form of democracy, or set of solutions will be viable around the world, the same is true of the content and pedagogy associated with ESD.

Several major caveats accompany the inclusion of sustainability issues in the curriculum. The issues need to be relevant, understandable, and appropriate to the audience's ability to understand and create solutions. It is not useful to frighten small children with global issues for which they have no control and for which they are not responsible. It is more useful to bring issues forward in locally relevant terms while seeking locally appropriate solutions. For example, the issue of nationalism can be approached in anti-racist programmes in a primary class. The issue of managing solid waste and sewage can be addressed locally in water conservation and waste management programmes.

The changes that will accompany locally relevant ESD – some small and others radically innovative – will be accelerated and enhanced by practitioners who share and exchange examples of their successes and failures. The use of new technologies (e.g., email and the Internet) will greatly speed the process of dissemination. The use of these technologies will help educators find examples of how their expertise could be creatively employed. Sharing these examples will help reinforce the professional development and in-service needs of the world's educators.

The strengths model

To complicate matters, the pedagogy necessary to teach the new curriculum may not be within the current repertoire of teachers. Usually, major changes in curriculum are accompanied by a call to retrain all practising teachers. These calls are based on a "needs model" in which a deficit is recognized and remediation recommended. However, it is unrealistic to expect nations to retrain over sixty million practising teachers and countless thousands of administrators to verse them in the broad scope of ESD. We need to find ways to harness the existing skills of the current educational labour force. We call such recognition and use of the skills, knowledge, and talents of current practitioners a "strengths model" for professional development and training. Once the concept of sustainability is broadly understood and the need to reorient education is accepted, the way forward will be greatly enhanced by combining the contributions of traditional disciplines and the experience and creativity of current teachers and administrators.

Many resources currently exist in the teaching and administrative labour pools. Talented educators in such fields as environmental education, population education, and human rights education can easily expand their focus to include concepts from sustainable development. Fortunately, every educator in every discipline has some existing expertise or strength to bring to ESD. In this approach, the strengths of each traditional discipline can be used and leveraged with the strengths of other disciplines to convey the associated knowledge, issues, skills, perceptions and values. Mathematics teachers can contribute the concept of relative risk; language teachers can teach media literacy and the role of advertising in addressing consumption; history teachers can include the concepts of time and change to help students put evolving issues such as climate change in perspective. However, use of this "strengths model" requires that someone be sufficiently well versed in the principles of ESD to pull together the pieces taught in the various disciplines to form a complete picture of the role of individuals, communities and nations in a sustainable world.

Teacher education

While the effort can begin with the current cadre of teaching professionals, it is clear that institutions of teacher education need to reorient pre-service teacher education to address ESD. Reorienting of teacher education institutions is a key element in the CSD work programme on ESD. The development of new professionals with ESD expertise will profoundly shorten the response time for achieving sustainability.

Two models of human resource development currently exist: in-service training and pre-service training. In the first, experienced professionals are provided with additional training. In turn, they reshape existing programmes by drawing on their new knowledge, previous expertise, and understanding of national and local systems. In pre-service training, concepts, principles, and methodologies are provided during initial training. The new professionals step into their jobs with ESD as part of their expertise. Due to the cost of replacing teachers during in-service training, pre-service training is generally more cost effective than retraining educators and administrators. For initial success, both in-service and pre-service programmes are necessary.

Moving forward

Many countries have delayed incorporating ESD into their formal education systems. Too often politicians, educators, and other decision-makers forget that 179 nations pledged to reorient their education system. This neglect has left UN Agencies, NGOs and interested individuals to undertake the reorientation effort with either little or no government assistance. Frequently, progress in ESD has been a difficult, uphill battle. In spite of this lack of assistance, some segments of the larger education community (e.g., environmental educators, population educators, and human rights groups) have contributed greatly to discussions and progress. Other ministries, such as environment, health, and development, are often much more attuned to the need for ESD. In many respects, these ministries could be great assets in the reorientation process.

The history of educational change, both successes and failures, shows that educators must be involved throughout the creation, development, and implementation of new educational programmes. Educators must be more than instruments of delivery for the ESD message. They must be centrally involved in developing the concepts, content, pedagogy, evaluation, and research that will support the creation of ESD.

The next steps in the evolution of ESD should engage all sectors of education to construct strategic plans. These strategic plans should lead to many small-scale experiments in curriculum development, sustainable building management, teacher training, community involvement, etc. Many of these experiments will succeed and some will fail. The successes can then be duplicated and the failures shared as valuable lessons. We suggest the following essential next steps:

- heads of State must recognize and shoulder the responsibility their nations accepted by signing *Agenda 21*;
- all ministries, especially education, must engage in addressing ESD;
- the decision-makers responsible for setting priorities and arranging corresponding budgets must affirm the importance of ESD;
- the government and educational community must involve traditional disciplines and concerned groups, such as environmental education, peace education, human rights education, and population education;
- administrators must allocate resources to develop strategic plans;
- the educational community must develop ESD leadership;
- ministries and school districts must assign responsibilities at all levels, and those who are responsible need to be held accountable;
- innovation must be encouraged;
- innovative practices must be disseminated;
- programme designers must establish research and evaluation techniques as part of the action plan;
- teacher training must incorporate pedagogy and content appropriate to ESD;
- educational institutions must model sustainability practices; and
- achievements should be recognized and celebrated.

These are but a few of the steps required to advance ESD.

The future of ESD will depend on how the concept is perceived in the next few years. If ESD is seen as yet another isolated societal issue to be squeezed into the curriculum, or yet another topic to be given as an elective, then little progress will be made. Without ESD, we will continue to create the crises that led us to envisage

sustainability in the first place. The question is not if we will address ESD but when and how we will address it. Obviously, the longer we wait, the more diminished our resources become and the fewer options open to future generations.

We know intuitively that the path we have been travelling will not lead to sustainability. We also know that we have not yet developed a common vision. Thoughtful, inclusive dialogue followed by educational experimentation is our hope for finding a new path to the yet elusive sustainability. To democratically move forward, in a time frame that will prevent massive human suffering and environmental degradation, we desperately need an informed and understanding populace. For this reason, the international community perceives education as essential to a sustainable future.

Notes

1. In 1992, the heads of various UN organizations, agencies, and programmes met in New York to coordinate follow-up to Rio. Each of the 40 chapters of Agenda 21 was given to a particular UN institution with expertise in the issue to act as Task Manager.

2. The United Nations Commission on Sustainable Development (CSD) was established in 1992 as part of the ongoing follow-up to Rio. This body of more than 50 elected nations meets yearly at the UN in New York to review the accomplishments of the implementation of Agenda 21 and to initiate ongoing efforts to achieve sustainable development.

3. We built on and adapted skills from earlier work on environmental literacy by others, including Milton McClaren, Chuck Roth, and Harold Hungerford.

References

Hopkins, C., J. Damlamian, and G. Lopez Ospina. (1996). "Evolving towards education for sustainable development: an international perspective" in *Nature and Resources*, 32(3):7.

UNESCO (1992). *United Nations Conference on Environment and Development: Agenda 21*. UNESCO: Switzerland.

United Nations Department of Public Information (1997). *Earth Summit: Agenda 21 The United Nations Programme of Action From Rio*. Chapter 36, pp. 264-269. DPI/1344/Rev.1-97-01888-February 1997-5m.

UNESCO – ACEID (1997). *Proceedings of the Third UNESCO-ACEID International Conference - Educational Innovation for Sustainable Development*. Principal Regional Office for Asia and the Pacific: Bangkok.

Part A

Asia-Pacific

Part A

Asia-Pacific: The context

John Fien

Asia and the Pacific is a region of great diversity, both in natural settings and in the cultural, social and economic activities of the people – nearly two-thirds of the world's population – who live there. Examples of this diversity are found in the following passage:

> *The Asia-Pacific region covers an outstanding array of geography and culture. The region is one of sharp contrasts. It has two of the world's most populous countries, China and India and some of the world's smallest countries, Nauru in the Pacific and the Maldives in the Indian Ocean. It has one of the world's richest countries, Japan, and the world's poorest, Cambodia and Bangladesh... [The] region's ethnic and linguistic diversity is greater than anywhere else in the world. Great cultures have left legacies such as the Great Wall of China... the legendary temples of Borobodor in Indonesia. A wealth of religions criss-cross the region, ranging from Buddhism, Hinduism, Christianity, Islam and Sikhism to other faiths such as Confucianism, Jainism and Taoism.*

(UNESCO 1996)

However, amidst this great diversity, many similarities may be found. Economically, Asia and the Pacific is the fastest growing region in the world, and there is a shared fear that modernization will imperil the traditional ways of belief and life that have ensured social and ecological sustainability for centuries. Indeed, the impacts of commercial agriculture, industrialization and the growth of service and tourism industries have already brought all-too-rapid and ill-planned urban growth and the associated problems of air, water and marine pollution, waste disposal, traffic congestion and social instability. As a result, and despite enormous pressures to entrench this descending spiral of unsustainable development, we find many families, communities, schools, non-governmental organizations and government agencies in every country in the region planning ways to live sustainably and create the structures that can encourage and empower others to do likewise.

Education has been identified as a critical driving force in this process, and many exciting and innovative programmes of education and sustainability, both in formal and non-formal education, are worthy of inclusion in this collection. Space limits allowed only five case studies – just over a quarter of the book – to represent this diversity of programmes. Thus there was not space to include the extensive work of the Centre for Environmental Education in India which, in just one of its projects, is developing a teacher education for sustainability programme for over seventy colleges. Similarly, there was not space to report on the UNESCO action research network for teacher educators, called the *Learning for a Sustainable Environment Project*, which operates in twenty countries in the region; the work of WWF in China to help embed issues of sustainability in national education policy; the work of the Population and Development Association in Thailand to provide professional development for teachers in remote areas; the South Pacific Regional Environment Programme to facilitate national and regional strategies for education and the sustainable development of small island states; or Christchurch College of Education in New Zealand to pioneer experiential learning approaches for developing an ethic of sustainability for student teachers – all would have made for excellent case studies of education for sustainability in the formal education sector in the region.

Then, there could have been case studies of the community education activities of the Australian "landcare" movement in encouraging catchment-scale responsibility for land and stream management, of the Grameen Bank in Bangladesh and its work to encourage small-scale entrepreneurial activities, especially among women, and of the Seikatsu Clubs of Japan which have entrenched sustainable consumption in the lives of over 225,000 participating families with total sales approaching one billion dollars annually.

So, the five case studies in this section stand as samples of the vibrancy and achievements, as well as the unresolved issues, of education for sustainability to be found in the Asia-Pacific region. Two of the case studies relate to formal education and three to non-formal education.

A major problem of schooling throughout the region is its overly-academic nature and lack of relevance to everyday rural and community life of the villages where most people in Asia and the Pacific live. The results is that the few students who succeed in schools move away to further education and paid employment in towns and cities while the majority of students attend school for the bare minimum of time that they can and leave to work on family plots. Traditional ways of educating young people to work the land sustainably have largely been destroyed by the imposition of schooling. The Uttapradesh Project was established to address problems such as these and is an outstanding model of the way that the school curriculum can be reoriented to empower young people to work for a sustainable future for themselves, their families and their communities. Miriam College in the Philippines is a "school" that takes students from primary school age right up to postgraduate classes. The curriculum at all these levels is grounded in principles of compassion and stewardship, but the case study of Miriam College is not about its curriculum or its campus green programmes, but of the outreach work of Miriam staff through their own NGO, Miriam-PEACE.

The third case study in the section explores the community-based theatre-in-education activities of Won Smalbag in Vanuatu in facilitating community discussion and action on issues of health, hygiene, domestic violence, conservation and appropriate development. This focus on environmental adult education is also seen in the case studies from Indonesia and Nepal. The dilemma of trying to promote sustainable community development and ecological responsibilitiy in a country once controlled by a military-backed regime and "crony-capitalism" is described in the case study from Indonesia which explores the work of Pusat Pendidikan Linkungan Hipup (PPHL) and its slowly expanding network of environmental education centres. Tourism provides a major proportion of the national income of Nepal but has also brought many negative social and environmental impacts. Early attempts to control tourists and demarcate areas as environmental reserves have had a severe impact on the livelihood of local communities. What is the alternative, and what role can education play in this? These questions are answered in the case study of the Annapurna Conservation Area Project (ACAP), which illustrates how community-based environmental education programmes that focus upon traditional cultural values have contributed to the ecological, economic and social sustainability of the Annapurna communities.

Reference

UNESCO (1996). *Celebrating Diversity, Cultivating Development, Creating Our Future Together: UNESCO in Asia and the Pacific.* UNESCO: Bangkok.

Chapter 3

Vanuatu

Turtles, trees, toilets and tourists: community theatre and environmental education

Stephen Passingham

Introduction

Communities in the Pacific have long used storytelling, music, song and dance to entertain and educate successive generations. Recently, the use of community theatre to explore issues and foster environmentally and socially responsible values, attitudes and practices has been enthusiastically embraced in several countries in the region. Vanuatu, an archipelago in the south-west Pacific, is home to several groups that use theatre, and other forms of communication, to entertain and educate people about a wide range of health, social and environmental issues.

Wan Smolbag Theatre was formed in 1989 as a small, part-time amateur drama group, taking its name from the one small bag in which actors carried their props. With much commitment by its members, and financial support from a range of external funding agencies, the group has grown dramatically and now has sixteen members, a studio-theatre and a widespread and enviable reputation. Wan Smolbag has contributed to the development of a number of other theatre groups, both within Vanuatu and elsewhere in the region. Some of these groups focus on a particular geographical area, some a particular range of issues, and others a particular target audience. In Vanuatu, Wuhuran and Haulua, for example, work mostly on their home islands of Ambrym and Pentecost, whereas Healthforce concentrates on plays with a health theme and Tua Theatre on issues of particular importance to women. While no theatre group focuses exclusively on environmental issues, those groups that do address such issues aim to collaborate with other organizations that have a concern for the environment as their primary responsibility. Together, they seek to encourage sustainable practices by promoting discussion, information-sharing and positive values and attitudes.

An untouched paradise?

Although tourist brochures promote Vanuatu as "the untouched paradise", the natural environment is increasingly coming under pressure. Rapid population growth and urbanization, and the over-exploitation of resources, have resulted in numerous threats to the environment, including coral reef degradation, deforestation, species depletion and pollution.

Traditionally, an intimate relationship existed between people and their natural environment, the resources of the land and sea not only being vital for subsistence and exchange but also as the foundation for kinship systems and spiritual values. Social and cultural diversity resulted in a wide range of techniques of exploitation, management and use of natural resources. Not surprisingly, immediate survival

requirements took precedence over any longer term notions of conservation. However, traditional practices, such as gender-specific food taboos, temporary bans on resource exploitation and the use of low-impact techniques, worked in favour of environmental sustainability by limiting the degree to which any one resource was exploited.

While traditions remain strong in some areas, traditional knowledge and ways of life are coming under threat. Ni-Vanuatu[1] are increasingly exposed to the wider world and many aspire to lifestyles that are radically different from those of their ancestors. Rapid urbanization is resulting in more people living in cramped squatter housing without access to clean water, sanitation and land for gardens. Malnutrition and environmental health hazards are increasingly evident in the two towns. The development of schooling, and the prevalence of boarding at secondary level, is resulting in young people being less rooted in traditional ways.

As Ni-Vanuatu are drawn into the money economy, the exploitation of resources increasingly employs high-impact tools, such as spear guns and chain saws, and has increasingly become commercialized, sometimes to the extent that future livelihoods are threatened. The exploitation of the coconut crab to meet the demands of restaurants in Port Vila has resulted in this large and late-maturing animal becoming depleted throughout even those islands furthest from the capital. Similarly, the over-exploitation of sea cucumbers, a delicacy in Chinese restaurants, threatens the diversity and future life of coral reefs.

While some communities are attempting to develop village-level initiatives to generate the resources needed to participate in the money economy, an increasing number is exposed to the promises of companies offering quick but often minimal rewards in return for allowing the exploitation of their resources. Some international companies, for example, have promoted the unsustainable logging of forests while others have illegally exported live coral. Gardening and gathering food and other resources from the forests and reefs remain vital for most people's livelihoods and a strong link between environmental degradation and poverty is increasingly apparent.

The wider context

Community theatre in Vanuatu is, of necessity, firmly rooted in its particular social-cultural, geographical and educational context. Approximately three-quarters of Ni-Vanuatu live in widely dispersed villages on over 60, mostly mountainous, islands. Transport and communication systems between villages and islands are poorly developed.

Vanuatu's social and cultural diversity is illustrated by the presence of 105 local languages, making the nation, on a per capita basis, the most linguistically complex country in the world. In addition, Vanuatu has three national languages, Bislama (the local dialect of Melanesian pidgin and the lingua franca), English and French. While data on adult literacy are disputed, it is likely that the rate in Vanuatu is below the average for least developed countries.

Although increasing numbers of children complete English or French medium primary education, many remain functionally illiterate. Less than thirty percent of children go to junior secondary school and there are few alternative sources of formal education for adolescents and adults. Children who drop out or who complete their formal education at the end of primary or junior secondary school,

increasingly have fewer employment opportunities and fewer ways of securing a livelihood in the formal economy.

While the primary curriculum includes "Environmental Studies", it is of relatively minor importance in the Primary School Leaving Examination and often does not receive the attention it deserves. At secondary level, the Science and Social Science curricula contain elements of environmental education but there is little focus on traditional knowledge of the environment. Rural Training Centres, the main providers of basic vocational skills training to rural adolescents, offer two year courses, in Bislama, that include a core course on environmental issues.

Vanuatu is very much an oral society and, for most Ni-Vanuatu, storytelling continues to be an important way in which information is shared. Access to information via the mass media is either limited or non-existent. Some communities have access to radio, much of which is in Bislama, and this is often the only source of news and information about social, health and environmental issues. The weekly newspapers have low production numbers and limited distribution, especially in rural areas. Use and understanding of English and French, the main languages of both newspapers and television and videos, is limited. Television coverage is very restricted although a growing number of people have occasional access to videos, mostly through the growth in "bush cinemas" in those villages that have generators. Videos are available for hire from private companies and are usually watched by all generations in a village. Most people have little or no access to media with a local development content other than very occasional radio programmes. Most television programmes and videos are imported and, despite their popularity, rarely have any sustainable development content. Perhaps the dominant message of most films is the promotion of an unattainable and unsustainable consumerism.

In such circumstances, where information is scarce, educational levels are low and communication is difficult, community theatre can be an accessible and appropriate means of education. While it often draws on the prevalent teaching methodology, by telling a story, transmitting information and being actor-centred, community theatre is also entertaining and thought-provoking. By being oral and highly visual, by providing a chance to identify with characters and empathize with the dilemmas they face and by active participation in pre- and post- performance discussions and sometimes in the plays themselves, theatre can make ideas and information available to a wide range of people including the poorest and the most disadvantaged. In doing so, it offers a realistic and meaningful exploration of the contexts in which people consider options and make choices and thus has the potential to be an effective teaching medium and a powerful means of achieving positive changes in knowledge, attitudes and practices. The *Tourists or Toilets?* play, for example, is a musical comedy that focuses on the dilemmas an outer island community faces in trying to answer the question "what is real development?" The play's use of song, dance and humour to explore a serious topic is a culturally appropriate way of encouraging such changes.

Theatre also has the advantage of being flexible. It is often easy to change information or to develop or adapt plays for particular audiences and situations. Wan Smolbag has, for example, developed several plays specifically for children. Such plays as *The Tale of Mighty Hawk and Magic Fish* (a pantomime about logging), *Invasion of the Litter Creatures* and *On the Reef* were developed primarily with children in mind but can be enjoyed by adults and used by teachers. Community theatre usually requires little equipment and plays can be performed in a variety of settings – under a tree, in a village meeting area, in a classroom or on a street corner.

Plays, sketches and skits can be developed and performed by the network of community theatre groups in a relatively short period of time, providing a quick and widespread response in times of need. Wan Smolbag's 1998 campaign to encourage people in Port Vila to destroy mosquito breeding sites, for example, is credited with preventing a serious outbreak of dengue fever.

Community theatre in practice

The repertoire of community theatre groups covers an increasing number of issues, including forest preservation, logging and reforestation, coral reef diversity, degradation and protection, litter, threatened species (turtles, sea cucumbers and koroliko birds), the potential environmental impact of tourism, cyclone preparedness, the impact of rapid population growth and environmental health concerns (ventilated improved pit (VIP) toilets, clean water, malaria and dengue fever).

Initially, theatre groups focused on providing information about environmental and other issues, mostly during infrequent visits to communities. More recently, most groups have extended their activities by using a range of more participatory and interactive ways of working where the development and performance of plays, sketches and skits is more a vehicle for shared learning. The most common practice is preceding and following performances with short presentations and question and answer sessions. These put the content of plays in a wider context and enable the audience to participate to the extent of clarifying and questioning issues raised. This practice ideally involves others, such as environmental outreach officers, both before and after performances and even as an integral part of a play.

Play development is usually proceeded by community-based research to explore knowledge, attitudes and practices. This is a more effective way of making plays meaningful and appropriate. It also allows sensitive issues to be addressed without causing offence. Wan Smolbag has placed a greater emphasis on post-initial performance activities such as disseminating information about activities, liaising between communities and other stakeholders, providing a variety of support and training to selected community members and assessing the influence and impact that their work has on particular issues and communities.

Turtle meat and eggs are a traditional and valued part of many people's diets, despite their consumption now being illegal. Wan Smolbag and Wuhuran performances of *I'm a Turtle* on turtle conservation clearly challenge food habits. The turtle campaign began in 1995 with theatre members visiting villages to learn about traditional beliefs and stories about turtles, older people's memories of species and numbers of turtles in the past compared with the present and people's current attitudes and practices towards turtles. This was not merely an extractive process for the purposes of making a play but the beginning of a relationship among villages, theatre groups and the Department of Fisheries. Given the illegality of turtle consumption and the involvement of a government department, it is a measure of the trust that developed that the campaign was able to proceed. In the initial phase, a number of villages on three islands decided to appoint turtle monitors. These people have received training from the Department of Fisheries on the life cycles of marine animals, marine resource management and the law regarding turtles and other species. They have also received training from the South Pacific Regional Environment Programme (SPREP) to tag turtles and report on turtle activity to SPREP and the Department of Fisheries. Wan Smolbag and Wuhuran have also

provided training in confidence-building basic drama skills. Many monitors have assisted the Department to release newly-hatched turtles from selected beaches. In some villages, chiefs have placed taboos on particular areas of beach and reef and supported requests by officials of the Department of Fisheries for compliance with the law. This campaign has resulted in the appointment of increasing numbers of turtle monitors throughout the archipelago.

Some theatre groups have also worked with communities to develop a play the community then performs. This methodology was used by Wan Smolbag on the *Em i Graon blong Yumi* (This is Our Land) video, where the group worked with people of Tongoa island to examine the situation of the koroliko, an endangered seabird that is hunted for food. More recently, over 60 members of the Blacksands community worked with Wan Smolbag to develop and perform a play about aspects of their lives in their densely populated squatter settlement on the edge of Port Vila. As well as developing a sense of self-worth and confidence, the play has also focused efforts to improve the quality of life in the settlement by establishing a family planning clinic staffed by nurses, providing basic sports facilities and sexual health education for young people, promoting the building and use of VIP latrines (rather than the bush or the beach) and organising rubbish collection and disposal.

Some theatre groups have experimented with the use of "forum theatre", where short plays require inputs and participation from the audience in the form of interventions to demonstrate alternative actions that enhance a sense of autonomy and empowerment. This has proved most useful in small-group situations rather than with the large audiences that theatre groups invariably attract when performing in public places.

Theatre groups have increasingly developed improvised and devised plays and sketches as well as using written scripts. The former are often more appropriate where oral communication is preferred and where participants are less confident in writing.

As well as developing over 50 plays and sketches, Wan Smolbag has produced a number of videos and users' guides, several radio dramas and spots, a book of plays and music cassettes of, for example, songs with environmental themes. These productions can be used repeatedly and widen the reach of community theatre's efforts to promote understanding of environmental issues. Many such products are distributed to schools to support ongoing work to enhance children's appreciation of their environment. As part of an effort to develop teachers' pedagogical skills, sessions on basic drama skills and on effective use of videos have been conducted during initial and in-service training courses and during school visits.

Continuing challenges

While theatre groups have learned many lessons they continue to face a number of challenges, most of which are inherent to the nature of community theatre rather than particular to any focus on environmental education. Key continuing challenges include the ongoing professional development of theatre members, the need for sound management practices and a concern and capacity for monitoring and evaluation.

Building professional development and training

Much of the success of community theatre to date is the result of the commitment and the skills of theatre members. The future success and technical sustainability of community theatre depends on their continuing professional development as actors, directors and play and sketch developers, on their understanding of particular issues and on their capacity to train, support and work with others.

Long-term members of Wan Smolbag have played a key role in inducting and training new members and in training and supporting many other theatre groups. Some members who started as fledgling actors are now confident and competent directors. Others specialize in particular skills such as music, song development and puppetry. While Wan Smolbag actors have received some external assistance, such as during the development of the animated *On the Reef* play, much progress has been made by repeated practice. Although no Ni-Vanuatu member of the group specializes in script-writing, at the time of writing, some have developed particular skills in improvising and devising plays and sketches, those used in the dengue fever campaign being but one example.

Managing project management

Community theatre groups have always relied on financial assistance from other organizations. Besides receiving support from a large number of external funding agencies, such as the South Pacific Regional Environment Programme (SPREP) and the World Wide Fund for Nature, Wan Smolbag has received substantial long-term financial support from the British Government's Department for International Development (DFID). This support has given the group a degree of security, within an agreed project framework, to focus on developing their skills and repertoire and to offer technical and small-scale financial support to other theatre groups. Secure funding also provides the flexibility to be both proactive and responsive by selecting priority issues and planning programmes of work rather than being forced to respond to *ad hoc* offers of support for particular initiatives. Support from an external source has also enabled the group to avoid being perceived as a politically partisan organization.

Reliance on such support requires a range of responsibilities in terms of project management that demand different skills from those usually held by actors and theatre directors. Wan Smolbag's growth initially placed great burdens on the actors and the director, all of whom undertook specific administrative and management tasks, with the latter assuming responsibility for such tasks as record-keeping, report-writing, accounting and liaison with other organizations, including funding agencies. More recently, the group's growth necessitated the recruitment of dedicated administration staff and may, in the future, require the recruitment of staff fully devoted to project management responsibilities. The continued development of management capacity is vital to maintaining funding agency support and thus to the financial sustainability of community theatre. Without external funding, community theatre would be forced to return to being no more than amateur drama groups with much less scope to educate people in areas beyond the immediate homes of each group.

Assessing influence and impact

The assessment of the effective delivery of activities and the achievement of immediate changes in knowledge and attitudes are fairly easy to organize. However, more in-depth evaluation of the impact of community theatre is problematic, particularly in terms of the assessment of theatre's influence on values and practices and in terms of what measure of any longer term success can be attributed to theatre.

Despite this, there is a wealth of evidence, at present largely anecdotal, of the effectiveness of community theatre in Vanuatu. Theatre groups have played a key role in raising awareness of issues and encouraging public discussion of important and often controversial concerns. They have, for example, instigated public discussion on attempts by logging companies to exploit forest resources for the minimal benefit of the communities concerned. This has led to much public debate about fair logging agreements and post-logging reforestation. Wan Smolbag, in collaboration with the Department of Forests, is currently involved in awareness-raising and promotion of a code of logging practice.

Wan Smolbag has increasingly focused on monitoring and evaluating the effectiveness of their work. Two members with specific responsibility for research and evaluation were appointed in 1996 and have undertaken a number of studies, including two on the turtle campaign and on the promotion of sanitation facilities in the Blacksands community, which have an environmental focus. To date, studies have largely focused on reporting activities and assessing their immediate impact. This has, for example, included pre- and post-performance assessments of people's knowledge and attitudes. Similarly, a recent assessment of the influence and impact of the *On the Reef* and *Kasis Road* videos was conducted in Vanuatu, Fiji and the Solomon Islands. The study, which reached quite positive conclusions, was based on pre- and post-viewing assessments with new audiences, interviews and focus group discussions. Assessments of the longer-term impact of community theatre require significant research capacity that may be beyond that available to theatre groups. While Wan Smolbag members responsible for research and evaluation were able to conduct an immediate assessment of the Blacksand's sanitation campaign, and may be able to periodically revisit the situation in that community, any assessment of turtle numbers requires long-term collaboration with organizations such as the Department of Fisheries and SPREP.

Perhaps the main lesson to be drawn from experience and from the studies of impact assessment conducted so far, is that community theatre is most effective when it is integrated with the work of other organizations. In terms of environmental issues, this requires groups to work with the Departments of Forestry and Fisheries, the Environment Unit, the Vanuatu Environment Organization and the Departments of Health and Education, Youth and Sports. In addition, liaison and collaboration is also required with community-based organizations such as churches, chiefs' associations, women's groups and youth clubs.

In seeking to maximize the appropriateness and effectiveness of community theatre, collaboration serves many purposes. This includes selecting priority issues for dramatic treatment, training theatre members on particular issues, organizing pre-performance research and other activities, checking the content of plays, agreeing, planning and organizing post-performance activities, gaining permission and making arrangements for visits and performances and monitoring the impact of particular initiatives. Collaboration also requires a more participatory approach and a people-centred concern for environmental, and other, issues.

The quality and scope of any collaboration is crucial to its success. While there have been many effective collaborations, experience to date has been mixed. In some cases, plays and associated activities are often best performed in the evenings when government extension officers, for example, are rarely working. In others, extension officers may not recognize a need for their continuing involvement, feeling that theatre groups alone are capable of achieving educational objectives. In some instances, initiatives have been so successful that government departments have not

had the capacity to cope. The regular radio broadcasting of the VIP toilet song, for example, resulted in the Department of Health's Rural Sanitation Programme being overwhelmed with requests for help in building such toilets.

Wan Smolbag's collaborations with the Departments of Fisheries and Health illustrate the factors that are important in achieving positive change. First, is the need for a joint understanding of tasks and responsibilities being vital to the success of any partnership. Other factors that are important include the need to start small and expand gradually, to base interventions on knowledge of local situations, to recognize the cultural context without simply accepting values and practices because they are traditional, to involve local people and develop a broad base of support from the start, to use a variety of approaches and to take risks and demonstrate a commitment to change. There is reasonably robust evidence that effective collaborations can make a significant difference both in terms of concern for the environment and for the quality of peoples' lives. Wan Smolbag's collaboration with the Department of Health in promoting VIP toilets in the Blacksands community suffered from several weaknesses but did result in a substantial increase in the number and use of these facilities in most areas of the settlement. Experience to date strongly demonstrates the case for continued support for community theatre and for maintaining government support for extension and outreach services. While theatre groups can support the work of extension officers, they cannot be effective substitutes. Their role is to enhance the scope and quality of extension work. This can only be achieved if the number of extension officers is maintained and if collaboration is properly planned and conducted.

Looking forward

While community theatre groups are not the only providers of environmental education in Vanuatu, they are indisputably high profile advocates of concern for the environment. They are some of the few organizations that consistently reach a large number and wide range of people, including some of the poorest and most disadvantaged people in both rural and urban areas. The fact that they do so in an entertaining, accessible and appropriate way means that effective partnerships among theatre groups, government departments, community organizations and external funding agencies have the potential to make a lasting difference both in terms of environmental sustainability and social justice. It is by promoting a sense of responsibility to care both for the environment and for people that community theatre can best contribute to the environmental well-being of Vanuatu.

Acknowledgements

The author would like to thank all members of Wan Smolbag Theatre and other theatre groups for their energy and commitment in making a vibrant and valuable educational resource available to a wide range of people both in Vanuatu and elsewhere in the Pacific. He also wishes to thank Peter Walker, Jo Dorras and Ian Collingwood for their comments on drafts of this text.

NB

The author worked as the United Kingdom's Department for International Development's Regional Education Adviser in the Pacific between 1995 and 1997. The views expressed in this text are entirely those of the author and do not necessarily represent those of theatre groups in Vanuatu or of the UK Department for International Development (DFID). Any errors, of omission or commission, are the responsibility of the author alone. Any discussion of the content of this text should therefore be addressed to the author and not to community theatre groups in Vanuatu or to DFID.

Contact

Wan Smolbag Theatre can be contacted at PO Box 1024, Port Vila, Vanuatu. Fax: + (678) 25308. Tel: + (678) 24397. Email: smolbag@vanuatu.com.vu

Notes

1. The term used for the indigenous people of Vanuatu

References

Bumseng, George (1995). *Tour report - Wuhuran Theatre*. Ambrym, Vanuatu.

Collingwood, Aleks and George Petro (1997). *North Efate Turtle Report*. Wan Smolbag Theatre: Port Vila, Vanuatu.

Corrigan, Helen (1977). *Promotion of Post-Logging Reforestation in Natural Forest in Vanuatu*. Department of Forests: Port Vila, Vanuatu.

Crocombe, Ron (1994). "Environmental Education in the South Pacific" in Walter Leal Filho, (ed.) *Environmental Education in Small Island Developing States*. Commonwealth of Learning: Vancouver, Canada.

CUSO (1992). *Emi Graun Blong Yumi - Popular Theatre and the Melanesian Environment*. CUSO: Port Vila, Vanuatu.

Dorras, Jo and Peter Walker (1995). *3 Plays for the Pacific (The Tale of Mighty Hawk and Magic Fish, Invasion of the Litter Creatures and On the Reef)*. Wan Smolbag Theatre: Port Vila, Vanuatu.

English, Kate, Alex Harper and Steve Passingham (1996). *Wan Smolbag Theatre for Development Project Memorandum*. Department for International Development: Suva, Fiji and London, England.

Nalial, Edward I.N. (1997). *Integration of Environmental, Social and Economic Sustainability for Vanuatu*. South Pacific Regional Environment Programme (SPREP): Apia, Samoa.

Petro, George (1997). *Blacksands Sanitation Report*. Wan Smolbag Theatre: Port Vila, Vanuatu.

Thomas, Pamela and Alex Mavrocordatos (1998). *Theatre for Development in the Pacific: the Wan Smolbag Theatre Experience (Mid-term review of the Wan Smolbag Theatre for Development Project)*.

Wan Smolbag Theatre (1993). *Environmental Songs music cassette and users guide*. Wan Smolbag Theatre: Port Vila, Vanuatu.

Wan Smolbag Theatre (1995). *Pacific Star video (Toilets or Tourists? play) and users guide*. Wan Smolbag Theatre: Port Vila, Vanuatu and Pasifika Communications: Suva, Fiji.

Wan Smolbag Theatre (1996). *Wan Smolbag Theatre's Turtle Campaign 1995-1996*. Wan Smolbag Theatre: Port Vila, Vanuatu.

Wan Smolbag Theatre (1996) *On the Reef: video and users guide*. Wan Smolbag Theatre: Port Vila, Vanuatu.

Wan Smolbag Theatre (1997). *Kasis Road: video and users guide*. Wan Smolbag Theatre: Port Vila, Vanuatu.

Chapter 4

The Philippines

Environmental education programmes at Miriam College

Angelina Galang

Introduction

The 1986 people-power revolution in the Philippines not only unleashed long-repressed political freedom; it inspired many of the citizenry to be actively involved in national issues, realizing that nation-building cannot be left to government alone. That new national vision also inspired the start of an environmental education network at Miriam College, a Catholic school in Manila.

Philippine history is punctuated by uprisings, the most notable being the revolution at the turn of the century. It was a war against Spain but was lost to the Americans because, under the Treaty of Paris, the Philippines was ceded by Spain to the United States for $20 million. However, while this tradition of courage could not be quenched, it also underscored the division between the rulers and the ruled. The relationship was either one of submissive compliance or tumultuous revolt.

A long history of colonization, by the Spaniards for 400 years, by the Americans for half a century and by the Japanese for four years, had created a populace accepting of top-down governance. Regulations, law enforcement, development and all other facets of life as a nation were left to government officials. The fate of the country rested on the benevolence and virtue or incompetence and corruption of those in power. Indeed, it was this colonial mentality that allowed Ferdinand Marcos to impose martial law in 1972 and supported his dictatorship until he was deposed. The manner by which Mr. Marcos exited is significant. He was overthrown not by another strongman with violence and bloodshed but by people massing in the streets, and stopping the army and its tanks with flowers, rosaries and sandwiches. It marked the start of assertive, rather than combative, citizenship. It was the spark that began genuine self-governance.

Miriam (then Maryknoll) College exemplifies this trend to self-governance. It was, like all other Catholic schools in the Philippines, owned and run by foreign missionaries, in this case the US-based Maryknoll Sisters' congregation. However, that changed in the 1970s when the Sisters turned over the school to be managed by Filipino laity. The school had had democratic traditions and participatory management structures that prepared the faculty for the transition. Administrators were chosen from the academic community. An alumna was appointed the first lay president in 1977, and the rite of passage was completed when in 1989 the institution's name was changed.

The school remains unique in Philippine education. All schools have been "Filipinized", i.e., are administered by Filipinos. However, all other Catholic schools are run by priests or nuns. While Miriam has religious/clerical personnel on its

Board of Trustees, it is the only private school which is a non-state, non-family, non-profit foundation partially managed by the employees themselves.

Miriam College teaches at all levels from pre-school to collegiate, which is not unusual in the Philippines. Internally, Miriam has a culture of faculty empowerment. This empowerment translated into an environmental outreach programme in 1986. That year was Miriam College's 60th anniversary and a year of national euphoria of freedom. With these twin inspirations, a group of faculty members established Miriam-PEACE, a voluntary organization that extends the college's environmental focus to the wider community.

Miriam-PEACE is now one part of Miriam College's environmental education (EE) programme. Another is its formal degree programmes: Bachelor of Science in Environmental Planning, Master of Science in Environmental Studies and Master of Arts in Environmental Education. Finally, there is the Curriculum Integration Programme, the deliberate infusion of the environmental perspective throughout the total curriculum at all levels from pre-school to collegiate levels.

The Organization

Miriam-PEACE started with a small group of faculty members from the departments of Science, Environmental Planning, Behavioural Science and Communication Arts. This combination was based on the philosophy that environmental concern should flow from scientific understanding of issues and must be communicated effectively. Likewise, behavioural scientists were needed because the goal of environmental education is behavioural change.

Today, Miriam-PEACE retains essentially the same character; Miriam College faculty members become participants and assistants in environmental projects or activities. There is no formal membership. The only permanent staff are the Director (who is from the school administration but who works on the environmental programme on a volunteer basis), the Executive Officer (whose work is given the equivalent of a number of teaching units but whose scope of work makes the job virtually a volunteer position), an administrative assistant-cum-secretary and a researcher. The financial and working arrangements are those of a non-government organization (NGO). Except for the salaries of the permanent staff, funds are resourced from outside grants or contracts. Staff work hours are flexible and, often well beyond eight hours per day. An informal Management Committee, consisting of the Director, the Executive Officer and heads of programmes and projects, meet to exchange information, formulate guidelines and discuss organizational activities.

Project proposals are prepared by the Director or the Executive Officer and when funds become available, a personnel-leader, a researcher, resource persons, teachers, etc., are recruited from those who have signified their interest to disseminate EE. When the project budget allows, these personnel are given honoraria, relative to the grant. The Miriam-PEACE "members" are happy when they receive honoraria; they are also happy to do the job when there are none.

The Focus

From its inception, Miriam-PEACE decided on education as its niche in the environmental movement. Its vision is that:

1. as children of God, all people are stewards of His creation;
2. as Filipino citizens, all people should be aware of and advocate the need for ecological balance and sustainable development; and
3. as individuals, all people should practice environmental protection in their daily lives.

Miriam-PEACE believes sustainable development requires a citizenry that has a holistic understanding of environmental problems with the motivation and skills necessary to address these issues. Furthermore, sustainable development of a country must be based on bio-physical features. The Philippines consists of tropical and mountainous islands and development must not tamper with but rather take advantage of these characteristics. Its development must not be forced to fit the mould of other nations, "advanced" though these may be. Each country has its own carrying capacity based on its population's use of natural resources. Finally, Miriam-PEACE believes that as environmental problems result from socio-economic, cultural and political factors in the context of the natural resources of a country, the pursuit of sustainable development must likewise address all these complex interactions.

The Programs

Miriam-PEACE programmes can be classified into environmental education, field projects, and networking and advocacy. However, these three are rarely mutually exclusive.

Environmental Education
The EE programme has three main targets: teacher education, specific public sectors and the general public. Teacher education training constitutes the bulk of the group's activities. It recognizes that teachers, while moulding the young, also influence parents indirectly. Furthermore, teachers are respected, especially in rural communities. They can be the only credible voices in places where local officials do not live up to people's expectations.

Teacher training workshops vary in length to suit the availability of those concerned and are offered in many parts of the Philippines. Summer is a busy period because both trainers and trainees are on "vacation". Three- to six-day workshops are a staple, covering Basic EE Training or Trainers' Training. Educational materials also are being produced within the programme. A 28-volume EE curriculum has been developed for elementary and high schools. Entry points for including EE have been identified in natural science and social studies at both levels, and values education and health at high school. The project also produced teachers' modules based on a matrix of topics and the environmental principles, concepts, values and skills taken up in the respective topics.

Workshops have also been given to business people, grassroots organizations, non-governmental organizations, homeowners' associations and religious orders. The basic EE and trainers' training modules are given context and emphasis relevant to the participants. For religious groups, emphasis is on the spiritual basis of stewardship. For NGOs, the socio-cultural-political implications of environmental conditions are discussed in depth. The focus for industrial or commercial groups depends on the main environmental impact of their activities; for example, waste management for an oil company, sustainable logging for woodcarvers, organic farming for agricultural workers.

The basic module revolves around seven principles or core messages. These are adapted from those popularized by the American environmentalist, Barry Commoner, and have been added to by discussions called by the Environmental Management Bureau and involving leading environmental educators. Miriam-PEACE believes that these principles not only capture most environmental issues but also point to solutions. These principles are:

- Balance of Nature – Nature Knows Best
- Diversity and Stability – All Forms of Life are Important
- Interdependence – Everything is Connected to Everything Else
- Change – Everything Changes
- Pollution – Everything Must Go Somewhere
- Finiteness of Resources – Ours is a Finite Earth
- Stewardship – Nature is Beautiful and we are Stewards of God's Creation

The first part of these pairs of statements are neutral statements, for example "Balance of Nature" and "Change". The second phrase suggests the direction in which action should be taken. For example, since "Nature knows Best", to follow nature is suggested as an undisputable guideline for action. This framework has been shown to be a very effective approach in planning teaching and learning materials.

The design and approach of the modules underscores that environmental education is *about, in, and for* the environment. Discussion is backed by a field trip that exposes the participants to the actual situation whenever possible. Even a one- or two-hour investigation of the items popularly bought in a neighbourhood supermarket can raise the environmental consciousness of consumers. Finally, the workshop's affective objective is pursued through exercises that raise and reinforce environmental attitudes and values. The workshop ends with a statement of commitment from the participants.

Student consciousness-raising activities have included the "Save Manila Bay" banner-painting contest. Here students gathered in the Luneta Park fronting the Bay one Sunday and, with paint donated by a sponsor, proceeded to interpret their messages in bold designs on three-metre lengths of white cloth. Their work was displayed in Roxas Boulevard for a few weeks, bringing the message to thousands of commuters. Miriam-PEACE coordinated the Philippine section of the United Nations Environment Programme (UNEP) contest for students. Staff arranged for the judging of student entries in photography, painting, short story and project-making categories and arranged a display in a public shopping mall. Then, in cooperation with colleagues from Indonesia, Singapore and Malaysia, Miriam-PEACE published an educational book *Let's Protect Our Seas*. The best poster entries in the region were also printed.

Nature awareness camps of varying lengths are run for various age groups using different locations. Miriam College grounds incorporate a tree park and pockets of lush vegetation and are often used for one-day and overnight camps for young children. Two-week camps have been run for college students, teachers and young professionals in national parks in Luzon.

For the public at large, Miriam-PEACE has run a one-hour, regular Sunday lunchtime radio programme for the past five years. It is aimed at parents and families so the programme is not heavily technical. The major item is a serious discussion of an environmental issue with an environmentalist, which is supported by environmental songs, trivia contests, news and a "radio patrol" where student

volunteers call in observations of the environment. Other community education campaigns include: a one-minute radio spot on certain Philippine endangered species, commissioned by another NGO; environmental concerts; t-shirts; and bumper stickers with the message "Mahalin Ang Kalikasan" to remind everyone to love nature. Miriam-PEACE and this NGO also are planning future cooperatively-produced TV spots.

An annual forum on a current environmental issue has been held since 1986, allowing a yearly reunion of friends and workers for the environment. The first was a consultative forum to determine the needs and gaps in the environmental movement. Subsequent issues have included: the environmental perspective in various academic disciplines; the new local government code and its environmental implications; business and the environment; smoke belching; solid waste management; and the Environmental Impact Assessment System of the Philippines.

Field Projects

Miriam-PEACE initiated field projects to contribute to the Philippine's ecological development and to promote environmental education. Hands-on experiences with issues in the field increase the organization's credibility for environmental education. Furthermore, environmental education training is always part and parcel of field projects.

Field projects have focused on reforestation and community-based resource management. In 1990 Miriam-PEACE joined a contract reforestation programme of the Department of Environment and Natural Resources to rehabilitate 50 hectares in a denuded portion of the Sierra Madre uplands in Dona Remedios Trinidad (DRT) Bulacan, a province adjacent to Metro Manila. The site is a two-hour ride and two-hour climb away, located in a thinly spread-out village. Rough as the ascent (and descent) is, all who have gone through the experience feel it is worth being close to nature, being exposed to life in the mountain communities and doing their bit through tree-planting and/or monitoring.

The bulk of reforestation tasks are done by community workers. However, Miriam College students, staff and other environmental groups are involved, to the extent that they can be in one-day field trips on, for example, seedling preparation, planting, re-planting, weeding, or monitoring. Miriam College also uses the area as one of its sites for ecological and social investigation. Reforestation is also undertaken for other groups, for example, the Manila Hotel, the International School, and Universal Motors Corporation.

The Miriam-PEACE project leader in DRT is also a community organizer. She is expected to facilitate the decision-making of the villager so as to improve their socio-economic conditions and at the same time ecologically manage their natural resources. One essential step has been the formation of a cooperative which will go into livelihood projects and help in the provision of credit. Miriam-PEACE teams have given environmental seminars for farmers, teachers, day care managers and women.

Miriam-PEACE was awarded the environmental management of Biak-na-Bato National Park, also in Bulacan. This area was the seat of the Revolutionary government in 1897. There, under cover of thick forests and the long and many-chambered caves, the revolutionaries formulated their strategies. The Park is also rich in natural resources. Most precious is clean, pure water from its many springs for drinking, domestic and agricultural purposes. There is also much in the way of

minerals, such as marble, limestone, guano and clay, as well as many fantastic cave formations, bat species and other flora and fauna that need protection. The site, although greatly denuded, could be used for business, industry, tourism and food production. The challenge is to reconcile the multiple interests, and to empower the rural community living in and around the park to arrive at a development plan that will improve their socio-economic conditions while protecting and rehabilitating their assets.

Miriam-PEACE is involved with the environmental aspects of the Department of Agriculture's Central Cordillera Agricultural Programme (CECAP), a project supported by the European Union. The area for the project includes the Banaue rice terraces, as well as forests valuable for their hardwoods and biodiversity, gushing springs and waterfalls and majestic vistas. It is home to upland communities with a rich and proud cultural heritage, including indigenous peoples who resisted with blood and tears the construction of the ecologically damaging Chico River dams. These upland dwellers are conscious of their victimization by a system insensitive to their traditional ways of sharing and living, but have seen and now desire the comfort and advantages that greater participation in the market economy can bring. While they grieve the damage done to their forests by big logging corporations, they continue their practice of slash-and-burn agriculture and their traditional woodcarving skills, which also have an effect on the forest.

How can these people reconcile their need for development with the need to sustain the natural resource base of survival? What is their vision of a brighter future? Miriam-PEACE hopes that a common vision of sustainable development can be reached through their community environmental education outreach to farmers, women, students, local government, CECAP staff and other sectors.

A recent grant from the World Bank-supported Brown Fund of the Department of Environment and Natural Resources will enable Miriam-PEACE to pilot a community-based solid waste management programme for an urban area, in the parish where it belongs. The objectives of the programme are the usual ones: aesthetics, health, alleviation of the dumpsite crisis, and the maximization of resource recovery. Many communities have gone into this type of programme. As an academic institution, however, we hope to undertake a more scientific investigation of the issue from waste generation to segregation and recycling to collection to final disposal. Another important objective is the measurement of the quantitative impact of a chosen and implemented scheme on the metropolitan garbage situation.

Networking and Advocacy
Miriam-PEACE went into networking and advocacy to influence public policy and public opinion. It links with other groups, usually non-government and grassroots organizations to increase the effectiveness of its campaigns. Miriam-PEACE volunteers make a point of delineating between their education and advocacy functions. In education, while they are transparent in promoting their environmental bias, trainees are encouraged to arrive at their own resolutions for action. Miriam-PEACE sees brainwashing as antithetical to its education goals. In its advocacy, Miriam-PEACE has lobbied with other groups for bills, policies and actions including the "Total Commercial Log Ban", "Ban the French Nuclear Tests in South Pacific", "Anti-Smoke Belching", "No to Nuclear Power in the Philippines" and "Balikbayong" (Return to Native or other Reusable Shopping Bags).

The Partners

Funding has come from a wide variety of sources – foreign and local foundations, business corporations, other groups and individuals. Students, parents and employees of Miriam are consistent supporters. Fund-raising projects have also been held from time to time. The whole school community has participated in two major raffles, buying and selling thousands of tickets. This raised half the cost of a new environmental education centre building with direct donations providing the rest.

In recent years, many Miriam-PEACE activities have been commissioned by people or organizations familiar with its track record and its credibility. These activities include staff training, ecology camps and consultancies in the preparation of education materials.

Has Miriam-Peace been Successful in its mission?

In quantitative terms, Miriam-PEACE's community environmental education work is unequivocally impressive. Countless talks and workshops have reached audiences ranging from eight to 200, but averaging 30. The annual conferences on environmental issues bring together around 150-200 friends active in the environmental movement. Its radio programme has been on air for six years. Miriam-PEACE has produced a 28-volume set of teachers' modules and other publications with collaboration from members. It is about to occupy a beautiful building that will serve as a centre of activity and networking for environmental organizations.

In terms of improving environmental quality, Miriam-PEACE can boast of contributing to the reforestation of about 75 hectares of denuded upland. Although the replanting scheme prescribed by DENR involved the use of exotic fast-growing trees of which some NGOs were critical, the forest succession has brought about the return of an indigenous ecosystem. In terms of structures that can lead to economically sustainable development, a cooperative formed in the reforestation area holds great potential. The people are interested in developing means of livelihood that are environmentally friendly and based on community management of their natural resources.

How meaningful are the above as indicators of success? Miriam-PEACE certainly has done much. Has it done well? Has it made a difference in environmental quality? Has environmental concern increased among the groups and sectors that Miriam-PEACE has reached?

A Personal Reflection

In terms of truly touching the hearts of those to whom Miriam-PEACE has given talks and workshops, we can only pray that the positive comments and high ratings on evaluation sheets are not just expressions of fleeting good feelings. Perhaps there are those for whom this is the case. Perhaps the seeds we have sown have not all fallen on fertile ground. Certainly there are some which have. A recent experience is highly inspiring and affirming. In connection with another project I was involved in, commissioned by the Asian Development Bank, I looked into the environmental education of a university. As I reviewed documents, the curriculum struck me as rather familiar. Furthermore, a teacher I observed was very competent in integrating

environmental concepts into her engineering subject. In our subsequent conversation, I was reminded that her school was one of the first that Miriam-PEACE had given a workshop to in 1992 and that she had attended. She had been motivated enough to develop a curriculum based on the approach of Miriam-PEACE and to work for the inclusion of a subject focusing on the environment in all the engineering majors in her university. That was one seed that fell on fertile ground and grew into a giant tree!

What Makes Miriam-Peace Work?

Miriam-PEACE's greatest strength is its volunteers, because sincerity and commitment are the marks of a volunteer. Also, the teachers have the security of an assured teaching salary at Miriam College, so the financial insecurity that plagues many NGOs is not a worry of Miriam-PEACE. However, this strength is also its weakness. Precisely because their teaching jobs have priority over outreach activities, they cannot readily be asked to serve in workshops. There is little problem when the training workshops can be done on weekends or in the evenings. Weekdays pose a problem. Although Miriam College does have a policy that allows faculty members to be out for a limited number of days on school-supported outreach activities, the match of schedules of trainers and trainees often presents difficulty. However, it is a difficulty that has always been handled through the cooperation of all concerned – the faculty, their supervisor(s) and Miriam-PEACE management.

A very important feature of Miriam-PEACE is the core group which finds support and inspiration in each other. Another is the position of the core group members in the college. There is no question that my position as Vice-president for academic affairs facilitated the growth of Miriam-PEACE. However, I did not go into this work initially in my official capacity. I went into it as the others did – an ordinary faculty member of the science and planning departments. The others come from other academic fields, and as such they could and did inject interest in their own areas. In time, a critical mass of concerned staff has made Miriam College's environmental programme what it is now – not the responsibility of one person, department or office but the mission of the entire institution. From the school President down, it has been given full support. As of last year, Miriam-PEACE was officially adopted as an office of the college. It is still dependent on outside sources for its projects and operations but the school has committed to supporting the administrative staff in lean times to keep alive its outreach work of caring for the Earth.

Miriam-PEACE and its impact on the internal community as well as on the larger society calls to mind what Margaret Mead once said, "Never doubt that a small group of thoughtful, committed citizens can change the world. Indeed, it is the only thing that ever has".

Chapter 5

Indonesia

Community environmental education at PPLH (Pusat Pendidikan Lingkungan Hidup)

Ulli Fuhker

Introduction

Pusat Pendidikan Linkgkungan Hidup (PPLH) is Bahasa Indonesia for Environmental Education Centre, and is the first such non-government centre in Indonesia. It is located near the village of Seloliman, a small village about one and a half hour's drive from Surabaya off the road to Malang in East Java. The centre was established in 1980 when its mother organization, Yayasan Indonesia Hijau (Greening Indonesia Foundation), in Jakarta realized that it needed a place Indonesian people could visit to learn about the environment. The centre gained initial funding from the World Wide Fund for Nature (WWF), various European governments and several foundations, including some that were supported by Regina Frey of the Bukit Lawang Orangutan Rehabilitation Centre. These organizations continue to support PPLH.

The PPLH centre recognizes the growing problems of environmental deterioration in Indonesia and the need to take action. It does this through programmes that catalyse public awareness and motivate people to care for their environment through their decision-making and daily life.

The services offered at PPLH are not limited to any one audience group, but are open to all levels of Indonesian society as well as to an international audience of visiting students, researchers, tourists and other experts. We also seek to include decision-makers and the young people who will become tomorrow's decision-makers. Great importance is given to training teachers, who can pass on their learning. Special programmes are also created for government administrators who implement and manage state policies, as well as for community-based organizations and representatives of the industrial sector. As the centre has become better established, general community education makes up over 75 percent of the work, with the balance being special interest workshops.

In all this work, PPLH looks to traditional Indonesian values that are based on a harmony between people and nature. An appreciation of these values and how they came to be supplanted by materialism in contemporary Indonesian society is central to understanding the environmental education work of PPLH.

Traditional perceptions of nature and the environment in Indonesia

Traditionally, environmental education starts in the very early stages of a Javanese childhood. At this stage the children experience society's relationships with nature

and built environments through their parents and the closest members of their family and neighbourhood. Within most Indonesian cultures, everyone is understood to share a common philosophy, belief and value system, and patterns of perception and responsibilities. These cultural patterns are not regarded as individual variables in Indonesia. Only in metropolitan and foreign-influenced areas has the very fast pace of change led people to alternative choices of values and lifestyles. In more traditional settings, environmental perceptions are still created within a heritage that is based on the longing for harmony between people and nature.

Ancient beliefs that nature's elements are inhabited by spirits, alive not only in a biological sense but also in a spiritual sense, have been passed on through the generations. Such a deep-rooted attitude of appreciation and love of nature originates from those times when peasants were dependent on it for their livelihood. While a rationalist might see this as based on a lack of access to scientific explanations of natural phenomena, others regard such perceptions as proof of a tremendous emotional wealth and sensitivity.

The natural elements are imbued with mythology and values through spiritual, religious and practical experiences. While there are many different Indonesian cultures, most view mountains, for example, as the realm of the gods or protective spirits. In this way, mountains become symbols of positive values and a conduit to the source of life because it is from there, from upstream, that clean water originates to feed the intensively used soils on the slopes of the volcanoes. In Java and Bali the river itself is not occupied by sacred values; only the springs, the source of the water, are places of such worship. Nevertheless, there is a concept of value that applies for upstream as positive and downstream as negative because of what is put into the river as it flows through settlements or agricultural and industrial estates. Sewage, sedimentation from erosion, pesticides and fertilizers, waste and factory dumping turn the river from a source of life into a threat to life. Similarly, the sea has no sacred connotation but is highly respected in Java and Bali where it is associated with fear. It is regarded as the counterpart of the mountains, occupied by the ruling goddess of the oceans.

A shift from this perception of nature began with irrigated agriculture and was accentuated by intensified agriculture. Gradually, nature began to be seen as able to be owned, dominated and exploited. A worldview in which nature was regarded as a threat to civilization which only the ruler could tame became established to support the power-base of developing feudal empires. The ruler came to be represented as a shaman with access to supernatural powers. Myths report the founding of kingdoms to which the ruler was brought by magical means such as a sacred tiger.

The most popular forms of cultural expressions, such as theatre, dance and shadow plays – which remain an important form of education – are based on the ancient Indian Mahabarata and Ramayana epics. These developed during the bloom of feudal kingdoms and help explain why a courtly view of nature is still present in some aspects of Javanese society today.

Contemporary perceptions of nature and the environment in Indonesia

Today, Islamic cosmology dominates Indonesian cultures, and the worldview is similar to Christian and western scientific views. Humans are seen as having dominance over nature; human civilization and nature are separate; and humans take

a rationalist approach to exploiting natural resources. These attitudes replaced the former attitude of respect for nature, and the feudal concept of fear. They are replaced by the naive wish that a civilization ought to emancipate itself from nature's threats and gain total control over the elements. Thus, culture is regarded as the antithesis of nature and nature is seen as uncultivated and (naturally) uncivilized. This viewpoint fits well with the growing trend of urbanization where nature is left little space and is to be controlled.

As the people become more and more estranged from the natural environment, a fear of nature is growing. The myths and legends are still alive. Fear is used as a tool for (mis-)educating children and to provoke good behaviour; frequently nature's elements and the spirits dwelling therein are misused to frighten children. Very few children brought up in towns and cities experience nature in their daily lives. Taken to a forest, the children will stand paralysed and full of fear, not daring to enter that strange territory, even though the most dangerous forest creatures are long since extinct.

Thus, most Indonesian citizens have had little experience of the natural environment and are unfamiliar with concepts of cycles, balance, beauty and diversity. Through this lack of direct experience, people develop the idea that tropical nature grows in an unlimited way and that no extra care or attention should be needed except to cut it back. This ignores the extent to which the water supply, rainforests, mangroves, agricultural soils or human settlements have been damaged. Decision-makers are growing up in cities and their value systems have been carried into each corner of this large archipelago by public media. Television programmes reach even the remotest of the two million people and show natural disasters threatening human settlements while industrialization, modernization and consumerism are screened in brilliant colours to significantly influence attitudes and opinions.

This "modern" perception of nature as a commodity has taken over and gains influence while all the former patterns still vividly exist within the diverse Indonesian cultures. The formerly vivid concept of communal responsibility, common sense and collective consciousness is being replaced by the desire for individual material advantage, and this is seen as the backbone of development. These changing attitudes coincide with increasing population pressures on the few remaining natural realms. The carrying capacity of the natural world is already stretched and results in threats to public health while the individual consumption of energy, water and consumer goods, although still far from western standards, is growing rapidly.

Rather than being a threat to civilization, nature itself is under threat in Indonesia. This situation is reflected in only one aspect of the national strategy for education; that is patriotism. Indonesia is the fourth biggest nation on the planet. A strong centralized state unites the many ethnic groups and protects that unity with force to preserve Pan-Indonesian Unity. A strong commitment to the nation is demanded. This involves an emotional appeal based on the heroic fight for independence and a heritage of great cultural as well as natural wealth.

The Indonesian government has declared its intention to conserve natural resources in order to preserve the nation's identity and national pride and to provide well being for the people who so far have not had much chance to enjoy the fruits of Indonesia's rapid development. However, this view is undermined by the modern Indonesian citizen's priority to take part in the process of industrial development, which promises never-before-experienced opportunities for economic prosperity and

consumption. Few people would embrace a shift in values from consumerism to sustainability if newly gained benefits were to be sacrificed in the process. Unfortunately, the effects that this development will have on nature, fellow citizens and the next generation are all too often ignored. Until the end of the Suharto era, contradictory views were not acceptable as these questioned a system that demanded total loyalty, and it remains to be seen whether the new, democratically elected government will be able to change the direction of national development. The pressures of globalization and trade liberalization that were imposed on Indonesia by the IMF during the economic crisis in the late 1990s leave little room for social and environmental reform.

The role of PPLH in working towards a solution

At PPLH, we believe that environmental education needs to start from another perspective. The emphasis needs to be on what can be gained by shifting to a concerned and responsible attitude to the environment rather than by dwelling on restrictions. The exponential growth of environmental deterioration has long been identified in Indonesia and millions of dollars have been spent on researching, analysing and monitoring these environmental threats, while enormous quantities of energy and human and natural resources have been expended. These have often only led to endless discussions during academic seminars, conferences and local district meetings; sadly, few of these seem to have led anywhere.

What is needed, in Indonesia as elsewhere, is the ability to recognize and identify the problems and to develop a sense of responsibility for the need to participate in the process of change. Building increased awareness allows us to see ourselves not only as victims, but also as creators and participants in the process of environmental and social renewal.

As the first environmental education centre in Indonesia, PPLH aims to raise that awareness and to encourage a balanced – or sustainable – lifestyle for each member of Indonesian society. Appreciation of both the natural and the social environment is encouraged, together with appropriate skills and knowledge to act as empowered, responsible citizens within and together with the community. The activities of PPLH work towards these sorts of changes at a number of levels – the experiential, the pedagogical, the transformative and the practical.

The experiential level

An educational centre has to be attractive and full of life. Easy access for a great number of people is as important as its unique location. The place itself, its orientation and surroundings, reflect the wealth and beauty of natural ecosystems as well as reflecting threats that act as examples. To go beyond mere intellectual perceptions of the environment, we must involve all our senses and strengthen our understanding of nature. If the environment is often perceived as a concentric defined space with us as the centre, the right choice for the place to initiate a change in attitude for that space is of extreme importance.

PPLH seeks to involve those who come to enjoy the beautiful surroundings rather than only participate in a programme. To attract a wider range of people, and to cater to the taste buds of participants and guests, PPLH has a restaurant that is open to the public. Prices for meals and drinks are designed not to exclude any group of people. The same principle applies to the sleeping facilities. In keeping with its inclusive approach to education, the Seloliman centre's auditorium is built as an

atrium, where everyone can have eye contact with everyone in the audience. There is no stage, nor any separation between speakers and audience. Steep steps on four sides provide seating for between 60 and 120 people.

The pedagogical approach

A fundamental belief at PPLH is that talking about abstract global matters only results in guilt and blaming others. Instead of stressing humanity's responsibility for environmental deterioration and invoking guilt, programmes at PPLH are based upon the human right to a healthy environment. Thus, rather than focusing on mistakes, we look for chances to act more positively. Programme participants have found this approach to be both enjoyable and enlightening and highly motivating in relation to improving their quality of life and environment. Neither in Asia nor anywhere else in the world will a demand for restrictions encourage a movement towards positive change.

Thus, one of the centre's basic tenets is never to blame a third party for their irresponsibility, but rather to find one's own way to protect and improve the environment. These start with one's own physical, mental and spiritual bodies – nutrition, clothing, housing, neighbourhood and the undefined space upon which one's activities may have an impact. It is our own personal and professional responsibility to identify, protect and improve upon whatever fields we can access.

To foster active participation from everyone in the programme, there is no separation between teaching and learning as everyone does both. Instead of teaching facts didactically and assuming an attitude of having to transfer know-how through lecturing, the centre invites all participants to share their experiences with the group. PPLH team members pose at least as many questions to the participants as the answers and solutions they provide. In this way, programme participants become resources for their own learning, and their efforts to provide answers for each other provoke a learning process at a deeper level. Rather than "teaching", the team facilitates discussions which allow the participants to investigate issues that interest them. In this way each individual plays a role in creating his or her own education.

Indigenous knowledge is increasingly being recognized as an underestimated resource in the attempt to find appropriate solutions to modern problems. Such traditions and indigenous skills are being neglected and lost in the rapid process of modernization, so PPLH welcomes and values all indigenous knowledge provided by participants.

The transformative level

A basic question we face is how can one change a person's attitudes? What is it that might really touch someone and motivate that person to actively participate in protecting and improving the environment? Changing someone's attitude has to start from one's personal interests. Key experiences that create awareness are sought. However, the appropriate experiences are often very different for people of varying cultures and personalities – religion, social class, formal education levels and family backgrounds all contribute to the personal perception of our living environment. For one person, nature's elements are perceived as a threat; to another, as love for all creatures; for someone else they might be seen as commodities that need to be marketed. Still, people of similar origins and social levels will have aspects of their perceptions in common and, as an environmental education centre, we must address this cultural background.

These personal interests can be catered for by designing programmes specific to people's needs and hopes. Our experience working with many participants has shown us that these include:

- improved personal wealth (ecological balance does not require spending more money);
- improved quality of living (a balanced environment is basic for a quality lifestyle);
- improved personal health (a healthy environment prevents illness).

Such simple, direct and immediate application of measures to protect and improve the environment can initiate real change, albeit on a small scale. For this reason, PPLH stresses practical experience. Starting with concrete steps allows the practitioners to see results that are convincing, encouraging and satisfying. Furthermore, those steps can be replicated, at home, in one's neighbourhood or within the professional sector.

The practical level

PPLH programmes give participants an opportunity to explore nature's ecosystems, cycles and inter-connections within the centre's vicinity. Practical experience is stressed, so the centre works closely and in cooperation with the villages in the vicinity. In this way we are able to demonstrate that traditional garden schemes (pekarangan), ecological farming concepts and appropriate technologies can be successful in everyday real life situations. In return, local farmers experience the benefits and income possible from ecological farming while a recently installed micro-hydro system at PPLH generates more than enough electricity for the centre's needs, and half is distributed to the villages.

Challenges

The Seloliman Environmental Education Centre (PPLH) is a non-governmental organization. It is a non-profit, non-commercial institution that is community-based. PPLH is totally independent and neither the government, nor business, nor any other institution, has access to its organizational and decision-making structure. Thus, we seek support, networking and exchange with institutions at all levels. Many cooperative activities have been conducted and are underway. A common experience for nearly all NGO's is the need for funding, thus their survival depends on the generosity of – in many cases, international – donor agencies. In numerous instances, not only will these sponsor institutions request an adoption of their rules, policies and principles, but they might also dictate or interfere with the design of the projects.

Sponsorship for running costs and building work is difficult to obtain, as it can be as dangerous as it is beneficial. An organization could easily become used to the regular income resulting in dependencies of spirit and substance. Aid may be suddenly cut without warning – political and economic changes happen in countries of origin as well as within the receiving states. Such a cut could prove devastating to the dependent NGO and result in a sudden end to the NGO's activities while the bulk of its dedicated work remains unfinished.

Maintaining self-reliance has always been the basic principle of PPLH. Thus, a variety of income generating activities have been designed to cover the majority of

the costs. Comfortable accommodation is provided and visitors are encouraged to stay overnight to gain the interaction, reflection and experiences outside the scheduled activities that can enhance the learning experience. There is an *asrama* or dormitory where over 60 people can stay at a very basic rate, as well as guesthouses and bungalows which offer more privacy and comfort at reasonable rates and contribute considerably to the centre's income.

The sales of books, brochures, educational material and souvenirs as well as sales of plants, vegetables and fruit, also provide income. Another major income generator is consultancy services in landscape and architectural planning, ecological farming, project cycle monitoring and evaluations, as well as projected environmental impact assessments offered by staff and friends of the centre. Apart from contributing to the centre's income, these services provide chances to take part in developing built environments that provide the first-hand experience useful for educational programmes.

Plans for the future

The Seloliman Centre wishes to set an example that can be transferred elsewhere. Having operated successfully since 1989, there are now numerous efforts to base new initiatives on the same concepts. Existing NGOs are keen to establish similar self-supporting facilities in their area and the Seloliman team is prepared to assist where needed. A network has been established with other NGOs working in environmental education to exchange experience in both the concepts and methodology of programmes, as well as the management of a centre and its facilities. A growing number of institutions from other Asian countries is also interested in working with us to develop mutual motivation and support.

The Seloliman Centre is now planning to set up a network of environmental education centres at various locations throughout Indonesia. A new centre in Puntundo, South Sulawesi, focuses on marine ecosystems. An Environmental Information Centre opened in Bali in June 1997 and will concentrate on water, health and the tourism industry. An Internet CafTheta provides access to worldwide information as well as communication. The Bali Information Centre is becoming the publishing, planning, and communication centre for the whole network. Other locations in West Java, Irian Jaya, Kalimantan and Sumatra are likely to be developed in the near future.

One of the more difficult parts of setting-up a network of NGO environmental education centres is a lack of staff who have the vision and initiative to join the team. The Seloliman Centre provides employment for over 70 full-time team-members and large numbers of part-timers and volunteers. There will soon be around 40 people working for the Puntundo Centre and an estimated 20 will manage the Information Centre in Bali, while the new centres will provide jobs for teams of young dedicated people. The challenge is to find, motivate and train these teams.

Chapter 6

Nepal

Ecotourism, sustainable development and environmental education: a case study of ACAP

Hum Bahadur Gurung

Background

The Annapurna Conservation Area Project (ACAP), under the aegis of the King Mahendra Trust for Nature Conservation, covers the largest protected area in Nepal. The 7,629 square kilometre Annapurna Conservation Area is arguably the most geographically and culturally diverse conservation area in the world. Over 120,000 people of diverse ethnic backgrounds inhabit its steep terraces and barren plateaus, where agriculture and trade have flourished for hundreds of years. Most of the people are subsistence farmers and poor. The area is also rich in habitats for a wide variety of flora and fauna that reflect the land's biological diversity.

The rapid growth of the local population and the influx of tourism in the Annapurna region have led to deteriorating environmental conditions. Concerned over this situation in 1985, His Majesty King Birendra Bir Bikram Shah Dev issued a directive to improve the development of tourism, while safeguarding the fragile environment and improving the living standard of the local people. Trekking tourism has grown rapidly, and over 50,000 international trekkers now visit the area which has led to the building of over 2,000 lodges, hotels and tea shops along the trails.

ACAP was launched in 1986 as an innovative concept in protected area management. This conservation innovation embraces the principles of multiple use resource management, combining environmental protection with sustainable community development. Traditional subsistence activities are woven into a framework of sound resource management, supplemented by small-scale conservation, development and alternative energy programmes to minimize the negative impacts of tourism on the local ecosystem and enhance the local standard of living.

Education for sustainable development

The formal education system of Nepal does not stress sustainable development issues. However, in traditional societies, the informal education system consists of various forms and means that have been practised through their existing cultural values and beliefs. For instance, Buddhism and Hinduism embrace many cultural beliefs related to nature conservation and sustainability issues. Informal beliefs such as worshipping sacred forests, mountains, animals, reptiles, lakes and waters, and stones, reflect a high respect for the natural world. In ACAP, these educational means have been greatly incorporated to promote sustainable development.

The paradigm of traditional environmental education has recently been shifted towards helping people to achieve the goal of sustainable human development. In the context of ACAP, environmental education supports the conservation and management of natural resources along with sustainable community development since rural livelihoods are so dependent on local natural resources. This is because the management and protection of the environment is strongly linked with the question of people's survival. Education itself is not a panacea for natural resources management or local environmental problems; rather it is a means for bringing people into the mainstream of sustainable development efforts.

Education processes become more effective with the formation of social capital in the communities through the institutionalization of local conservation and development committees and women's groups. The issues and understanding *about*, *in* and *for* sustainable development by the communities have been translated into sustainable actions. The actions are carried out on an individual and collective basis. People work collectively when they see the benefits through empowerment of their traditional resource management systems. Furthermore, the education process is strengthened by alternative and complementary strategies linked to the basic needs of people. This has been experimented with in Nepal where environmental concerns and development issues are critical. In ACAP, conservation education and environmental education are used interchangeably and linked with extension strategies.

Conservation education and extension programme

ACAP's grassroots philosophy involves local people in all aspects of the conservation and development process, empowering them with appropriate skills, knowledge, and technical and financial assistance, with the goal of improving their quality of life.

The heart of the ACAP is the Conservation Education and Extension Programme (CEEP). CEEP is a driving force to generate awareness and win the hearts and minds of people toward resource conservation, tourism management and sustainable community development. The success of ACAP depends on the strength of CEEP (Thakali 1995) which is the vehicle through which all of ACAP's activities attain relevance (Gurung et.al. 1995).

CEEP is linked to other programmes of ACAP and involves a wide range of activities in both formal and non-formal education. These activities play a key role in the success of ACAP's major programmes and include conservation and outdoor education, adult education, clean up campaigns, conservation awareness and tree plantations.

Since the inception of ACAP, conservation education has been used as a vehicle for educating the local people in protected area management. Unless and until local people become fully aware of the need for biodiversity conservation, government efforts alone cannot be successful. Support for conservation can be achieved through various educational activities. In Nepal, instead of forcing through rules and regulations, local people cooperate via educational means and the provision of alternatives.

Principles of ACAP

ACAP takes a people-centred approach to protected area management, different from those of traditional parks management systems. Traditionally, protected area management was solely concerned with the protection of wildlife and biological species with no regard for the welfare or the role of indigenous people. This innovative project was one of the first to recognize the role local people need to play in conservation and sustainable development. Local people have been regarded as both the executors and beneficiaries of the conservation area.

The following three principles have guided ACAP:

1) People's participation. To effect long lasting efforts in integrated conservation and development, it was recognized that the local people needed to be active participants and their basic needs had to be considered. Unless the local people became both participants in and beneficiaries of the project, the lasting goal of the project could not be achieved. Thus, ACAP includes the local people in all levels of decision-making and delegates management responsibilities for the conservation area to them.

2) Catalyst approach. One of ACAP's main objectives is to enhance the quality of life of the local people. ACAP sees itself as a lami, a facilitator to bring resources from outside the area to meet their needs, while harnessing the potential of local people for effective mobilization of locally available resources.

3) Sustainability. ACAP embraces the concept of sustainability to benefit the local people. Many developments that rely on foreign aid fail because no provision is made for sustaining them once the donor agencies leave. The completed projects can be neither maintained nor managed by the local people or the government, resulting in a great loss of resources, time and effort. In ACAP, sustainability has been guaranteed by ensuring local participation and contributions in cash or kind for conservation and development activities. For the sustainability of the organization, the government has levied a conservation area entry fee of rupees 1,000 (US$17) for each international trekker who visits the region.

ACAP's programmes

ACAP promotes integrated conservation and development programmes (ICDP) that gradually enhance the quality of the life of the local people without depleting the natural resources. In developing countries people's survival comes first and conservation comes second, although conservation and development are two sides of the same coin (Gurung 1992). For this reason ACAP includes the following major programmes:

Resource conservation
The natural and cultural resources of the Annapurna Conservation Area must be protected for the benefit of the present and future generations. To this end, forest nurseries have been set up, local conservation workers trained, wildlife protection mechanisms set up, and indigenous forest management practices promoted. The promotion of nature conservation has been supplemented through appropriate technology such as solar water heaters, back-boilers, low-wattage cookers and micro-hydro electricity. To save the forest, kerosene and gases have also been used in areas where the demands for energy have been high to cater to trekkers' needs.

Community-based integrated conservation and development programmes have been promoted through the formation of grassroots institutions such as Conservation and Development Committees. Indigenous resource management practices also include programmes to increase the skills and knowledge of the people to allow equitable participation at all levels of decision-making.

The Annapurna region is unique for its rich biological diversity. The status of the biodiversity profile of the region (Table 1) demonstrates the need for protection and preservation of biological resources, which have both local and global significance.

Species	Estimated Number of Species in World	Number of Species in Nepal	Number of Species in ACA
Plants	248428	7000	1226
Mammals	4000	175	101
Birds	9040	861	474
Reptiles	6300	71	39
Amphibians	4184	30	22

Table 1: The Biodiversity profile of the Annapurna Conservation Area (BCP, 1994).

The ACA is also rich in cultural diversity. Restoration of sites of historical, cultural, religious and archaeological importance has been carried out. Traditional and local culture has been promoted through awareness programmes and special events. Restoration of Buddhist monasteries in Upper Mustang, for instance, is a priority programme and the establishment of a monastic school for local people are important ways for conserving the cultural heritage.

Sustainable community development

The community-managed development programme encourages nature and environmental conservation. Experience from Nepal's protected area management system has repeatedly taught that local people's basic needs must be addressed first to encourage maximum participation in conserving biodiversity. ACAP has shared its experience of integrated conservation and development programmes with international conservation communities. An example from Gurung (1993) in a report on the way the project has developed describes how in the first year " we went there, we never talk[ed] about forest protection. We never talk[ed] about the animal protection. We talk[ed] about drinking water". (Gurung 1993, p.23).

In considering the needs of local communities, the ACAP project has become an alternative model, putting people first and insisting on conservation for, of and by the people. ACAP supports local people's initiatives for environmentally sustainable, small-scale development programmes such as provision of drinking water, trail construction and repair, irrigation projects, health posts, and the provision of easy loans for the development of local enterprises and income generation. Women are encouraged in the mainstream of conservation and development, creating a greater role within the conservation movement. For example, adult education and skills

development are provided for illiterate women. Women's groups such as Ama Tolis have demonstrated major works that have benefited many people, including children and socially and economically deprived women.

Adult environmental education is designed for women who have been considered as the primary managers of natural resources. They have the dual responsibility of looking after the family and children, as well as of collecting firewood and fodder, and doing agricultural work to sustain their livelihoods. The six-month course is usually conducted at night, which is the only free time for women. The adult education programme has two major objectives: (i) to develop literacy among the women so that they can read and write; and (ii) to learn more about environmental concerns, women's development, environmental management and sustainable development. Experiences have shown that they have made a tremendous impact on improving their livelihoods by carrying out various community development activities such as tree plantations, trail repair and construction, and establishment of child day-care centres, carpet weaving, vegetable farming, and village clean-up. Many of these activities have been income generating. Their collective actions have contributed considerably to local sustainable development initiatives.

Tourism management

Community-based tourism management is promoted through the formation of local Lodge Management Committees (LMCs). The LMCs are responsible for promoting quality tourism through environmentally friendly services. ACAP also supports the production of educational materials such as brochures, posters, T-shirts and video films to generate awareness among domestic and international trekkers, and to provide hotel and lodge management training for lodge owners. ACAP has set up over sixteen tourist information and interpretation centres throughout the major tourist routes. The growth of tourism demands better management of the environment through community education and waste management.

ACAP's tourism management programme has demonstrated that the adverse impact of tourism on the environment can be greatly reduced. Environmental problems like deforestation and pollution were much more severe in the mid-1980s when only about 25,000 trekkers visited. In 1996, the number of trekkers reached 49,318 but the negative effects were greatly controlled (Adhikari and Lama 1996). Gurung (1995) pointed out that experience has proved that tourism itself is not the problem; the problem is poor management of tourism.

Living sustainably: putting people first

Conservation and development are two sides of the same coin. The notion of sustainable development in the Annapurna region has long been practised through careful and well thought through practical strategies along with the use of indigenous knowledge and wisdom. Being environmentally sound in the modern world means meeting people's needs with conservation solutions (Shah 1997). Conservation of biodiversity is a difficult task, but the people of the Annapurna region, encouraged and helped by ACAP, are saving that magnificent part of the Himalayas from the destructive activities which, not long ago, threatened to ruin it for ever (Pye-Smith et. al 1994).

ACAP's efforts in the past decade have brought a lot of changes in the lives of the poor people and have helped achieve sustainability both ecologically and socially.

The following activities are carried out by ACAP in keeping with a number of principles of sustainable living (Gurung and Macleod 1996).

Principles of Sustainable Living	What ACAP Does
Qualitative Development	The project focuses on community development programmes and uses basic needs of the people as its mission. ACAP recognizes that environmental and social problems are inseparable. ACAP's philosophy is one of conservation for people. Qualitative baseline data used to evaluate the project.
Adopting a Global Perspective	Its ecotourism project uses expertise from around the world.
Ensuring Efficiency	ACAP encourages the use of alternative energy such as kerosene, gas, micro-hydro electricity and solar power schemes as well as more efficient stoves for firewood burning, bijuli dekchis and back-boilers.
Ensuring a Resilient Economy	ACAP's philosophy of people participation in change means that the changes will be self-sustaining. Fees from trekkers ensure that the project will not require a constant injection of funds from other sources.
Ensuring an Externally Balanced Economy	ACAP focuses on education programmes for trekkers to encourage the use of local goods and so reduce dependency on imports.
Community Participation	ACAP's grassroots philosophy of people participation ensures empowerment of the local people to manage their own affairs. Success is noticeable with ACAP's introduction of drinking water schemes, which have been more successful than a previous government-imposed scheme. Local people are encouraged to bring suggestions for improvement to locally developed committees.
Ensuring Social Equity	ACAP's Women Development Programme ensures that women have gained more involvement in decision-making on environmental issues. Community Development Committees are representative of all castes.
Ensuring Intergenerational Equity	ACAP's forest conservation and regeneration programmes, with the establishment of tree nurseries, mean sustainable forest resources. Education and training programmes provide skills for conservation for future generations.

Principles of Sustainable Living	What ACAP Does
Preserving Constant Natural Capital and Sustainable Income	Forest nurseries allow local people to live off the interest of the forest. Micro-hydro electricity, schemes rather than large-scale hydro electricity power, provide a sustainable source of alternative energy. The use of trekkers' fees sustains ACAP's projects.
Supporting an Anticipatory and Precautionary Policy Approach	The traditional committee structure and people participation ensure long term and equitable planning. ACAP's methodology of dialogue with the people ensures a "slow" approach to projects but with more sustainable outcomes.
Limiting Natural Resources Use	ACAP has many programmes to focus on: - Alternative energy and conservation - Educational programmes for trekkers - Reduction of the use of open wood fires. ACAP has also promoted a change in traditional behaviours to reduce the use of fuel wood, e.g., smaller households and the use of warm clothes.
Ensuring Cultural Equity	ACAP's educational programmes encourage trekkers to respect cultural practices. ACAP also manages a number of projects to restore and promote cultural heritage, e.g., the Upper Mustang Conservation and Development Project and the maintenance and repair of Buddhist temples. The philosophy of conservation for development also encourages the revival of traditional resource management practices.

Table 2: Principles of sustainable living within ACAP activities.

The ACAP approach to community-based conservation has received worldwide recognition. This is because the conservation strategies were designed with people in mind. Shah (1997, p. 5) says:

> *No conservation program can succeed if it is divorced from the lives of those it directly affects. It is their well being which must be the ultimate goal of all environment and development policies.*

In the past, the hardship of lives forced people in many rural communities to migrate to urban areas. However, after the establishment of ACAP, local people's efforts have brought dramatic changes. The Ghandruk's Conservation and Development Committee chairperson described these changes:

> *... there was no high school, no health clinic, no electricity; the trails were dangerous and the bridges were poor. Now things are much better. Ten years ago, when the Gurkha soldiers retired from the army, they didn't want to come back here; they stayed in Pokhara. But now they are returning and buying land they sold before. They can see that Pokhara is polluted and Ghandruk is prospering. In material terms, we might not be a lot better off, but the facilities health-care, education, water are far better than they were before.*
>
> (Smith-Pye 1994, p. 35)

Conclusion

The Annapurna region's multifaceted environmental problems have been addressed through integrated, community-based conservation and development programmes. These programmes have helped promote the concept of a Conservation Area and integrated conservation and development programmes in Nepal and abroad. Rural communities have benefited from the promotion of ecotourism and the distribution of income, in particular entry fees from international trekkers, which have permitted small scale and environmentally sound community development activities.

Education for sustainable development has become a driving force in mobilizing the local communities. Capacity-building of the local communities through various educational programmes has enhanced their ability to manage their resources. It has helped them to understand the process of achieving sustainability through sound management of their ecology and environment. Development becomes sustainable when people feel ownership and fulfil their needs without destroying the resource base. ACAP is an outstanding example of how local initiatives can lead to a society that can sustain itself through environmentally sustainable local development efforts. It is important that these initiatives have long-term support, but to obtain this commitment is a slow process. Local communities must put their trust in the programme before making such a commitment. However, the success so far demonstrates that biodiversity, conservation and ecotourism management, combined with community-based environmental education can generate sustainable actions that enable communities to help themselves and safeguard their environment. The ability to manage the environment for sustainable development by the people of the Annapurna region is perhaps one of the greatest impacts of education for sustainability.

References

Adhikari, J. and T. Lama, (eds.) (1996). *A new approach in protected area management: a decade of conservation for development (1986-1996)*, King Mahendra Trust for Nature Conservation/Annapurna Conservation Area Project: Pokhara.

Annapurna Conservation Area Project (1994). *Biodiversity conservation profile*. King Mahendra Trust for Nature Conservation: Kathmandu.

Gurung, C.P. (1993). *The view from Airlie, community based conservation in perspective*. Liz Claiborne and Art Ortenberg Foundation.

Gurung, H.B. (1992). "Environmental Education in Nepal: A mechanism for resource conservation" in *World Leisure and Recreation*, 34(2):18-22.

Gurung, H.B. (1995). *Eco-trekking in the Southern Annapurna Himal*. King Mahendra Trust for Nature Conservation: Kathmandu.

Gurung, H.B. and H. Macleod (1996). "Culture and religion: Important lessons for sustainable living" in J. Fien (ed.), *Teaching for a Sustainable World*. UNEP/ UNESCO/ IEEP: Brisbane.

Shah, Gyanendra Bir Bikram, Keynote Address to the Workshop on "Exploring Conservation Strategies", National Planning Commission and King Mahendra Trust for Nature Conservation, Kathmandu, 20 August 1997.

Sherpa, M.N., B. Coburn and C.P. Gurung (1986). *Annapurna Conservation Area Operational Plan*. King Mahendra Trust for Nature Conservation: Kathmandu.

Smith-Pye, Charlie and Grazia Borrini-Feyerabend (1994). *The wealth of communities: stories of success in local environmental management*. Earthscan Publications: London.

Thakali, Shailendra, "King Mahendra Trust for Nature Conservation's Experience with the Annapurna Conservation Area Project on Assessing the Environmental Impact in the Annapurna Conservation Area". Paper presented at ADIPA Eleventh General Meeting, 25-27 October 1995, Sabah, Malyasia, 1995.

Thakali, Shailendra (ed.) (1997). *Annual Report 1996*. King Mahendra Trust for Nature Conservation: Kathmandu.

World Commission on Environment and Development (1987). *Our Common Future*. Oxford University Press: Oxford.

Chapter 7

India

Our Land, Our Life: an innovative approach to environmental education in the central Himalayas

Lalit Pande

Introduction

The region of the central Himalayas in the northern part of the state of Uttar Pradesh, India, bounded by Nepal in the east and China (Tibet) in the north, is known as Uttarakhand. Uttarakhand covers an area of 51,125 km2 of which rises from 210 to 7,817 m, interspersed with valleys and high ridges. It contains a population of approximately six million people who live in predominantly rural areas. This article deals with the permanent human settlements in the mid-altitude zone (1,000 – 3,500 m).

Though diverse in origin, people that have inhabited Uttarakhand for thousands of years have evolved distinctive life-styles, attitudes and practices with an in-depth understanding of the complex inter-relationships between the mountain ecosystem and the economy of rural societies. The literature, dance, music, narratives and traditional practices therefore reflect an eco-conservation orientation and high ecological literacy.

The natural vegetation is oak (Quercus incana) which allows humus and undergrowth, along with thick canopies and other mixed species, to grow. However, in many areas this has been replaced by a monoculture of commercially useful trees. Thus, not only is biodiversity lost, but soil erosion is accelerated. Greater harm results from the runoff of rainwater which would normally soak into the thick forests and form springs. The oak forests ensure fodder for animals which provide draught power for ploughing and manure to be used as compost in agricultural fields (artificial fertilizers are of little use as most of the land is not irrigated).

The need for timber for railroads in the lowlands, packaging and paper pulp led to the clear felling of forests from the colonial period onwards. A system of forest administration was introduced, alienating the local people from their land. Forests, that had previously been under village management, were demarcated as reserved areas and access to forest produce was denied. There are several cases of peasant uprisings and the spontaneous emergence of women's groups when village resources, especially forests, were tampered with both by the government and private agencies.

The region is the source of the major river systems of the Indian subcontinent and receives abundant rainfall (averaging between 100-200 cm each year), yet the local villages face a scarcity of water. The growth of population and the breakdown of traditional livelihood practices have not only decreased the crop yield (per capita) but have increased demands for fuel wood, fodder, timber and water. The men migrate to the cities in search of jobs. The young look to education as a means of

obtaining "office jobs". Women sustain the economy and perform all tasks both in agricultural fields and in the home. In the wake of a deepening ecological crisis, women's drudgery is increasing.

Several development projects have failed due to "top-down" approaches and the area being remote, hilly and difficult to access. This has led to cynicism and apathy amongst the local people. The advent of a market economy and money coming in as subsidies and remittances from migrant workers has also contributed to the breakdown of communities. Superficial indicators of economic development in the form of ready-made clothes, more imported food and market goods hide the real poverty of the region. It needs to be emphasized that a natural life support system, such as water, cannot really be imported and that the real wealth of a region is in its own productivity.

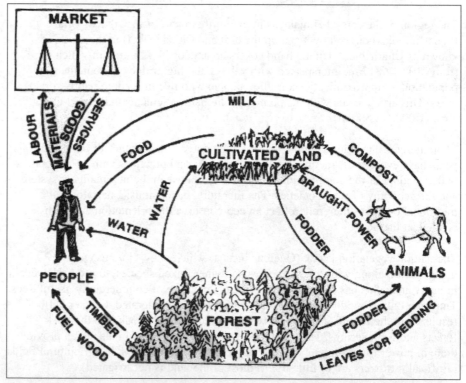

Figure 1: A village ecosystem. Since the forest, or uncultivated land, provides commodities that support crop yields as well as fuel wood, fodder and water, it is described as the support area. The major problem has been identified as land degradation and a breakdown in the sustainable relationships between the various components of the village ecosystem.

It was felt that educational intervention was most desirable in order to develop programmes which examined the livelihood issue in a holistic manner (Figure 1). The aim of these programmes was to help change people's attitudes and behaviour towards their environment by creating awareness about the harmful effects of the present situation and then to help them acquire the knowledge and skills necessary to effectively solve environmental problems, particularly in rural areas. The new educational policy of the Government of India (1986) recognized the need for environmental education and has provided such opportunities. The Uttarakhand Seva Nidhi, a voluntary organization, was selected as a nodal agency for this purpose. The Uttarakhand Environment Education Centre is a part of this organization.

An important methodology that was adopted was the involvement of communities through local village-based non-governmental organizations (NGOs), as well as through the formal education system with the introduction of relevant environmental concepts through schools.

The work can be broadly identified under the following headings, although there are strong links between them:

1. Environmental Education (EE) in schools.
2. Community education support programmes through local NGOs – include pre-primary education, natural resource management, safe sanitation, water harvesting, health education, women's empowerment, gender equity and awareness programmes.
3. Development of educational material, publications, research and training for the above programmes.

Environmental education in schools

We envisaged that the environmental education course for school children should be local-specific, practical and activity-based. We were also aware of the pitfalls of simplistic approaches, such as treating environmental education merely as nature study, tree planting or pollution control. Environmental education had to be something more than general knowledge and had to address the issue of the inter-relatedness of different academic disciplines, whilst simultaneously dealing with various components of a village ecosystem. The village, both as an ecosystem and a social entity, was considered the most appropriate starting point. The inter-relationships of energy and mass flows could be explained in practical terms by the commodities that people use everyday. We avoided the use of watersheds, commonly used in many development programmes, because in our setting a single watershed normally contains many villages.

The existing school curriculum was critically reviewed and discussed. In India, textbooks are prepared centrally and a standard curriculum is taught in the country. In recent years there has been an effort to incorporate some environmental topics into the existing curriculum. However, this is not entirely satisfactory. For example, standard textbooks on agriculture emphasize the use of pesticides and how they have increased production. However, elsewhere, the harmful effects of pesticides are enumerated. Such conflicting messages are unlikely to alter behaviour. As another example, in science textbooks deforestation is cited as a major problem and students are advised to plant more trees. However, this advice is somewhat simplistic. Where are the saplings to be planted? What species? Where will the seeds and saplings be obtained? How will they be protected from cattle or fire?

Similarly, global problems are given prominence. To a child who has never left Uttarakhand or his village, where only one or two buses pass each day on the nearest road a few miles away, addressing the issues of vehicular or industrial pollution will only encourage memorization. Only when students begin to understand their local environment will some action be generated to address their own situation. This will ultimately help restore the global environment.

In designing the environmental education course, we have taken a cue from the grassroots work of various local organizations, especially women's groups.

Furthermore, an attempt was made to identify practices that lead to unsustainable management of the ecosystem and the changes needed to reverse this. It was envisaged that the local people should be able to understand the relationships between various components of the system and themselves suggest ways for resources to be sustainably managed. In practical terms, this meant a quantitative assessment of resources in the village and changing existing misconceptions.

The village is the laboratory for students to learn and experiment. Using basic measurement concepts, students learn to quantify their village resources and calculate how many people and animals could be supported, how much is produced under existing management practices and how much could be produced under improved systems. The theoretical understanding of concepts relating to soil, water flows, compost, population dynamics, ecological concepts, land rehabilitation, types of trees, and so on, is followed by practical exercises in the study village. Towards the end of each exercise, all information is assembled to assess the situation. The whole course is built on the concepts of sustainability and the carrying capacity of the village ecosystem.

The first trial was an18-month course, as an extra subject in Classes 9-10 (age group 14-16 years) in 39 schools over a period of four years and involving some 3,700 students and nearly 80 teachers. Training camps for selected principals and teachers were organized in collaboration with the state education department. Frequent visits were made to schools. Soon these visits became the means of establishing rapport with the students and teachers, giving the researchers a feel for the level of understanding of the students and the problems faced by teachers. This also helped us to learn about classroom pedagogy and educational practices. The programme provided free workbooks to students and minimal equipment like hand tools and measuring equipment. It was important to keep the costs of the programme low due to the financial strain on the school system.

Feedback from the schools and suggestions made by the evaluation committee of the Government of India in 1991 revealed that the course needed simplification. Two things became evident – first, that the programme should be lengthened to five years beginning in Class 6 (post-primary) and second, that it was necessary to make the course examinable. Placing the programme in the regular school curriculum was another important issue.

The Government approved the idea of introducing the course in Class 6 as a separate subject replacing the existing crafts/agriculture period in the school curriculum. A teaching manual and a set of workbooks entitled *Our Land, Our Life* were developed for Classes 6-10. The course is now examinable in Classes 6-8. As usual there are competing claims for recognition and the issue of environmental education has not been resolved. As a result, it has not yet been possible to put the programme in place in Classes 9-10. However, after starting with only 23 schools in 1992, the programme is currently in place in 318 schools and involves some 35,000 students and 600 in-service teachers.

A discussion mode of teaching is encouraged. To facilitate practical exercises, the teacher divides the class into 10 teams. In each team, one student becomes the leader and helps the others complete the work. Children first go through an investigative phase in which they identify and structure the information and collect data from the village. When back in the classroom, all teams pool data to estimate the situation of the whole village. Gradually, based on the database and observations, a plan for restoration and improvement of the productivity of the village ecosystem is prepared and discussed with the local community.

In-service teachers from government and aided schools teach the subject. Since the envisaged discussion method is a departure from the conventional teaching methods in schools, teachers had to be shown this new method in training courses. Review meetings and refresher courses for teachers and principals were also held. Training is provided by our staff and selected teachers who have shown great aptitude and interest in the subject.

It has been our experience that young teachers (age group 25-40 years) are more receptive to new ideas and are therefore easier to motivate. Additionally, middle school teachers (Classes 6-8) indicated that they have more difficulty in grasping concepts during training. However, when they return to schools, these teachers perform better than the teachers of the higher classes. This is probably due to more supervision and monitoring by the education department in middle schools. Supervisory staff in the education department have been trained in monitoring environmental education in schools to encourage their active participation.

Local communities, especially women, are not only requested to provide information but also to help students in the quantitative assessment of available resources. Old people are tapped to narrate the past history of the village and parents become resource persons, providing information on production and consumption rates of fuel wood, fodder, water, milk and food grains. The local administrative bodies provide data relating to landholdings and the forest areas.

For the parents and other community members, an annual work display day is organized in schools, wherein students present their work in the form of models of the village, charts, posters, debates, puppet shows, songs, plays and skits. The villagers are encouraged to question the schools about their work, teaching practices, relevance and the validity of the course on environmental education. If possible, slide shows and video films are screened in villages.

The progress of the course is monitored and evaluated by visits of our staff to schools, the monthly progress reports of teachers, the reports of the education department, review meetings, exams in schools and an analysis of the completed workbooks. The fact that many schools are voluntarily approaching us to join the programme is an indication of its acceptance by teachers. Innovations from schools are also starting to emerge. For example, a middle school teacher developed a method of teaching the concept of altitude to children. This model has since been incorporated in the workbook as well as in the training programmes. The course is reinforcing what students learn in other subjects like geography, maths, science and popular education. The performance of teachers seems almost independent of their academic background, and is more a function of their interest. It is also not necessarily the case that only science teachers can be effective in teaching environmental education.

Community support programme

Along with the course in schools, the project envisages capacity building among local village-based NGOs and community organizers. For too long villagers have been treated as illiterate, ignorant people, identified only as recipients of development projects. Their latent talents, leadership and organizational capabilities have not been given space and recognition to grow and expand.

The approach adopted by us for development is somewhat different to the conventional projects. To build up the capacities of small village groups, people are

encouraged to choose their own projects and learn by doing. As a part of this strategy, we never contact any village community with a "laid-out" project for them. Instead, people contact us with some idea of the work they want to do in their own villages and if the project is found to be feasible, grants are released immediately so as to retain the initial enthusiasm and motivation. The working philosophy demands that the work should not be the implementation of an idea developed somewhere else and forced upon people as a project. Instead, it should evolve with the willing cooperation and leadership of the local people. For example, when the sanitation programme was initiated with the help of village-based voluntary organizations, people were apprehensive about the idea of using it. One woman said, "this is something that only the city dwellers have". Another said, "I thought environment deals only with trees". Meetings were then organized to spread the message of cleanliness and the inter-linkages between water, health and sanitation were discussed. The village women themselves acquired the role of catalysts and helped spread the message of the need for safe sanitation in villages.

When a perceived need for safe sanitation became clear, we had two options. Either we could employ a team of masons and contractors who could install toilets in villages or we could let the people themselves take on the job. We chose the latter option and over 5,000 toilets have been constructed in 10 years in about 1,000 villages. These have not been given as outright gifts, as the peoples' own contribution is significant. This example also gives an indication of the rate at which change can be achieved.

Having seen that local groups themselves can manage projects without "professional input", many of these groups take up new activities with our assistance. There has, therefore, been a long process of partnerships. Some of the local organizations that we supported during initial stages are now pursuing large projects independently and from other funding agencies. We feel this is not only educational, but a true step towards the goal of sustainable development, as these people have developed confidence in their own abilities and now feel that they can manage such projects on their own.

By providing small grants and guidance, more than 200 groups have been assisted in work related to the environment and education. Failures, in general, have been insignificant. A wide range of activities have been included, as experience has shown that a single, or "one-off", activity is often not very effective.

Pre-primary education centres

Pre-primary education centres are run by the village-based voluntary organizations. When the educational programme for children in the age group 3-6 years was initiated, a centre was conceived as a place in the village where children would gather for four hours under the supervision of a trained local girl. Since then, the programme has evolved in such a manner that these canters are now considered as a means of social change, as an entry point to the villages, as community development centres, as a means of creating gender sensitivity and as instruments for promoting individual and social learning. Also, 3-6 years is the best age to lay the foundations for environmental education.

There are added dimensions that make it necessary for such centres to be extremely flexible. Because the villages are scattered and the terrain is very rugged, a school located one to two kilometres from the village may become inaccessible to young

children. As a result, many children start attending school late or never enrol at all. Therefore, the pre-primary centres are also attended by older children, especially girls who bring along younger siblings. The same centre then has to serve as both a play school and a primary school.

Each centre is a community institution and the villagers have donated land, a building/room and even food. We do not provide midday meals to children, instead the parents are asked to provide food for their children which is then shared with others, irrespective of caste and creed.

All of the organizations involved in the programme share common goals (social change and environmental improvement), and this common thread makes it possible to consider some joint action. We provide training and other assistance to all workers belonging to different organizations and there is also a common system of monitoring and supervision. Due to marriage, there is a high turnover of young girls who teach in the pre-primary schools. Despite this, we feel that the effort is not wasted because these women have been trained in issues that help them to become environmentally sensitive citizens.

From only four centres in 1987, 350 centres are now being run by 28, usually, village girls or women. Young men run the centres in villages where educated girls are not available. Supervisors receive training from us and monitor the activities in each centre. They are accountable to the women's group in each village and to the local voluntary organization.

The learning method adopted in all centres is the same – the "playway" method. Children are grouped according to their age and capabilities. The younger children are primarily engaged in activities such as clay work, stories, action songs, language development, numeracy, cleanliness, etc., while the older children are prepared for lateral entry into primary school.

The curriculum adheres to an environmental orientation. Children attending the centres are engaged in activities rich in environmental values and ethics. Children sow seeds, take care of seedlings, observe plant growth, learn to collect and recycle waste material and learn about wild and domestic animals, birds, village resources and so on. Materials for language and numeracy development, songs, stories, poems, slogans and games are rich in environmental messages. These have been developed by us in collaboration with the teachers.

Instruments of sustainable development

In our setting, the best target groups for environmental education are children and women. The pre-primary education centres provide a unique opportunity to reach and influence both.

The experience of these centres gives a clue as to the process that people's participation can achieve and provides a forum where other issues can be discussed. When a centre is established, the teachers and supervisors organize several meetings to help women form groups in the villages. Once the women are ready to act in a collective way, they set their own priorities. Strategies are devised by women themselves to find solutions to their common problems. Included in such strategies are management of resources, education of the girl-child, health and gender relationships, both within the household and at community level. Currently, nearly

350 women's groups are active in environmental and educational activities in the villages of Uttarakhand. The young girls and women have not only developed skills and confidence, but have become motivated community workers.

As the women's groups grow in strength, they begin to identify and take up environmental and socio-economic issues. In response to a need articulated by women themselves, we started providing assistance for afforestation programmes. Many groups started raising their own nurseries to meet the demand for fuel wood and fodder tree species. The people themselves provided the land and labour. The saplings are planted on the village's common land and people take time off to protect and maintain the afforestation sites.

Several women's groups are now shouldering the responsibility of providing guidance to the villagers for installing toilets and spreading the message of cleanliness and hygiene. They identify the beneficiaries, decide on the pattern of assistance and monitor the programme. Projects like rain-water harvesting and revitalizing traditional water sources have also been adopted. There have been several cases of informal forest protection and better management of natural resources. Some have changed the traditional system of open grazing for cattle to stall-feeding and evolved equitable distribution of increased fodder production from protected community land.

The issue here is not the educational centre, plantation or sanitation work in itself, which do have their own benefits, but the process by which the local communities, especially the women, are trying to achieve the goal of people-centred development.

It was a conscious decision to provide no midday meals to the children at the centre. Our strategy is to motivate the parents and create mechanisms to help them understand why the crop yields in the fields are declining, why smaller families are required and how to promote self-sufficiency in the village with least dependence on external feeding agencies. Suitable interventions are then suggested to improve upon the situation.

Recognizing the great shortage of locally relevant materials, 60 booklets, pamphlets and posters have been preparedin simple language and printed for use in schools and communities. Logistical difficulties of transport and electricity have prevented the large-scale use of audio-visual aids. A video for teacher training has been developed. An atlas of the region showing administrative units, land use, relief, watersheds, population density and other data has been prepared. We have been able to tap the knowledge of several local professionals because, as one of them put it, "I am doing this work because I get a sense of fulfilment different from merely academic research".

Reflections

There is an in-built system of monitoring and evaluation of the programmes. Projects are evaluated both at the field sites and within the organization on a regular basis. The programme has also been evaluated by three high-powered committees from the Department of Education, Government of India in 1989, 1991 and 1996. These have helped to guide and develop the programme.

In practice, the development of a grassroots movement towards the goal of sustainable development is not an easy task. There is a close relationship between

rural poverty and environmental degradation. Evolving meaningful strategies to create awareness and develop skills in people struggling for their daily existence requires a sensitivity and empathy for the human situation to help catalyse changes.

Linking classroom theory with actual environmental problems, identifying links between issues reflecting the real world situation and relating environmental education to the local community in a broader social and ecological context are some of the issues that need to be discussed in international fora in relation to projects on environmental education. In an age of increasing consumerism influencing social attitudes and with the international nature of industry and business competing for markets, environmental and ethical issues receive low priority.

Acceptance and encouragement from governments, as well as recognition from examination boards and school committees, are important for the reach and viability of any educational programme. The recognition of environmental education as a discipline will go a long way in its effectiveness. Similarly, it is worth considering the desirability of the "sharp focus" achieved by introducing environmental education as a separate subject as opposed to an "infusion" approach. The impact of educational activity can be perceived only over time and this requires the programmes to be continuous instead of sporadic.

The experience of working on this programme has also revealed certain lacunae. For example, an environmental education curriculum for primary schools (Classes 1-5) needs to be developed, its placement in Classes 9-10 has to be sought and developing models and materials is an ongoing process that requires experimentation and testing. Widening the network of environmental education to include other regions is desirable. We also need better methods for assessing impact and attitudinal changes, both in schools and communities.

The success of the programme in Uttarakhand has supported our approach. The most import gain has been the emergence of several groups and individuals who are active in environmental issues and who therefore act as agents of change in villages and schools. The approach presented here has the potential for adaptation by other mountain ecosystems, particularly in the Third World, but the concepts are relevant to any agrarian society dependent on its surrounding environment for daily requirements.

Acknowledgements

The generous support of the Ministry of Human Resource Development, Department of Education, Government of India for allowing us to innovate, is gratefully acknowledged. The guidance of the late Sri Madhava Ashish, M.G. Jackson, B.D. Pande, Anil Bordia and Radha Bhatt, amongst others, enabled the programme to evolve. Several individuals, organizations, teachers and students have, by their motivation and work, made the ideas a reality.

Part B

Europe

Part B

Europe: The context

Daniella Tilbury

The vocabulary associated with sustainable development does not have a strong presence in education policy in Europe. In contrast, terms such as 'education for sustainability' and 'sustainable development education' figure prominently in environmental strategies at the local, national and European government level. This may reflect the fact that much of the innovative work in the field is driven by environment (and development) groups such as the IUCN CEC European Committee for Environmental Education, the World Wide Fund for Nature (WWF) Mediterranean Programme Office or the OECD Environment and Schools Initiative (ENSI) Group rather than by curriculum, examination or adult education organizations.

The Organisation for Economic Cooperation and Development, otherwise known as OCED, have through ENSI, promoted action-research based approaches to curriculum and professonal development. It has supported projects that have redefined notions of environmental education towards more action-orientated and critical perspectives in countries including Austria, Belgium, Denmark, Finland, France, Germany, Hungary, Italy, The Netherlands, Norway, Portugal, Scotland, Spain, Sweden and Switzerland. ENSI has encouraged the development of 'dynamic qualities' such a initiative, independenance, commitment and readiness to accept responsibility, influencing teacher education approaches to environmental education in Europe over the past fifteen years (see Kyburz-Graber and Robottom 1999). The WWF Mediterranean Programme has also poineered developments in environmental education in the region, mostly in the area of community education for sustainable development. WWF MedPO has worked closely with local NGOs to build partnerships and capacity in communities around Europe and the Mediterranean for almost ten years (see WWF MedPO 2001). The IUCN's European Committee for Environmental Education is another active group which also works in partnership with stakeholders (e.g. with the World Commission on Protected Areas, Europe) promoting education for sustainability in protected areas across Europe (see IUCN 1999 and IUCN 2000).

The concept of educating for an improved environment has been gaining ground in Europe, both at the national and European policy level, since 1988 when environmental education was recognized by the Ministers of the European Union as vital to environmental improvement and declared "an integral and essential part of every European citizen's upbringing" (1988). Futhermore, the European Union's Fifth Action Plan for the Environment (1995) has interpreted education as critical to the successful implementation of environmental policy. The Commission of the European Union considers education and training to be the responsibility of Member States (Hesselink 2000) and does not currently fund international projects in environmental education. However, funds are available to support institutional projects, for example, in Spring 2001 it released $US 1 million funds, via the European Regional Development Fund, to support the development of a further education courses on sustainability (EEEN 2001). It is also promoting education about and for sustainability within higher education through the COPERNICUS

program. The COPERNICUS University Charter for Sustainable Development initiative commits university management, teachers and students to the adoption and implementation of guidelines on sustainability.

At the national level, cases can be cited, from across Europe, to illustrate how government agencies have also spearheaded initiatives in environmental education. For example, in The Netherlands, six Dutch ministries have joint forces to promote sustainable development education through an Interdepartmental Steering Group for Environmental Education. The objectives of their 'Learning for Sustainability' initiative include: bridging the gap between the Dutch policy with regard to Education for Sustainable Development (ESD) and the international practice of ESD; providing Dutch experts opportunities to deepen their thinking about ESD by exposing them to exchanges with international experts; and, contributing to the ongoing international debate on ESD managed by UNESCO and the Commission on Sustainable Development (Hesselink et al 2000). The Group is working on developing new policies and initiatives through a co-operative approach involving several ministries, provinces, municipalities, NGOs, businesses and active community networks.

Other national initiatives, across Europe, include the integration of environmental education within environmental policies. This has lead many countries such as Belgium, England, Finland, France, Germany, Italy, Norway, Scotland, Spain and Wales to design national strategies or action plans for environmental education. Increases in the sources and levels of funding available for practical projects in environmental education from the national and local governments have arisen from these initiatives. There has also been growing financial support for environmental studies and education projects from the business sector, with multi-national companies such as Shell International, BP (recently renamed to 'Beyond Petroleum') and the Ford Motor Company providing the largest sums for schools, youth and community education projects across Europe for environmental education projects. Simultaneously, the corporate sector has began to engage in a learning process towards sustainability - with organisations such as The Natural Step, providing educational programmes and support for businesses wishing to make changes towards more sustainable practices.

Local Agenda 21 initiatives have also increased the profile and opportunities for educating about and for sustainability at the local level in Europe. Local authorities are building the capacity of community stakeholders to engage in social change processes. The Report of the Pan European Expert Meeting (1999) illustrates how local authorities are making environmental education their concern, as they recognise it to be key to stakeholder engagement in strategic planning and actions for sustainability.

It is within this context that community groups, local authorities, non-governmental organizations, national park authorities, schools and universities have developed their own educational responses to the challenge of sustainability. The European contributions presented in the book document some of these responses. The first story is about an initiative developed in a national park in Wales that encouraged students and their teachers to consider planning issues through Sustainability for Real. Children's participation in environmental planning, particularly at the community level, is a vital component of this project. Participation is also a key theme in the second story that describes how a university involved those who use its campus in making changes towards a sustainable environment. It documents how the greening of higher education can go beyond the infusion of environmental

concepts in the curriculum and involve students, lecturers and administrators through action research processes in managing and sustaining their indoor and outdoor learning environments. The third European story documents a Hungarian initiative, funded jointly by the Ministry for the Environment, the Municipality of Budapest and the Soros Foundation. It seeks to promote a sustainable future through curriculum and pedagogical change in environmental education. The experiences documented in this European section reveal that committed and creative efforts in educating for sustainability do exist. They also remind us of the value of sharing our experiences and reflecting upon lessons learnt.

References

European Commission (1998). Environmental Education Resolution 88/C 177/03, in *Official Journal of the European Commission Resolution*.

European Commission (1995). Fifth Action Plan for the Environment 95/C 345/87, in *Official Journal of the European Commission Resolution*.

European Environmental Education Education Newsletter (2001) *COPERNICUS Network on Higher Education for Sustainabiity Continues to Grow*, Hamburg: Technical University of Hamburg-Harburg, Spring 2001

Hesselink, F. and van Kempen, P. and Wals, A. (2000) *ESDebate: International debate on education for sustainable development* IUCN Commission on Education and Communication (CEC), Gland, Switzerland

Hesselink, F. (2000) *Education for Sustainable Development Europe* IUCN: Gland, Switzerland http://iucn.org/cec/

IUCN Commission on Education and Communication (CEC) (1999) *Learning in Protected Areas – How to Assess Quality* IUCN CEC, European Committee for Environmental Education, IUCN: Gland, Switzerland

IUCN Commission on Education and Communication (CEC) (2000) *Learning to Sustain – Promoting Understanding in Protected Areas*. IUCN CEC, European Committee for Environmental Education, IUCN: Gland, Switzerland

Kyburz-Graber, R and Robottom, I (1999) *The OECD-ENSI Project and its Relevance for Teacher Training Concepts in Environmental Education* Environmental Education Research 5(3)273-291.

World Wide Fund for Nature Meditteranean Programme Office (2001) *Across the Waters Project*. Mediterranean Programme Office Barcelona: WWF MedPO.

Pan European Expert Meeting (1999) *Environmental Education and Sustainable Development*. Soesterberg 27-29 January 1999, Dutch Council for Sustainable Development, Amsterdam.

Chapter 8

Wales

Sustainability for real: a national park initiative in environmental education

David Brinn and Jane Wright

Introduction

The concept of a "National Park" was first put into practice in 1872 when the United States established Yellowstone as a protected area. Since then, the National Park concept has spread throughout the world with most countries now having areas designated as protected landscapes. However, these areas vary in the way they are established and managed.

The English and Welsh National Parks, established under the 1949 Act of Parliament, differ from the earlier American Yellowstone model in a number of ways:

- they are cultural landscapes rather than uninhabited natural areas and the National Park environments have been considerably modified through human activity over thousands of years;
- they are places where people live and work, as well as places where people visit;
- most of the land is in private ownership; and
- decisions which affect the use of the Park are not vested exclusively in the National Park Authority.

The above circumstances have meant that the successful management of these National Parks greatly depends upon the understanding and support of their local communities. It is now widely recognized that a form of partnership between those who manage the Parks and those who live in them is essential if the aims of the National Parks are to be achieved. These aims include nature conservation, promoting opportunities for the understanding and enjoyment of the Park, together with fostering the economic and social well-being of the local communities (Environment Act 1995, pp. 86-87).

Sustainable Development: a participatory concept

The experiences presented in this chapter are the result of a Brecon Beacons National Park initiative in environmental education. This educational initiative intends to provide a foundation for students in environmental planning, decision-making and participation at the local level. It is based on the belief that sustainable development requires citizens who understand and care for the environment and play an active role in its management.

Roger Hart (1997) believes that children's environmental education needs to be brought into line with the principles and practice of local community participation in all countries and with all communities. He argues that:

> Only through direct participation can children develop a genuine appreciation of democracy and a sense of their own competence and responsibility to participate. The planning, design, monitoring and management of the physical environment is an ideal domain for the practice of children's participation; it seems to be clear for children to see and understand many social problems. We need children to become highly reflective, even critical participants in environmental issues in their own communities. We need them to think as well as act local while also being aware of the global issues.
>
> (Hart 1997, p. 3)

Sustainability for Real embraces these environmental education principles and explores how children can begin to play an active role in the management of their environments. It does this through developing active learning strategies which elicit individual responses from each pupil and encourage participatory learning.

Participation in the national park context

The Brecon Beacons National Park, which was designated in 1957, covers an area of 519 square miles. It is unusual in that its southern edge traces the boundary of the South Wales industrial belt, and its northern edge is in rural mid-Wales. Brecon, which has a population of 7,500, is the Park's largest town. Over 32,000 people live in the Brecon Beacons National Park. Agriculture exerts a dominant influence on the Brecon Beacon's landscape with almost one million sheep in the Park. Traditionally, the tourist industry, the Armed Forces and forestry business have been important employers, although now many Park residents are increasingly finding work in the commercial sector and choosing to commute to nearby towns and cities outside the Park.

The Brecon Beacons National Park Authority approves or rejects planning applications for development. In common with other national parks, it has experienced problems in its relationship with the local communities. Many local people perceive the system as unnecessarily restrictive – although there are, in fact, very few differences between the development control powers of the National Park Authority and other local authorities in England and Wales. The problem is exacerbated by the fact that many people do not understand the planning system, often mistrust it and generally feel excluded from the decision-making processes which underpin it. The National Park Authority, well aware of this situation, is determined to do what it can to democratize the system not just through public consultation, but through public participation.

One of the key responsibilities of the National Park Authority is the production of the Local Plan for its area. This document sets out policies for managing the Park and guides the future use and development of land. The document is consulted when planning applications are considered.

In 1993, the Brecon Beacons National Park Authority produced a new Local Plan, which established the strategies for running the Park over a five-year period. The document set out a vision for the future based on:

> a harmony between the protection and enhancement of the environment and the
> economic, social, cultural and recreational requirements of residents and visitors.
> (Brecon Beacons National Park Committee 1993, p. 6)

It drew upon important international documents such as Caring for the Earth (IUCN,
UNEP, WWF 1991) to develop its concept of sustainability. Underlying the new
Local Plan is a recognition that living sustainably depends on accepting a duty to
seek harmony with other people and with nature (IUCN, UNEP, WWF 1991, p.8).
In qualifying its vision statement the Local Plan stated that:

> Achieving this harmony will require a commitment to environmentally sustainable
> development and the highest standards of land management.
> (Brecon Beacons National Park Committee 1993, p. 6)

The Fourth World Congress on National Parks and Protected Areas, held in
Venezuela in 1992 culminated in the Caracas Declaration. This Declaration was a
commitment to support protected areas and included an action plan to guide
managers toward achieving this objective. One Action Point was to:

> Seek the support of local communities in promoting protected areas by offering
> opportunities for influencing decision-making, for example through representation
> on local protected area management boards and at public debates on management
> issues.
>
> (IUCN 1993, p. 224)

The Local Plan acknowledges the importance of community participation in
working toward sustainable development, recognizing that it is critical for the
successful and harmonious management of the Park. It cites:

> Communities and citizens' groups provide the most readily accessible means for
> people to take socially valuable action as well as to express their concerns.
> Properly mandated, empowered and informed communities can contribute to
> decisions that affect them and play an indispensable part in creating a securely
> based sustainable society.
>
> (IUCN, UNEP, WWF 1991, p. 11)

Towards sustainable development: planning for real

In 1994, and in response to the new Local Plan, the Brecon Beacons National Park
Authority set up a Sustainability Working Group to consider how best to develop
and promote the concept of sustainable development in its operations. However,
progress was slow as a result of a major re-organization of local government and so
the pre-occupation was with restructuring, rather than with the development of local
Agenda 21 initiatives.

Subsequently, at one of its meetings the Sustainability Working Group agreed that it
was desirable to start at least one practical project whilst it continued to discuss
strategic initiatives. A project involving school children was seen as a useful
springboard for initiating activities in a wider context. The National Park Authority
had recently undertaken a Planning for Real initiative which was an attempt at
involving the local community in decision-making processes. It was felt that a
similar programme could be used for introducing sustainability issues into planning.

A technique known as Planning for Real was developed to improve the process by
which communities are involved with Local Plan preparation. The method was

pioneered during a consultative exercise in the Dalmarnock Estate in Glasgow, Scotland and has since been developed by the Neighbourhood Initiatives Foundation (1977). In 1993, the Brecon Beacons National Park adapted this method to suit local contexts and used it in 39 communities during the preparation of the Local Plan. The National Park Authority's Planning for Real initiative involved inviting people to the local community centre, village hall or school. A large-scale map was laid out on a table in the centre of the hall, and a series of posters placed on the walls helped guide discussion toward particularly relevant issues. Residents were asked to tick boxes on the posters and attach coloured pins, flags and small model houses to the map to indicate their opinions about the various issues. Some examples of these issues were: whether there was a need for additional housing in the village; whether the village was experiencing problems with traffic; and whether tourism should be encouraged in the area. By the end of each meeting there was a better understanding of local feelings towards development, which allowed for a more focused Local Plan (Jones and Thomas 1995).

Some schoolteachers who had participated in the Planning for Real meetings asked if their pupils could be shown how the initiative worked. As a result, the Park's Education Officer and Local Plan Officer developed a children's version of Planning for Real. The programme was piloted in a local junior school where it became clear that the children understood the issues and had important contributions to make to the planning debate. The pupils quickly exhausted the children's version and turned their attention to the adult one, which proved to be more to their interest. In considering local housing needs, for example, the children proposed that there should be: houses for people who have just got married and have not got much money but want to stay in the village. In discussing local shops they recognized that a chemist's shop was important because old people need to get pills and medicines. Subsequently, Planning for Real with school children was used in a number of schools across the National Park. The experience demonstrated how children of nine and ten years of age are capable of thinking about their local area, its problems and potential in a mature way (Brinn and Wright 1996a). They also enjoyed the challenge and experience of discussing real situations.

Sustainability for real: the thinking

In the early 1990s, consultants were engaged to study the effectiveness of various aspects of management in the National Parks (Kayes and Flood 1994). Education Services formed part of this brief and it soon discovered that measuring the efficiency and impact of the education activities was problematic. This raised questions about the achievements and effectiveness of education activities within the Brecon Beacons National Park.

Traditionally the park's educational role was concerned with providing information about the park and its management (which would, hopefully, foster understanding and support) and developing understanding of the countryside through formal and informal activities. The impact of the park's educational efforts in this field had not been assessed. There were, however, grounds for questioning whether much was being achieved. First, academics had drawn attention to the failure of conventional environmental education approaches in addressing environmental problems. They were questioning existing forms of environmental education and argued that it needed to evolve into a broader focus that incorporated notions of sustainability (Orr 1992; Tilbury 1995). Others such as Ian Mercer, a former National Park Officer at the Dartmoor National Park who had recently become Chief Executive of the

Countryside Council for Wales, also voiced concern about the impact of environmental education:

> After all the efforts by thousands of teachers across the educational spectrum, from generalists in primary school to specialists at university – and even more specialised effort in field centres and, say, agricultural colleges, where have we got to with universal environmental understanding? The answer is not far – or certainly not far enough.
>
> (Mercer 1994, p.26)

Second, at a more fundamental level, it was clear that knowledge and understanding alone were not sufficient to promote appropriate environmental decisions. Evidence from other fields such as energy conservation behaviour (Constanzo et al 1986), breast cancer examination (Bennett et al 1983) and clean air legislation (Berry 1993) has illustrated this point.

As a result, a number of Park Education Officers began to question the effectiveness of conventional environmental education programmes – both in the national and in the Park-specific context. The existing programmes had produced some notable successes: countryside visits generally increased children's understanding of and appreciation for the countryside; field-studies enhanced scientific knowledge; the role of the National Parks was better understood; and the behaviour of school and university groups visiting the countryside had improved. However, there was no obvious correlation between increased awareness and understanding and commitments to taking positive action to address environmental problems at the local level. Although the programmes have raised the standards of knowledge and understanding amongst pupils and students, young people do not seem to join the park's volunteer groups nor do they turn up to community consultation meetings. Some Education Officers felt that education programmes were failing to persuade young people to participate.

From the National Park perspective, there seemed to be merit in adopting a new approach. Planning for Real with school children had been a successful first step toward addressing some of the above issues and the time had now come to develop this initiative further, so as to incorporate sustainability issues.

Sustainability for real: the programme

In 1995, the Park's Education Officer prepared a short discussion paper for the Sustainability Working Group which outlined some suggestions as to how children could be introduced to sustainability issues (Brinn 1995). The paper drew upon new educational approaches that favoured an integrated approach to environment and development concerns. Associated with this approach was a new term: environmental education for sustainability (Meadows 1990; Fien 1995; Smyth 1995; Tilbury 1995). It was within this context that techniques were developed that would enable children to explore the connections between development and the environment in a way that was not just enjoyable, but also relevant to the children in their everyday lives. Activities were piloted in local junior schools with support and advice from the teachers. After several months of trials the most successful of the activities were distilled into a programme which became known as Sustainability for Real. The programme was fine-tuned following its successful use in nine primary schools (Wright 1995; Brinn 1996; Brinn & Wright 1996b). Sustainability for Real was conducted in three steps: an introductory session, an environmental forum, and a debriefing session.

Introductory session

This session opened with a questionnaire for pupils which explored their knowledge and perceptions of environmental issues. The purpose of this exercise was to obtain a snapshot of the children's understanding, attitudes and dispositions before any activities took place. The pupils also provided a benchmark for comparison at the end of the final session when the questionnaire was repeated.

Immediately after this session the children were invited to discuss a number of environmental concepts that were raised in the questionnaire. The teacher (or activity leader) introduced the concepts and facilitated a discussion, asking the children to consider their feelings about the local environment, the links between their lifestyles and what happens in other countries, their thinking about how to begin to solve environmental problems and their attitudes toward taking action themselves.

The children were then given an illustrated presentation that explained some of the issues that were raised during the Rio Earth Summit. These included pollution, biodiversity loss, methods of food production, poverty and consumerism. The presentation was interactive and the children made observations and asked questions. The aim of this talk was to encourage children to interpret the environment in a multi-dimensional way, incorporating physical, economic and social considerations.

The linkages between what is done locally and what happens globally were explored. The teacher went on to discuss how our choices affect not just our own lifestyles but those of all people throughout the world. This was an attempt to make connections between personal actions and global environmental problems.

The energy activity that followed was designed to show the children that balancing development and environmental concerns can be complex and that even the best option is unlikely to be a perfect one. The children were introduced to issues related to electricity generation, including nuclear, fossil fuel and wind-power options, as well as to energy conservation measures. They were encouraged to make the connection between their use of electricity as they watched TV or played computer games, and other events such as strip-mining of coal, oil tankers plying the oceans, acid precipitation and wind turbines being built on hilltops. The children were then divided into four teams (Nuclear Team, Fossil Fuel Team, Wind Energy Team and Energy Conservation Team) to play a card game based on energy options. The game was developed with assistance from the University of Hertfordshire. Essentially, each team had to claim cards appropriate to its energy option. Some cards highlighted advantages, others disadvantages and an environmental costing mechanism illustrated the lack of a single perfect choice.

The environmental forum

The next component of our programme, the Environmental Forum, sought to encourage action. An Environmental Forum is a mechanism that allows citizens to influence decisions relating to environmental issues. Our aim was to give children the opportunity to think about their own values and those of others through a participatory activity. We also intended to stimulate pupils' desire to participate in consultative processes in the future.

On the day of the Environmental Forum, a large-scale map that clearly showed the sites of some proposed developments was set up. Small wooden models of windmills and a factory building were used to pinpoint the development sites.

Before the session started, the teacher explained to the children what an Environmental Forum was. In this particular case, it was a mechanism for gauging local opinion about three proposed developments that would impact upon the local environment if they were allowed to be built. The teacher took the role of a Councillor and initiated the Forum by explaining that the National Park Authority or Local Council would use their decisions to help the Planning Committee deliberate over the proposals. The first proposal was then discussed and the child who was role-playing the developer was invited to explain the scheme using the map and models. The other children, in role, then questioned the developer, making points for and against the scheme. After a reasonable debate, when all viewpoints had been expressed, a vote was taken to determine whether the majority view was for, or against, the proposal. The Councillor then promised to convey the results of the vote to the Planning Committee. The other proposals were then considered in the same fashion. The three proposals were:

- the construction of a wind farm on a hillside above the town;
- building a plant in the town for recycling metal, glass and plastic; and
- using European funding to either extend the town car park or to subsidize a passenger bus service.

Great care was taken over the selection of characters for the role-play. A plausible cross-section of people, from deeply concerned conservationists to young people anxious to secure employment from the proposed developments, were represented in the roles.

The debriefing

At the end of the Environmental Forum, the children were asked to reflect upon the sessions, and identify what they had learned and whether or not the experience had influenced their inclination to take action to help remedy some of the problems. At the end, as a final activity, the children were asked to complete the questionnaire once more.

During the debriefing sessions the children commented on how much they enjoyed expressing their views to adults who not only listened carefully to what they said but also wrote down many of their comments. This is an important point, as Satterthwaite et al (1996), have indicated:

> ... as long as the children feel that adults listen to their conclusions and engage in a dialogue, the benefits to their sense of "ownership" of the community are great.

One child said, "I understand more about politics now". When questioned further about this statement she explained that ordinary people could take part in making decisions. Another child said, "I feel more for the environment", and many of them said that they would take action; for example, through recycling the things that they used as a step toward helping to improve the environment.

Sustainability for real: children's responses

The questionnaire produced some interesting responses. In general, the children were worried about environmental problems and were pessimistic about the likelihood of improvement. It was also noticeable both from the questionnaire results and the subsequent discussions that children feel what Cullingford (1996) has described as "personal animosity" towards some conditions. Dog dirt and broken

glass in their playground seem to be more of an issue for some children than the loss of tropical rainforest. School and television were cited as important sources of information about the environment.

The open discussions that took place after the questionnaire had been answered suggest that a degree of caution needs to be exercised over the interpretation of results of the questionnaires. For example, according to the results, children tend to regard the environment as the "green horizon" around their school or home. People and socio-economic concerns do not seem to figure much in their perceptions. However, in open discussion, the children soon show that they can understand the connections among the physical, social and economic environments.

Conclusion

From the National Park's point of view, Sustainability for Real has been successful in a number of ways. First, it introduced children to some of the environmental problems that we are facing within the Park, especially common conflicts of interest. It does so in a way that addresses the complexities involved through giving consideration to environmental, economic and social factors. It also demonstrates that solutions are not straightforward and should be approached in a holistic way.

Second, the children said that they enjoyed the role-playing and that they would like to be involved in consultation exercises such as an Environmental Forum when they grew up. They have been exposed to some of the skills involved and could be seen to be growing in confidence as the exercise unfolded. The development is a feature of active or participatory learning in which confidence "creates a climate within the classroom that explicitly values and affirms each individual and encourages pupils to take responsibility for their own learning" (Tilbury 1995, p. 204).

Finally, this type of activity contributes to education for empowerment. Empowerment is critical for any dynamic to improve local and global environments. As Hart explains:

> ... children need to understand the right of all persons to have a voice in establishing a healthy and meaningful life for themselves on this planet... this can be achieved only through frequent experiences with direct democratic participation in institutional settings . . . in this way, children can come gradually to construct authentic participatory democracies as adults.
>
> (Hart 1997, p. 192)

We are aware that this project has been tested in a relatively small number of schools in one part of the country and that it is difficult to evaluate its impact in other local areas. However, we think it is a potentially exciting and effective programme which can provide a way into teaching about action for the environment rather than simply about the environment. For this reason, we are investing in the development of a teaching pack based on Sustainability for Real. We also hope that our experience might encourage others to develop the project further.

References

Bennett, S.E., R.S. Lawrence, K.H. Fleischmann, C.S. Gifford, and W.V. Slack (1983). "Profile of Women Practicing Breast Self-examination" in *Journal of the American Medical Association*, (249):488-491.

Berry, R.J. (1993). "Ethics, Attitudes and Environmental Understanding for All" in *Field Studies*, 8 (2):245-255.

Brecon Beacons National Park Committee (1993). *National Park Plan* Third Edition (1993 - 98). Brecon Beacons National Park Committee: Brecon, UK.

Brinn, D. (1995). Agenda 21: *A project for schools. Annex 7 National Park Officer's Report to Committee*. Brecon Beacons National Park Committee: Brecon, UK.

Brinn, D. (1996). "Sustainability for Real: An initiative for raising environmental understanding in children" in *Environmental Education*, 51, Spring, 29.

Brinn, D. and J. Wright (1996a). *Environmental Education for Sustainability: A view from the National Park Authority*. Education Service Report 1996/1. Brecon Beacons National Park Authority: Brecon, UK.

Brinn, D. and J. Wright (1996b). "Sustainability for Real" in *European Bulletin Nature and National Parks*, 34 (128):9-11.

Constanzo, M., D. Archer, E. Aronson and T. Pettigrew (1986). "Energy Conservation Behaviour: the difficult path from information to action" in *American Psychologist*, 41(5):521-528.

Cullingford, C. (1996). "Children's Attitudes to the Environment" in G. Harris and C. Blackwell, *Environmental Issues in Education*. Arena Publishing: Aldershot, UK.

Fien, J. (1995). "Teaching for a Sustainable World: The environmental and development education project for teacher education" in *Environmental Education Research*, 1(1):21-33.

Hart, R. (1997). *Children's Participation: The theory and practice of involving young citizens in community development and environmental care*. UNICEF/Earthscan: London.

IUCN (1993). *Parks and progress: 4th world congress on national parks and protected areas*. IUCN: Washington D.C., USA.

IUCN (1994). "Creating the climate for success: public support for protected areas" in *Parks for Life: action for protected areas in Europe*. IUCN: Gland, Switzerland.

IUCN, UNEP, WWF (1980). *World conservation strategy: living resource conservation for sustainable development*. IUCN: Gland, Switzerland.

IUCN, UNEP, WWF (1991). *Caring for the earth: a strategy for sustainable living*. IUCN: Gland, Switzerland.

Jones, T. and H. Thomas (1995). "Beacons Planners Get Real in Rural Plan Consultation" in *Planning*, Feb 1104.

Kayes, R and M. Flood (1994). "Final Report of the PIMS Pilot Project" in *Critical Environment Review Consultancy*. Oxford.

Meadows, D. (1990). *Harvesting one-hundredfold*. UNEP (United Nations Environment Programme): Kenya.

Mercer, I. (1994). "The Sole Arena in Which All Else Happens" in S. Sterling, *Annual Review of Environmental Education: On the fringe of the machine*. Council for Environmental Education, Reading. 26.

Neighbourhood Initiatives Foundation (1977). *Planning for real pack*. NIF: Telford.

Orr, D. (1992). *Ecological literacy: education and the transition to a post-modern world*. State University of New York Press: New York.

Satterthwaite, D., R. Hart, C. Levy, D. Mitlin, D. Ross, J. Smit and C. Stephens (1996). *The environment for children*. UNICEF/Earthscan: London.

Smyth, J.C. (1995). "Environment and Education: A view of a changing scene" in *Environmental Education Research*, 1 (1):3-20.

Tilbury, D. (1995). "Environmental Education for Sustainability: Defining the new focus of environmental education in the 1990s" in *Environmental Education Research*, 1(2):195-212.

Wright, J. (1995). "Environmental Education" in *Planning*, (8), 10. Wales.

Chapter 9

Spain

Learning in sustainable environments: the greening of higher education

Susana Calvo Roy, Javier Benayas and José Gutiérrez Pérez

Introduction

To improve environmental quality and standards of socio-economic development, we need to critically reflect upon and promote lifestyles that respect nature's cycles and resources. The process of environmental education provides us with a tool for questioning and reflecting upon our lifestyle choices, professional activities as well as social and institutional structures.

Despite its potential for transformation, environmental education at the university level is mostly interpreted as the infusion of environmental concepts into the curriculum. Few universities involve the learner in a critical reflective process to assess their environmental footprints or in actively improving their environments. This chapter describes an eco-auditing initiative which attempted to actively involve the learner in assessing, managing and improving their indoor and outdoor learning areas.

The potential of eco-audits in educational institutions

Institutions can monitor and attempt to lighten their impact on the physical environment through eco-auditing. This process is an important educational tool that can benefit the teaching and management of change towards sustainable development in educational institutions. Although similar to business audits, eco-audits adopt more process and participatory objectives. Through them, schools and universities can become models for the promotion of sustainable development in wider society.

The goal of environmental auditing in the management of universities, and other learning institutions, is to develop and establish environmentally friendly practices that can be sustained through quality control procedures. On the other hand, an educational audit is considered an intrinsically pedagogical procedure, directed towards the improvement of: environmental conditions, management processes and organizational patterns. In this type of auditing, it is essential that all the individuals who live, work or use these environments are involved in participatory processes to achieve environmental standards.

The auditing of learning institutions described here as eco-audits, goes beyond a mere validation of the existence of mechanisms which reach environmentally friendly standards. The audit identifies guidelines for change within the organization's management patterns. It attempts to develop strategies for the management of change towards the intended transformation, based on the analysis

of needs and the action priorities chosen. They are systematic research-and-action processes that require all those involved to plan and think together. Figure 1 depicts the different stages of eco-auditing, starting with an initial diagnosis, followed by the planning and design of strategies; this leads to the appropriate environmental actions and the evaluation of achievements.

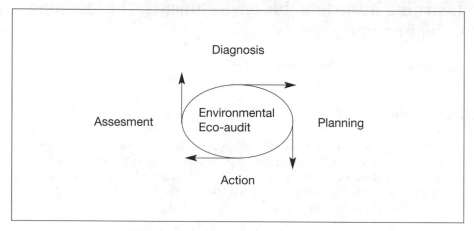

Figure 1: The different stages of eco-auditing

At the first stage participants work on the diagnosis of the institution's environmental performance. They examine the institution's use and management of spaces and their impact on bio-climatic parameters. They consider how the design of buildings influences performance and look at the use of adequate building materials, examine ergonomic criteria for furniture and the control of variables such as cleanliness, lighting, ventilation, soundproofing and availability of green areas. This initial stage also requires a review of the inputs and resources used so as to arrive at an overall assessment of the environmental impact of the institution. It also involves an examination of how environmental issues are dealt with in curricular and extracurricular activities.

Generally, eco-audits tackle the examination of the following environmental aspects in educational institutions:

- the use of water;
- power consumption;
- mobility and transportation;
- material consumption and waste production;
- the institution's facilities: furniture, equipment;
- building design;
- characteristics of the outside spaces;
- noise levels;
- social life and relationships within the institution.

At the second stage, participants work on planning and design within the areas of activity identified. This results in the development of a feasibility plan with operational management strategies to assess the efficiency, impact and popularity of such actions. Limitations and possible obstacles to change need to be anticipated. The plan, which emerges as a result of negotiation and agreement with stakeholders, will set out clearly defined responsibilities for all the parties involved.

This stage is followed by an implementation phase, which is guided by an action plan. This plan should be flexible and yet consistent with decisions taken by the group.

The fourth stage focuses on monitoring and assessment of the new initiatives. This assessment is based on the systematic observation and gathering of data which analyses the physical performance, as well as changes in decision-making processes, which have resulted from the actions undertaken. This is followed by a reflection process, where all who are involved in the management of change reflect upon the achievements and existing problems and work on overcoming the constraints. This stage needs to generate new courses of action and new criteria to feedback into the audit cycle. Since this process of change is a form of action research, all who participate in this process are given responsibilities in the auditing function and are involved in the change programme.

During the eco-auditing process, these four stages produce a series of responsibilities and tasks which can be structured under three main headings: pre-audit, audit and post-audit (see Table 1).

In recent years a variety of eco-auditing initiatives have been developed in Spain. Among these is the Ecological School Project, developed in Basque schools under the direction of the Centre for Didactic Environmental Education and Research (CEIDA) (see Fernandez 1996). There have also been other simultaneous initiatives in the Balearic Islands (Sureda & Calvo 1996), in Barcelona (Franquesa 1997) and in the Universidad Autónoma, Madrid. This Chapter will limit itself to describing the experience of eco-auditing at the Universidad Autónoma de Madrid.

The eco-auditing experience at the Universidad Autónoma, Madrid

The Universidad Autónoma de Madrid is a relatively young (1968) and middle-sized University. It currently has over 36,000 students, 2,000 academic personnel and approximately 800 staff in administration and services. The campus is 15 kilometres north of Madrid, surrounded by the Higher Manzanares Regional Park Biosphere Reserve and the Mediterranean forest of "El Pardo". Its remote location persuaded its planners to develop it as a small town, which included services necessary to carry out all educational, research and social activities. This "small town" campus provides an ideal opportunity for the design and implementation of a comprehensive environmental management plan

The University campus, which is still expanding, currently covers 220 hectares (556 acres), of which 302,000 square metres are built environment. The construction of an additional 2,600,000 square metres is planned. This further development will provide an ideal opportunity for the introduction of environmental considerations within the planning and execution stage. Although initially, when the campus was built, little thought was given to environmental factors, the institution is now becoming increasingly aware of the need to address environmental concerns. For instance, all new students' and teachers' residences are built according to bio-climatic criteria.

PREAUDIT

Diagnosis of the Situation in the Educational Centre

- Preliminary data gathering stages.
- Recruitment of contributors.
- Preliminary information to students.
- Motivation and encouragement of other agents' involvement.
- Register of elements and procedures to be audited.
- Definition of spheres and determination of priorities regarding the interventions.
- Design of operational instruments for data garthering.

AUDIT

Planning, Actions, Design and Intervention

- Elaboration of schedules by spheres of intervention.
- Definition of responsibilities and assumption of individual commitments.
- Development of awareness-creating campaigns.
- Call for cooperation from other agents.
- Comparison of documents and analysis of results.
- Proposal of corrective measurements and study of their feasibility.
- Planning of interventions by sectors.

PROSTAUDIT

Assessment and Feedback

- Design of instruments to follow up on actions.
- Assignment of evaluating responsibilities.
- Strategies for joint review and comparison of achievements.
- Assessment of obstacles and hindrances.
- Definition of new ways of implementation.
- Dissemination of results through informative meetings both inside and outside the educational centre.
- Independent evaluation by participating agents and contributors.

Table 1: Environmental pre-audit, audit and post-audit

The Charter: an environmental commitment to *Agenda 21*

At the end of 1997, representatives of approximately 160 countries came together at the Kyoto Summit in Japan, with the objective of signing several agreements to restrict the release of greenhouse gases into the atmosphere. Such events and corresponding agreements have placed universities in a position where they can no longer limit themselves to contributing by researching and monitoring climatic change. Universities are public institutions, which must assume a leading role in creating environmental awareness and in promoting possible solutions to existing problems. This can be achieved by changing their management practices as well as curriculum content. Universities can become model centres for sustainable practice and set an example to other public and private institutions.

Within this context the Universidad Autónoma de Madrid's Senate, which is its top decision-making body, announced during its meeting in April 1997 that it had unanimously approved a University Charter of Environmental Commitment to *Agenda 21*. To support this Charter, the Senate launched an environmental management project entitled "Ecocampus".

The University Charter of Environmental commitment has two main goals: first, to establish points of reference that will reduce the environmental impact of the university and, second, to promote the involvement of the university community in the debate and search for solutions to environmental conflicts. It detailed a commitment to several objectives, such as the gradual replacement of products causing damage to the ozone layer; the consideration of environmental criteria in the design of new buildings; an increase in biodiversity within the campus; the development of a plan for reduction, recycling and re-use of waste; the gradual implementation of systems for the treatment and minimization of toxic, hazardous, biological and radioactive waste; the decrease of energy consumption; the application of environmental criteria to the assessment of suppliers and service companies; the gradual decrease of water consumption and the encouragement and promotion of fair trade products, which respect the environment and promote good working conditions.

The definition of an environmental management model: eco-audits on campus

In order to achieve the ambitious objectives delineated in the new Charter, the university needs to identify and correct those practices and actions that degrade and pollute its environment on a daily basis. The development of appropriate tools and methodologies is necessary to allow for a continuous assessment of the main environmental variables. The first step involves a comprehensive diagnosis establishing reference points that can be used to determine whether the conditions become better or worse. Fortunately, the university had previous experience in this area. In 1993, the university had commissioned an environmental audit at both the Cartoblanco campus and Medical School Campus. The purpose of this study was to prepare a preliminary environmental inventory of all teaching and research activities, in order to identify and propose solutions to the main problems concerning toxic and hazardous gas release, water and atmosphere effluents and the assessment of energy efficiency.

The audit provided a framework for a plan establishing required investments and setting priority actions for the short term. The first actions worked towards controlling and removing toxic and hazardous waste (1994-1996), mainly in the Science School and later in the Medical School. During 1996, 14 tones of "special" waste were collected in these two centres, and for the first time a budget of approximately six million pesetas (US$ 38,400) was assigned to this concern. Now, as a direct result of the university's environmental commitment, a yearly report is to be prepared, identifying toxic products and producers.

In order to assess the annual progress of the University's environmental performance, a survey was prepared to gather basic information concerning environmental indicators for toxic and hazardous waste, water, solid waste, pest control amongst others. The gathering of data has been the responsibility of the Eco-Campus Office, in cooperation with some students and teachers. Collecting information from different sources and various departments is a complex job, however, the yearly experience of compiling this data has created more efficient communication channels among all involved.

An education model in environmental management for the university community

The elaboration and achievement of environmental management plans (and procedures) need to be based on the involvement and active contribution of every person who works, studies and/or resides in this environment. Management, if supported only by administrative and technical bodies is likely to encounter difficulties. The community's involvement in the campus's environmental management is valuable not only because of the positive effects it may produce but mostly because it can set in motion environmental education processes for those who take part in it. Direct intervention in decision-making and cooperation in every action becomes an educational process that tends to commit students and teachers to their centre's sustainable development. For these reasons the university paid particular attention to involving the university community in these environmental management process.

One of the first actions was the creation of an Environmental Commission approved in March 1992, by the university's senate. This commission consisted of representatives from the individuals who are involved in every level of university life and included students, administration and service staff, teachers from every school, representatives from the community services department, employees from the works and maintenance department, amongst others. The commission has monthly meetings during the academic year and already has a good record of supporting and engaging numerous actions. It has played an important role in the follow-up and assessment of the environmental issues that have emerged in the institution's daily activities. It has also fulfilled a remarkable task preparing environmental studies and audits on specific subjects in order to elaborate future action plans. One of its first initiatives was a campaign to create environmental awareness within the university community. Posters and stickers were targeted at issues of consumption, waste management, including the sustainable use of water, energy and paper.

A competition on ideas for the environmental improvement of the university campus was also developed. The main purpose of this initiative has been to encourage participation in the change towards more sustainable forms of management. Nine

projects were presented and assessed according to their originality and practical value. The commission is currently working on executing the winning projects which include the elaboration of a campus botanical catalogue, guide and itinerary; the development of a campaign to optimize the university's environmental management computer systems and the construction of a pond in the campus's green areas.

The Universidad Autónoma de Madrid has research teams that specialize in environmental subjects of a national and international importance but whose focuses are very distant from the concerns of the campus. There is now an effort to encourage these scientists to become involved in studies on the Campus' environment as has been done elsewhere (see Gómez Mendoza et al. 1987; Corraliza 1987; Génova 1985; also see chapter 16) and a series of monographs have been published presenting the results of their work. There is also an attempt to get research teams involved in monitoring environmental indicators. A mobile analysis unit makes this possible by gathering samples and data on air, water and soil parameters.

The best results are being achieved when practical studies are linked with the eco-auditing procedures. For example, biology students use their Limnology and Microbial Ecology to work with their teachers in gathering samples to measure the effect of changes on sewage levels. Other students work on quantifying energy and material flows produced on campus, as part of Human Ecology. The new degree in Environmental Sciences has allowed a group of students of environmental physics to measure sound levels in different university schools and situations – including several libraries. More recently, another group of students has prepared an analysis of the environmental management model and structure being applied at the University, as part of the Environmental Policy module.

These examples illustrate the potential of integrating environmental management of the university into the curriculum. Often university education is accused of being too theoretical and irrelevant to everyday concerns. More efforts are necessary to get teachers and students to apply the knowledge obtained from practical projects on environmental management of the campus to environmental concerns in their particular fields.

The University also promotes the involvement of students' associations in extracurricular tasks, which can contribute, to sustainable environmental change within the Campus. The student bodies cooperate with the university administration to encourage projects in this area. For example, support was given to students at the Business School when organizing a Green Week (with lectures, debates and several awareness raising activities). On another occasion, the Environmental Sciences Faculty gave assistance to the student association that was promoting a car-sharing scheme.

Learning from the experience

All these actions contribute to raising awareness and involvement levels of those who use the campus. However, the implementation of such programmes often encounters many hurdles and difficulties, which delay their development and reduce their effectiveness. The main problems we have faced in recent years stem from:

(a) The educational institution's own inertia – some universities often have little flexibility for bringing any changes into its working systems. Environmental concerns are not always regarded as a priority.
(b) The lack of economic and human resources to develop actions. This means that many of the initiatives rely heavily on volunteers.
(c) Heavy student workloads leaves little time for the student to get involved in extracurricular activities such as those required by this programme.
(d) The unwillingness of college students to give up practices that are environmentally unsustainable but which they consider important such as the use of private transportation to get to campus, overuse of photocopies and canned drinks, etc.
(e) The difficulty of influencing the works and maintenance staff, so that they are able to include criteria on environmentally sustainable actions into their work.

Despite these difficulties it is important to continue to pursue greening initiatives in higher education. Learning in environmentally friendly and sustainable environments is a powerful way of communicating the message of sustainability. Higher education institutions need to engage in environmental research to address sustainable development issues but also must provide opportunities for those who teach and learn in these environments to learn how to make changes to improve their environmental impact. For example, when action research processes are involved individuals embark on reflecting and taking action for change. In our experience, these processes are resulting in the improvement of the campus environmental performance, as well as in changes in wider social practice as students take on other responsibilities outside the university.

References

Corraliza, J. A. (1987). La Experiencia Del Ambiente. *Percepción Y Significado Del Medio Construido*. Tecnos Ed.:Madrid. p. 269.

Fernández Ostolaza, Mª A. (1996). *EcoauditorPhia Escolar*. Departamento de Ordenación del Territorio, Vivienda y Medio Ambiente del Gobierno Vasco. Servicio de Publicaciones del Gobierno Vasco: Vitoria. p. 104.

Franquesa, T. (1997). *Centres Ecologics. Guia per fer L'eco Auditoria del Centre Educatiu*. M°M. (1985) degree dissertation. Pla d'Educació Ambiental, Institut d'Educació, Ajuntament de Barcelona: Génova.

Gómez Mendoza, J., G. Luna, R. Más, M. Mollá, E. Saez (1987). *Ghettos Universitarios*. El Campus de la Universidad Autónoma de Madrid, Ediciones de la UAM: Madrid. p.196.

Sureda, J. and A. Calvo (1996) "Educación Ambiental y Escuela: Apuntes Para la Implantación de Estrategias Organizativas" in *Educación Abierta* 124. pp. 37-76.

Chapter 10

Hungary

An Education Initiative for a sustainable future

Eva Csobod

Introduction

In recent years, the Hungarian education system has undergone dramatic changes as a result of a broader political and socio-economic transformation. Power and organizational structures are being redefined as Hungary moves towards a market economy and mature forms of democracy. These changes are offering opportunities, as well as increasing the need, for education for sustainability in Hungary. They have paved the way for an environmental education initiative which attempts to make education for sustainability part of the formal learning experience of Hungarian school children.

Education for sustainability is a process through which teachers and students learn about the concept of power in society and how citizens can actively contribute to social and environmental changes, through democratic means (Huckle 1995; 1998). Education for sustainability provides an opportunity for Hungarians to consider what sustainable development would mean in their context and how it can be achieved through exercising their social and political rights. It develops critical thinking, encourages learners to question dominant ideologies and supports those who are working towards a sustainable future.

I begin this chapter by briefly summarizing the key aspects of curriculum reform, which were introduced through the Hungarian National Basic Curriculum (1996). I then focus upon an initiative known as "The Renewal of Environmental Education in Hungary" that emerged in response to this new national curriculum. The initiative encourages citizens to engage with democratic processes to build a sustainable future. It promotes participation, integration and community action for sustainable development. I end the chapter by reviewing the achievements of this initiative to date and reflecting upon the lessons learnt.

Educational reform in Hungary

Education for sustainability poses many challenges to curriculum innovators particularly when it is interpreted as an agent of change and not as a content-based discipline. However, Huckle (1995) points out how curriculum reform can provide a context and opportunity for education for sustainability and facilitate opportunities for its inclusion into formal education.

Hungary's education system is currently undergoing reform. Through the new National Basic Curriculum (1996), the Ministry of Culture and Education is shifting a discipline-oriented curriculum towards a competency-based model organized around a number of themes and areas of learning. This national curriculum determines 60% of the core content and essential teaching strategies for formal

education in Hungary. It outlines basic education principles, identified by the National Council of Public Education, and curriculum guidelines, issued by the Ministry, to assist schools with the reform.

The importance of the National Basic Curriculum lies not only in its aim to modernize the school system but also in its potential to influence Hungarian culture in the coming decades. Perhaps its most significant contribution is its attempt at decentralizing formal education. At one level, the Ministry has determined that formal education is now the shared responsibility of central and local public administrations, thereby decentralizing the decision-making powers of the national government. At another level, it has granted schools the freedom to develop their own educational programmes within the frame of the National Basic Curriculum and to determine the remaining 40% of the curriculum. Teachers can plan, teach and evaluate their own programmes. This greater responsibility will encourage teachers to be reflective, cooperative and to feel ownership of the teaching process. The moves to decentralize decision-making powers and increase teacher autonomy are seen as necessary steps towards a democratic society. They provide great opportunities for education for sustainability in Hungary.

Environmental education within the National Basic Curriculum

Environmental education is regarded as a cross-curricular area within the National Basic Curriculum. Its primary goal is to encourage children to be actively involved in preserving and improving their immediate surroundings and to promote a sense of responsibility towards the environment. Through this area of learning, the Ministry for Education and Culture aims to develop a new generation that will prevent the environmental crisis from deepening, protect nature, and promote a healthy society.

This cross-curricular area relates to three themes within the National Basic Curriculum: "Man and Nature", "Earth and Environment" and "Man and Society". "Man and Nature" is a science education theme that considers the interrelationship between humans and the natural world and their interdependence. Students are introduced to global environmental thinking and to the fragility of the global ecosystem through the "Earth and Environment" theme. They are encouraged to establish connections between developments in one part of the earth and global change. Through the "Man and Society" theme students engage in learning activities which aim to help them form their own opinions and participate actively in the school community's life. They are given opportunities to experience real environment and development issues and are exposed to democratic attitudes and behaviour. Students are encouraged to reflect upon personal, national and civic identity, race and age issues, social and environmental rights and responsibilities. The approach to environmental education promoted by the "Man and Society" theme of the National Basic Curriculum is sometimes referred to as "education for sustainability".

Education for sustainability

The label "education for sustainability" is now often used to describe work carried out through environmental education. Those who use the label rarely describe what it is or how it differs from other environmental education approaches. In this section, I will outline some basic characteristics of this approach which were promoted by

"The Renewal of Environmental Education" initiative developed in Hungarian schools.

It could be argued that education for sustainability combines the goals of environmental protection and improvement associated with environmental education of humankind, with those of development education which focus on improving the quality of life. However, the meeting of environmental and development education is complex. They cannot simply be added together to form education for sustainable development. Environmental education has many approaches which include education *about* the environment that focuses on increasing levels of knowledge and awareness of the environment, to education in the environment that involves developing attitudes and skills through experiencing the natural environment, and the more radical education *for* the environment approach that analyses power bases and social structures, incorporates Southern voices and sees the environment as socially determined (Downs 1994; Tilbury 1995). Development education deals with similar themes to education *for* the environment but places a higher priority on issues associated, with human rights, social environment, global inequality and conflict (Tilbury 1997). These differences of interest arise from development education's concern for people and environmental education's focus on people's environment. However, underlying these differences is a common goal, that of attaining sustainable development and a common belief in education as an important tool for social change (Downs 1994).

Sustainable development is linked to a change in social paradigm or what is sometimes referred to as a new worldview. It involves a transition towards social systems and institutions which respect the natural and social limits to growth and which work through careful planning and management to minimize the threats to nature and the quality of life. There are different perspectives on how education can help bring about sustainable development. Two prominent views are expressed in *Education for Sustainability* (Routledge 1996) in which Huckle outlines his "red-green" position and Sterling puts forward his "deeper-green" perspective. These different views reveal differences in environmental and political ideology.

The renewal of environmental education initiative

The "Renewal of Environmental Education" initiative borrows heavily from Huckle's (1996) "red-green" perspective on education for sustainability. Huckle believes that different forms of economic production and social reproduction are more or less ecologically (and socially) sustainable. He interprets education for sustainability as the process that promotes shared reflection and action on forms of political economy. He argues for a clearer understanding of political power and its social relations to everyday life and advocates teaching approaches which link environmental education to critical theory and social change. Huckle (1995) views education for sustainability as a future-oriented process which engages pupils in visualizing sustainable futures. Through engaging in this learning process teachers and students learn about the concept of power in society and how citizens can actively contribute to social and environmental changes through democratic means.

The Renewal of Environmental Education initiative attempts to achieve Huckle's objectives through developing the "action competence" of the learner. Jensen and Schnack (1997) define action competence as the capacity to act and be responsible for one's actions today and in the future. The action competence model was developed by the Royal Danish School of Educational Studies in their work on

environmental and health education (see Royal Danish School of Educational Studies 1990, 1991; Breiting 1994; Jensen and Schnack 1997). This model places great emphasis on developing students' ability to envision a better future and to take responsibility for their own learning so that they can achieve the desired outcome. The learning takes place in teams, where the students plan, act and reflect upon their decisions to influence the future.

When understood in this way, education for sustainability can provide the context and skills for Hungarians to reflect upon the concept of sustainable development – what it would mean in their context and how it can be achieved through exercising their social and political rights. This approach, which was promoted by the Renewal of Environmental Education Initiative, develops critical thinking, encourages learners to question dominant ideologies and supports those who are working towards a sustainable future.

The Renewal of Environmental Education in Hungary initiative is developed and funded by the Ministry for the Environment, Hungary, Municipality of Budapest and the Soros Foundation. It aims to incorporate education for sustainability into formal education, but also in an indirect way, attempts to assist teachers with implementing broader curriculum reforms in Hungary. Teachers are encouraged and supported to develop democratic approaches to teaching by fostering participatory, problem-solving, community-oriented, cross-curricular learning.

This three-year initiative has four objectives:

1. to increase the presence of environmental education within the formal curriculum in Hungarian schools;

2. to improve the provision of environmental education through integrating environmental issues across a number of disciplines;

3. to increase the interest and experience of teachers in democratic ideas and participation through environmental education methodologies; and

4. to encourage teachers and students to become actively involved in improving and protecting the environment.

The initiative focuses on developing the planned curriculum, as well as teachers' competencies in teaching for sustainability. It assumes that through gaining practical experience with this new environmental education approach, teachers will develop democratic and participatory methodologies, thereby supporting broader education reform.

Developing the initiative
Ten pilot schools (four secondary and six primary) were chosen to participate in this initiative. The schools were selected on the basis of their previous experience in environmental education and receptivity to innovative projects. Four or five teachers from each of these schools volunteered to work in teams and develop plans to realize the objectives of the initiative.

Initially, all participating teachers and school head teachers met at a preparatory meeting where they developed a three-year action plan. The action plan followed the critical reflective practitioner model, where teachers plan, act, gather information, reflect, report and evaluate their progress to inform the next stage of the initiative.

The teachers were asked to design small environmental education projects that would develop the action competence of the learner in addressing environmental issues. The projects had to provide curricular opportunities that would increase students' confidence and ability to be active and responsible citizens in a democratic society. Activities had to be designed so students could learn decision-making, cooperation and participation skills necessary for addressing environmental and social challenges. It was important that teachers developed their own projects as responsibility was seen as vital to establishing teachers' interest and commitment and necessary for building their competence in curriculum development. Teachers were also required to work across curriculum areas. This meant that teachers needed to develop collaborative skills and find ways of working with colleagues from other subjects.

The content

Waste management was chosen as the core theme of this initiative. Topics such as "the use of natural resources" and "waste reduction and recycling" were treated cross-curricularly with teachers from different subject areas planning and teaching in teams.There were various reasons why waste management was chosen as the focus of this initiative. First, the Municipality of Budapest had decided to promote waste and recycling issues as a priority through school programmes. The Ministry of Culture and Education and the Ministry of Environmental Protection saw this as an opportunity to enable cooperation between different levels of government. The second reason was that waste issues provide an ideal theme for the development of democratic and community-oriented approaches to learning within the formal curriculum. They are community based and the collective responsibility of families, schools and municipalities which need to take action to address this environmental problem. The direct relevance of waste management issues to children's daily experiences was another reason why this theme was selected.

The implementation

The primary and secondary teachers involved in the initiative were given new teaching materials to assist them with the task of integrating waste management issues across a number of school disciplines. The materials supported teachers in developing activities across different levels and outside the school environment. They promoted democratic approaches and assisted with the development of action competence. The teachers were expected to critically reflect on the materials and revise them to suit their needs.

Support was also offered through workshops where the teachers from the 10 different schools met twice a year for four days. These workshops served as an important context for teachers to learn and exchange ideas about teamwork and cross-curricular planning and to build a support network. Few had experience or training in solving problems in this area. The workshops encouraged teachers to experiment with their own ideas away from their school environment. The teachers also were supported through visits during the different stages of the initiative.

The evaluation

The impact of the innovation was assessed through a questionnaire and a series of interviews. The questionnaire sought to appraise the teachers' understanding of environmental education and teaching competence in this area. It collected information on the impact of the initiative on school curriculum development, particularly with regard to changes in teaching style and democratic approaches to learning. The interviews were specifically aimed at collecting data on teachers' experiences in environmental education and documenting successful teaching strategies.

The questionnaire results indicated that the teachers had developed new understandings of environmental education and had become more confident in the use of active and democratic learning approaches. Some teachers apparently had recognized the need to act as facilitators rather than instructors to improve the quality of learning and had begun to develop their thinking on the teaching-learning process and need for more democratic teaching approaches. The questionnaire revealed that teachers were recognizing the importance of developing the students' critical reflection, participation and action.

The interviews reinforced the above findings and highlighted the importance of giving teachers space and flexibility to make curricular and pedagogical changes. Teachers greatly appreciated the opportunity to reflect on how best to use the new materials and to be given the freedom to adapt the activities to fit their own circumstances and needs. The interviews revealed that the old curriculum with its traditional teaching approaches made teachers feel regulated and constrained. The autonomy provided by the initiative, increased their involvement, valued their professional judgements and released creative energy. This finding supported Schermer's (1994) belief that teacher involvement in environmental education innovation is essential to its successful implementation. Teachers need to be part of the curriculum development team and not treated as technicians implementing new ideas. This was an important finding which could inform other initiatives and programmes stemming from the National Basic Curriculum.

The evaluation also revealed that curriculum planning at the school level developed the capacity of teachers to work in teams and taught them how to integrate environmental education into different subjects. The interviews suggested that networking with other teachers who were experiencing similar difficulties provided important support which sustained the teachers' efforts.

A number of OECD experts evaluated the initiative during a visit to Hungary in 1994 soon after the initiative had began and again in 1996 after it had been running for three years. They found that the school principals had played an active and important part in the development of this initiative (ENSI-OECD 1996). They acknowledged that teachers could not make major or long-lasting changes without the principal's approval and support. Actively involving the school principals was seen as another significant achievement of the initiative.

Lessons learnt
A dialectical relationship existed between the Renewal of Environmental Education initiative and the curriculum reform which was taking place at the time. Government moves towards democratic schools and support for newer pedagogical approaches motivated the teachers to participate in this new environmental education initiative. The initiative provided an opportunity (as well as freedom) for teachers to explore the implications of new active and democratic approaches at the classroom level. It therefore supported not only the development of education for sustainability, but also broader curriculum reform.

The evaluation suggests that the success of the project can also be linked to the way in which teachers participated in the management and development of the initiative. Although difficulties emerged at different stages of the initiative (mainly because of the lack of teacher preparation in curriculum development and lack of teamwork experience), the active and collective responsibility given to teachers engaged their interests and stretched their abilities. The result was that teachers felt confident and

competent to develop more participatory, problem-solving, community-oriented and cross-curricular approaches to learning.

> The future is not some place we are going to, but one we are creating; The paths to it are not found but made; The making of those pathways changes both the maker and the destination.
>
> (Australian Commission for the Future, cited in Ali Khan 1995)

Environmental education is a tool for educational change which can assist in the transition towards a democratic society. The initiative described in this chapter is based upon a new generation of environmental education approaches (Breiting 1994) which attempts to improve the quality of life and build a sustainable future for Hungarians. It has led to the "renewal" of local environmental education programmes in some Hungarian schools and has assisted with reforming the curriculum. These initiatives have a great role to play in developing an active citizenship which supports political and socio-economic transformation towards mature forms of democracy.

References

Ali Khan, (1995). "Approaches to curriculum development" in *The Environmental Agenda-Taking Responsibility*. WWF, Pluto Press. pp. 222-227.

Breiting, S (1994). "Towards a New Concept of Environmental Education" in *Proceedings of the Conference on the Exchange of Promising Experiences in Environmental Education in Britain and the Nordic Countries, Karlslunde, Denmark, 11-13 November*. European Research and Training Centre on Environmental Education, 5-17: Bradford.

Downs, E. (1994). "Education for sustainability: is the whole more or less than the sum of the parts?" in *Development Education Journal*, Issue 2, December 5-8.

ENSI-OECD (1996). *Environmental education in Europe report*. OCED: Paris.

Fien, J and T. Trainer (1993). *Environmental Education – Pathways to Sustainability*. Deakin University: Geelong.

Huckle J., (1995). *Reaching Out*. WWF: Godalming.

Huckle, J. (1996). "Realizing Sustainability in Changing Times" in J. Huckle, S. Sterling, (1996). *Education for sustainability*. Earthscan, WWF UK: London. pp. 3-17.

Huckle J, (1998). *The Objectives for Global Citizenship Education*. Paper presented to the Development Education Commission, UK.

Huckle, J and S. Sterling (1996). *Education for sustainability*. Earthscan,WWF UK: London.

IUCN, UNEP, WWF (1991). *Caring for the earth: a strategy for sustainable living*. IUCN: Gland, Switzerland.

Jansen B, and K. Schnack (1997). "The action competence approach in environmental education" in *Environmental Education Research*, 3(2):163-178.

Ministry of Culture and Education, (1996). *A guide to the Hungarian national core curriculum*. Ministry of Culture and Education: Budapest.

Posch, P. (1995). *Curriculum change and school development*. European Conference on Educational Research, 10-15 September. Bath University, UK.

Royal Danish School of Educational Studies (1991). *Environmental Education and Health Education: International Contributions 1990 Proceedings from the Research Centre for Environmental and Health Education*. No.15 Royal Danish School of Educational Studies: Copenhagen.

Royal Danish School of Educational Studies (1992). *Environmental Education and Health Education: International Contributions 1991 Proceedings from the Research Centre for Environmental and Health Education*. No.17. Royal Danish School of Educational Studies: Copenhagen.

Schermer, A, (1994). *Planned assisted institutionalisation of environmental education*. 19th ATEE Conference, 5-9 September. Prague, Czech Republic.

Tilbury, D (1995). "Environmental education for sustainability: defining the new focus of environmental education in 1990s" in *Environmental education research*, 1(2):195-212.

Tilbury, D. (1997). "Environmental education and development education: teaching geography for a sustainable world" in D. Tilbury and M. Williams (eds). *Teaching and Learning Geography*. Routledge: London. pp. 105-116.

Part C

Southern Africa

Part C

Southern Africa: The context

Danie Schreuder

A relatively peaceful second democratic election in South Africa, economic turmoil, and confrontations between government and organized labour mark the end of the millennium for Southern Africa. A rampant AIDS crisis coupled with renewed malaria outbreaks and prevailing droughts also shape the landscape. Socially the emergent democracies struggle to find their feet and all too frequent violence, fraud and abuse of power and public funding fill newspaper columns daily.

As a result of what appears to be turmoil, violence and instability in many sectors, many professional people are leaving Southern Africa to settle elsewhere. This is demonstrated best by the political instability which followed the farm invasions in Zimbabwe. Since the contribution in Chapter 13 was written, the author (Kathy Stiles) also left the country for reasons of personal safety. However, for many others, the last two decades of this millennium has presented opportunities to reflect critically on the real causes of the turbulence in nearly all the sectors of the local landscape. For those, it has become clear that sweeping changes are inevitable, and the opportunities for transformation are immense. In a sense, this puts Southern Africa in a privileged position. In many ways, and not unlike most countries, our economy, agriculture, education and many other social constructs could be described as unsustainable – it just could not continue in its old ways. Our transition to democracy has offered the opportunity to make this vividly clear, and offered the opportunity to rethink.

Is there a common cause for the unsustainability of these sectors? For nearly 400 years, colonial powers have been transposing western principles, ideologies and patterns of thinking in the "development" of this sub-continent. Over the past decade especially, the inappropriateness of many forms of technology, politics, legislation, economy, agriculture and education has become vividly evident – we cannot continue along existing paths. Finding new, more sustainable and contextually appropriate pathways will be the task of the present generation, and many people view these seemingly enormous challenges with hope and expectation. A new consciousness seems to be dawning that the Southern African context demands approaches that are responsive to the unique character of the community, the landscape, and the history. There are already indications that new patterns are emerging in the economic sector, while land use and agriculture and conservation are following suit.

The South African Education Ministry has adopted a system based upon equity in education provision, contextually appropriate curricula and life-long learning. The contribution towards transformation in education by the environmental education community has been significant. Long before the first democratic election in 1994, an Environmental Education Policy Initiative (EEPI) was formed with a view to influencing education policy-making processes. After the election, this group was re-constituted to form the Environmental Education Curriculum Initiative (EECI) which had been working very closely with education authorities in developing curricula in an outcomes-based education system. In the new Curriculum 2005 many of the principles and ideas emanating from the environmental education community

have been embraced. This is a culmination of what has been believed about environmental education in South Africa for a long time: Environmental education should lead, and not follow education reconstruction. In this spirit, the National Minister of Education made a commitment in June 2000 to develop a strong emphasis on environmental education for South Africa when the National Environmental Education Programme (NEEP) was launched. One of the early priorities of this programme was a research phase, which culminated in the widely consultative and inclusive "Learning for Sustainability" process. Currently, the process is in the professional development phase where strategic involvement of many stakeholders is being sought to develop strategies to develop practitioner skills in outcome-based education within an environmental framework.

Many of these developments are having important influences in a number of neighbouring countries and of course, vice versa. For instance, the Southern African Environmental Education Association – founded in 1982 in Natal – has changed its constitution in order to allow a maximum of two council members from any SADC country. This means most of these countries are regularly represented on the EEASA Council, and that many positive developments in environmental education are shared across many countries in Southern Africa. Over the past decade annual EESA conferences have been organized by Namibia, South Africa, Botswana, Lesotho, Swaziland and in 2002 Zimbabwe will host the event. This enables a sharing of rich and contextualized stories of environmental education.

One of these is related in Chapter 13. It tells the story of how local inhabitants are educated on aspects of biodiversity and sustainability using camp facilities on the banks of the Zambezi River, the author running courses, which supplement school curricula. Heavy emphasis is being placed on the conservation of the rich biodiversity of the region, and its role in the sustainability of the area's ecosystems. A significant feature of this programme is how traditional values and knowledge are integrated into the courses during the Rifa camp experience. Learners from predominantly western-style schools get the opportunity to discover the principles of sustainable land management through biodiversity conservation.

Another recent development illustrating the use of collaborative networking processes in Southern Africa is the establishment, by SADC-ELMS (Southern African Development Community – Environment and Land Management Sector) of a Regional Environmental Education Programme. This programme, which is focusing on enhanced networking, training and resource material development, as well as support for local policy development processes is being undertaken by the Wildlife and Environmental Society of Southern Africa (WESSA) and is based at the Umgeni Valley Nature Reserve in Kwa-Zulu Natal. Through this network, the ties with environmental education colleagues in neighbouring countries have been strengthened, more than 100 participants have received training in environmental education, and more than 200 resource materials responding to specific local needs have been developed and published.

Environmental education in Southern Africa is characterized by firstly its critical nature, and secondly by the well established and functional networking processes in the area. Both these features should be understood against the background of political change over the past two decades; many people lost faith and confidence in ideologies influencing social structures, such as government, church and education, and developed alternative theories and patterns of thinking. In chapter 12 this critical disposition is illustrated by the innovative approaches to the development of environmental education curriculum materials through the Share-Net process. The

paper presents a strong critique of modernist approaches to materials and curriculum development, and relates a unique interpretation and implementation of the principles of authentic, practical participation and networking in the production of low-cost, appropriate resources.

Chapter 14 tells the story of how an imaginative interpretation of the concept of sustainability is applied in developing a unifying theme for science resource materials to be used within an outcomes-base framework. Again, the critical nature of environmental education in South Africa is illustrated when the authors critique some widely accepted approaches to "education for sustainability". The role of national networks and the formation of partnerships in research, funding, materials and curriculum development, dissemination and evaluation are portrayed.

Chapter 11

Southern Africa

Share-Net: environmental education resource networking in a risk society

Jim Taylor and Eureta Janse van Rensburg

Introduction

Share-Net developed in the late 1980s as an informal, collaborative network through which individuals, projects and agencies can both contribute to, and benefit from, the development and use of environmental education resources (Taylor 1997, p. 137). It seeks to encourage grass-roots, participatory materials development in Southern Africa for supporting teachers and other community members in environmental education processes. This loose network functions around a low-cost printing and distribution office housed at the Umgeni Valley Project by the Wildlife and Environment Society of South Africa (WESSA) in the province of KwaZulu-Natal.

The influence that Share-Net materials and processes have had on environmental education in South Africa, and indeed more widely, has been disproportional to the project's modest aims, premises and budgets. Today, as the project is poised to support the Regional Environmental Education Centre for the Southern African Developing Community, it is useful to review the assumptions guiding the Share-Net initiative. By doing so here, we not only wish to share what we have learned, but we also hope to continue clarifying how best to support meaningful networking and productive resource development processes as Share-Net develops beyond the "small functional node" it has represented thus far.

A key feature of the early development of Share-Net was the collaboration between WESSA and the Natal Parks Board (now KwaZulu-Natal Nature Conservation Service) with the objective of supporting teachers so as to enable them to conduct their own fieldwork with confidence. Teacher workshops and appropriate resource materials were needed which teachers could use to support their fieldwork processes. The early materials were developed at the Umgeni Valley Project which has developed as a functional node of Share-Net.

We start the discussion with an introduction to the notion of a small, functional node, how it operates in Share-Net, and how it characterizes the orientation of the project. A descriptive analysis of a selection of environmental education resources which have been developed through Share-Net follows in the body of the chapter. In the final sections we describe a perspective on networking, before concluding with a summary of the critique of modernist assumptions and ideas about social change which emerge from this project.

Share-Net: from small functional units to cooperating nodes in a network

We talk of the Share-Net "node" at the Umgeni Valley Project to distinguish it from a "centre" of control. While the project's main printing facility and mail order support service are based at WESSA offices at the Umgeni Valley Project, Share-Net's developers see the project as a network of collaborating resource developers and users, rather than a controlling centre of excellence. The printing and mailing hub is at the service of the entire environmental education community in the region, members of which often visit it for advice, to review resources on sale or to discuss and print materials which they have developed in their own work setting. Copyright-free materials, available on computer disk or as cut-and-paste photocopy masters, support the selective adaptation of materials to local contexts and needs. It was indeed a disillusionment with centralized develop-and-disseminate approaches to materials' development that led to the establishment of Share-Net in the first place (O'Donoghue and Taylor 1988).

The project started small and still employs only two full-time staff on modest salaries (to manage the printers and sales and a small internship programme to enable others to develop skills). It is supported by limited donor funding well below the average funding budget of projects with far smaller outputs. This is made possible by the input of staff time by WESSA, but also by the fact that all materials produced are sold. At prices well within reach of South African teachers, Share-Net sales cover up to two-thirds of the project running costs. The policy to sell rather than hand out materials contradicts the approach of many funders who prefer to sponsor once-off print-runs of resources and then distribute them freely to "resource-poor" areas. However, the "handout" mentality which prevails among many donors and recipients alike tends to perpetuate the myth of Africans being unable to develop themselves. In the case of environmental education, for example, it does not contribute much to the resource production capacity of teachers and other environmental educators.

We describe Share-Net as "functional", in reference to its very productive output of materials and the service it provides to the environmental education community through active and responsive networking, but also to distinguish it from a structural-functionalist orientation to social change through educational resources. The project orientation is reflected in the ways in which developments in Share-Net help reveal the myths of modernity which seem to misguide many environmental education activities. Although Share-Net is not free from modernist assumptions, ongoing reflection within the action of the project provides the clarity to prevent the project from falling victim to grand narratives of rationalist social change through communication techniques and educational technologies. This reflexive orientation to knowledge in the context of environmental issues distinguishes the initiative from rationalistic notions of progress and change which characterize the shadow side of modernity (Beck 1992), and has come to depict Share-Net as an educational response within a risk society.

From field guides to how-to pamphlets

By reviewing the nature of the range of Share-Net materials which are developed both at the Umgeni Valley node and elsewhere in Southern Africa, we notice some significant trends in environmental education in the region. Some of the earliest materials developed through Share-Net are the *Hands-On series* of field guides to

ecosystems, such as grasslands, forests, rocky shores, soil, streams and ponds. With the growing realization that "environment" was more than the great outdoors, these field guides were joined by Mba Manqele's guide to common household organisms. The *Hands-On* field guides, with their black-and-white line drawings of the organisms learners are most likely to encounter, enable even inexperienced teachers to conduct water and soil studies with little more than a nearby pond, puddle of water or a spade-full of compost to supplement the guides. The format for these booklets was used to develop a complementary series of *Beginners' Field Guides* to specific species, including spiders, butterflies and water birds. These black-and-white, A5-size booklets are inexpensive and small enough for teachers to use with pupils in the field. As the emphasis on active, outdoor learning rather than rote, classroom-based learning grew in South Africa, the *Beginners' and Hands-On* guides were particularly popular with teachers and field officers working for NGO's and governmental conservation agencies.

As elsewhere in the world, South African environmental educators wanted to broaden teaching "about" and "in" the natural environment with educational processes that would encourage action to address local environmental issues (see O'Donoghue & Janse van Rensburg 1995). This trend is reflected in the development of a set of "How-To" pamphlets (that can be folded to fit a pocket) on a range of practical environmental actions, from how to make recycled paper to how to build a "chicken tractor" or a pit latrine which does not smell. Another set of more substantial booklets, aptly named the Action series, gives information on topics like the re-vegetation of stream banks and the cultivation of scarce plants for traditional healers in *muti* (medicine) nurseries.

By sharing information about environmental issues, supporting teaching and study in the physical environment, and encouraging learning for environmental action, the library of Share-Net resources enables teachers to overcome limitations of text-driven rote learning inside the classroom. They thus also help to make a connection between classroom learning and community action. A Share-Net project which has focused strongly on appropriate resource materials to support a local engagement with environmental problems, through "action research and community problem-solving processes" (Wals 1994), involved the countrywide development of water kits.

Water kits: giving away the tools of science

After encountering *GREEN* (Global Rivers Environmental Education Network) in the USA, Rob O'Donoghue started to develop, through Share-Net, educational water quality monitoring materials for South Africa. The aim was to "give away the tools of science" (Taylor 1993) but this, as well as local conditions, meant that the equipment had to be cheaper and simpler than the apparatus used in the USA (or in *WaterWatch* in Australia). Jam tins and small cardboard boxes were thus distributed, packed with simple tools to test for coliform (sewage) contamination, turbidity (soil erosion), nitrates (fertilizer levels), pH and so on. A booklet with instructions for using the kit to monitor water catchment quality was included in the box. It used the acronym ACTION to guide learners through the processes of Asking (local residents about the changing quality of their river or stream); Checking (various visible features of the catchment); Testing (using the apparatus provided); Informing (residents and authorities of the findings); Outlining (a catchment conservation plan); and Networking (involving others in catchment action).

As research related to the water kits proceeded, common myths in environmental education were revealed. Among them was the assumption that rich learning processes can be reduced to a "thing", a technique or technology to cause change in others. This assumption seems to drive a national water conservation education campaign initiated by the South African government in 1997, aimed at raising school children's and teachers' awareness of water wastage and changing their consumption patterns. Taking the form of water audits to be conducted in schools, the government project is based on expensive buckets of sophisticated water monitoring and saving devices which could mystify rather than encourage teachers and learners (Masuku, pers. comm. 1997). To overcome this weakness, the planners of the project have gone to great lengths to foster local workshop support and interaction around the materials.

The limited educational success of message-centred awareness campaigns throws into sharp relief the "spiralling-out" nature of the water project, in which we learned that sharing the tools of science requires educational materials which will allow learners themselves to contribute to the process of developing knowledge about their environmental problems. Large-scale awareness-raising initiatives, on the other hand, are based on a social engineering intent which is at times counter-productive to environmental education processes.

The water kit itself can be used with a similar intent to rationally change learners' behaviour: for some, the ACTION acronym appears to provide a systematic procedure, a structure for learners' actions, that will lead to particular outcomes. When used with such technicist expectations the kit may seem to be, therefore, an ideal tool to cause change. Thus teachers, field officers and researchers at times reported, with some disappointment, that pupils had not always followed the acronym routine accurately and that the testing of water quality had not necessarily led to the desired local action. The kit, they would claim, does not always "work"! But ironically, it was the underlying assumptions about the directing of social change that couldn't work.

Where field officers and teachers were able to give up the idea of using the water quality monitoring materials to manipulate change in others and simply got on with constructive fieldwork, the learning appeared to proceed with less contrived effort. Enthusiasm to find out jointly with participants, rather than field work to cause change in the participants, usually led to richer field work that appeared to be more meaningful to all concerned.

The desire to cause change in others by managing social processes leads to a rhetoric which is often credible in planning committees or board rooms. But it is the teachers and field workers who have to make the concepts work in practice who may become disillusioned when the change in the "target group" fails to go according to plan. Levin (1980, p.34) makes the following point about expectations of change agents:

> If planners and reformers use such terminology as change agents, managed change and planned change, they and their followers tend to believe that the use of language and the logic of rational change imply a control of the change process itself. In contrast a review of educational reform and implementation literature suggests that the rhetoric of reform is probably its most important manifestation, rather than the change it claims to produce.

Such "grand narrative" planning routines (often evident in international policy and planning documents for environmental education) can disempower people at a local

level as we become subsumed by a bigger picture with apparently better, more progressive, rhetoric.

Water testing kits and other techniques and technologies taught us about the importance of the social habitue and the assumptions with/in which resources are used. The resources may be used to support better education processes, but the expectation that they can cause and direct social change is doubtful. Rather, they are potentially useful as supportive tools for learning to be given away or shared (Taylor 1993). To assume that resources can operate as systematic procedures to direct outcomes is a technicist error that is, unfortunately, prevalent in environmental education. The expectation that a kit (or any educational material, computer or media, for that matter) can cause the desired change in the users, fails to accommodate the non-rational nature of social change or the importance of the social habitue in which the materials are used, which includes the people, places and histories involved (O'Donoghue 1997; Papaciannis et al 1982; Popkewitz 1984).

Enviro-Facts: disputing the "facts"

Action without information is often inappropriate, and while learners should be encouraged to access local sources of information, including their own experiences and community resources, there is also a need to seek expert scientific opinion. The Enviro-Facts is a series of 60 pamphlets developed through Share-Net to provide concise, up-to-date technical information on a range of topics (Paxton 1994). The topics varied from an earlier focus on endangered species, such as the Blue Swallow and the Black Rhino, to broader socio-ecological topics like Sustainable Development and Integrated Environmental Management.

The first aspect of the Enviro-Facts series which reflects the orientation guiding ShareNet is the approach to knowledge evident in their format. The fact sheets, though quite simple in language and style, do not present knowledge as a given and do not shirk the contentious nature of much scientific information. One contributing scientist commented that contradictory theories about the ozone hole over the southern hemisphere should be withheld from the fact sheet on this topic, as it could create the impression that scientists are unsure about the issue. Instead of delivering plain and simple facts, users of the pamphlets were introduced to many sides of every story and encouraged to discuss difficult issues with others in a section called "Issues for Debate".

It is often the grappling with the meanings of words that is important for learning and a complex problem presented as a simplified abstraction may detract from greater understanding. This issue is addressed by Popkewitz (1991) in his critique of "popularism and critical theory traditions". He notes that, while at one level writing should be made to be understandable, the argument about language is more complex because of the values and interests carried in discursive practices. He concludes that "claims about making language accessible should be scrutinised" (1991, p. 234). Spivak, in Lather, (1996, p. 544) is more forthright "we know plain prose cheats".

The second aspect of the Enviro-Facts to highlight here is the way in which the materials were developed. Each fact sheet was written by the series editor, Linda Paxton, based on inputs solicited from a number of specialists in the particular field. Although Share-Net was developed to encourage participatory resource development, the success of this "top-down" project, which provided a wealth of relevant information in a ready-to-use format, for example to students working on

projects, made us re-think the apparent dichotomy between "top-down" and "grassroots" resource development. Sometimes there was a place for the former, as the processing of a vast body of information was best handled by a single, dedicated author. The products of such top-down materials development processes were no less able to support and inform grassroots action, and a lack of ownership' did not prevent learners and teachers from using them. Finally, as a science teacher who straddled the domains of scientific-expert and educator-using-materials, the editor could also not be readily placed at either the "top" (experts) or the "bottom" (users or materials).

What we did find useful in several courses we run for environmental educators from South, Southern and Eastern Africa, was to challenge participants to learn to develop their own fact sheets, starting with a cut-and-paste adaptation of an existing Enviro-Fact sheet. This was usually a very encouraging activity, as learners not only developed basic resource development skills, but also encountered the notion of socially constructed knowledge. Past educational experiences in highly authoritarian education systems made this a very significant learning activity for many who participated.

A combination of expert-driven and collaborative resource development was also evident in the field guides discussed at the start. Here the format for the booklets was developed through the participation of a number of teachers and other environmental educators, who also developed some booklets. The same format was then given to various subject specialists who expressed an interest in developing educational field guides in their own special interest areas. Whereas our scepticism of RDDA (research-develop-disseminate-adoption) approaches to environmental education resources remained, we refined our promotion of participatory resource development so that it no longer advocated the opposite extreme to "top-down" development any more. Rather, we came to value both broad participation and expert-based inputs into resource development processes.

A network needs tangible work

Having reviewed materials developed through Share-Net as a means of illustrating some of the guiding assumptions of the project, we now move to a discussion of networking. The popularity of the notion of networking in recent years has come to trivialize the concept somewhat. In Share-Net we have come to identify features that allow networking to work as the meaningful enabling function it can be. The first set of features encompasses the voluntary, informal, open-ended and low-key structure which lacks a controlling centre, but which is sufficiently well informed to provide a rich pool of resources, ideas and human contacts to those who participate in it. It is these participants, their ideas and their resources shared amongst functional nodes which make the network work; not a budget, a coordinator or a well-appointed office, although good communication tools are important. An early networking resource produced at Share-Net was an address and telephone directory of participants active in various aspects of educational resource production in environmental education. The directory is still regularly updated by asking those listed in it to add the details of others with whom they work closely in their environmental education activities. Thus the directory grows in and through the network.

These local experiences brought into focus dubious assumptions underpinning orientations to networking initiatives. Questionnaire surveys from funding agencies and other centres interested in initiating and coordinating networking in Southern Africa, are often highly contradictory. Questions like: What are the target groups of the network? (European Research and Training Centre on Environmental Education, 1995), for example, reflect a well intentioned but arrogant "outside-inside" intent to facilitate others to network. An underlying structural-functionalist agenda is clearly evident, although an attempt is made to mask this desire with progressive terms like "network".

The substance around which such engineered networking is to take place is, despite large budgets and supporting research projects, often absent. Networking processes need to take place around tangible issues, problems, tasks and actual production – in the case of Share-Net, around viable resource materials among interacting functional nodes. People get in touch with each other to have a booklet proofread, to find out the margin settings for printing, to solicit expertise for the content of their materials, to seek better understanding of new curriculum frameworks, to offer their resource to someone else's pilot project. In the process many unintended outcomes may develop.

The final point is about the non-colonizing orientation of good networking processes. Share-Net works as a low-budget but productive network because it links in with and supports other networks. It has been developed, for example, under the auspices of EEASA, the Environmental Education Association of Southern Africa, to whom many new environmental educators are introduced who could then also benefit from EEASA's annual conference and publications (and vice versa). The significant role of WESSA, a national NGO with many branches around South Africa, has been alluded to in the discussions above. Share-Net shares staff with the extension services of WESSA. Courses run by WESSA and various educational institutions around the country, including Rhodes University, benefit from the resources produced cheaply and copyright-free through Share-Net, as well as from the ongoing reflection which is such an integral part of the project processes. In turn, resource materials produced on these courses can become very popular Share-Net resources. An example is the booklet *Justice, Peace and the Environment: A Year of Special Days* (Davies 1997), which contains readings, prayers and resource materials for celebrating special days in the year. This resource was developed and produced through Share-Net by Kate Davies while on an introductory course for environmental educators certificated by Rhodes University. Mumsie Gumede of Durban Metro later adapted this resource by adding Local Agenda 21 information, thereby making it appropriate to the community workers and teachers she works with in the greater Durban metropolitan area.

Share-Net will, in future, be closely involved with the SADC Regional Environmental Education Centre to be based at the Umgeni Valley Project of WESSA. As a network of environmental education resource producers Share-Net will undoubtedly be influenced by this grand-scale project which links an international donor aid budget and centralized coordination of training and networking to the localized action and low-cost resource production thus far characterizing much of the work at Umgeni Valley. In looking at ways in which Share-Net can best serve this initiative, it is useful to review the modernist assumptions that have been revealed through the research on and within this open-ended network.

Share-Net and the challenge to modernist assumptions

Ongoing research in the practice of everyday environmental education processes in South Africa have helped inform our understanding of the modernist assumptions that permeate our work. Modernism is a dominating global outlook of the 20th century that is characterized by an unquestioning belief in progress through certain models –"grand narratives" – of intellectual, social and political "advance" (Stout 1992, p. 4). The direction of progress is said to be towards a better quality of life for all – often expressed as (capitalist) economic development, technological expertise, individual rights, democracy, equality, control over natural phenomena and enlightenment from the irrational myths of the pre-modern era. We have come to believe that the orientations associated with modernism present a major challenge in environmental education generally (Janse van Rensburg 1995) and in the production and use of resource materials in environmental learning in particular (Taylor 1997).

Some years back the *Journal of Environmental Education* published a paper in which Kastenholz and Erdemann (1994, p. 116) noted that "the achievements of the Enlightenment are often ignored or considered to be the reason for today's crisis". Ulrich Beck's work too, is helpful in understanding that a critique of modernist assumptions represents neither a call for environmental educators to embrace "post-modernism" nor a return to a pre-industrial world. Beck, along with many environmental educators, pointed out that the ideal of a better life for all is not actually being met, despite astronomical economic growth and technological advances, mass education, science, and numerous "first-world/third-world" development projects. At the same time our uncritical efforts to do so are resulting in the socio-ecological issues which characterize the risk society of our times. Beck's sociological analysis reveals the emergence of reflexive orientations within modernization; how an ongoing, critical reflection-in-action of our assumptions about how a better life for all – in a healthy environment – is to be achieved.

The first assumption challenged through reflections within the action of Share-Net is that behavioural change can be caused from the outside, in controlled ways, through rational techniques and technologies, including educational materials. We find it useful to label this assumption "technicist", a narrow and uncritical preoccupation with technique and technology, and a feature of a modernist worldview which sees the world, and how people relate to it, as involving rational processes that can be addressed in a mechanistic manner (Nel 1987; Lyotard 1993). Technicism shares features of structural-functionalism, a dominant mode of thought characterized by linear and causal perspectives on education and social change. "Structures" with particular "functions" are assumed to have direct causal effects on learning and social change. But social change is seldom a linear process (Popkewitz 1984) and structural functionalist orientations to education are invariably based on inappropriate expectations and often lead to disillusionment.

Much international policy documentation demonstrates a structural-functionalist, technicist orientation to environmental education as a tool to communicate environmental messages and cause behaviour change. Such planning documents often demonstrate a preoccupation with structures and systems that are designed to effect or coordinate rational change on a grand scale. These assumptions are predictably prevalent in an environmental context that is dominated by principles inspired by the rationalist logic of positivistic or naturalistic philosophies of natural science (Giddens 1982, p.1; see Robottom 1991, for a critique of "technocratic rationality" in environmental education). Structural-functionalism also has its roots in a North American "frontier" outlook, and resonates with a similar social

disposition in apartheid South Africa (Sparks 1990). Within this web of centre-to-periphery social change the technical and administrative reform of institutions are seen as the techniques and technologies to effect change on/for others.

Instead, we came to see that environmental educators can only engage with learners in processes of change, that the outcomes of these educational and social change processes are not predefined in predictable routines, but that educational resources can help to enrich, stimulate, inform and support them. Thus the resources produced through Share-Net are seen as tools to support encounters (with environment and environmental issues, for example the field guides to support field work or the water kits to assess water quality), dialogue (to discuss what is being learned, for example the "Issues for Debate" section in the Enviro-Facts) and reflection (a critical review of learning, stimulated, for example, by the ACTION acronym which encourages the development of catchment conservation plans). Encounter-dialogue-reflection provides an open-ended model of processes of learning which avoids the assumption of rationalist, causal relationships between knowledge, attitude and positive environmental behaviour.

A second orientation we came to question involves two seemingly opposed approaches to social change. While Share-Net was established to foster participatory resource development in the wake of disillusionment with RDDA approaches, experiences in the project revealed that "top-down" and "participatory" do not necessarily form a dichotomy and that both can have value as long as the assumptions driving them are clarified. While sceptical of grand scale top-down initiatives, we also started to question the popularist preoccupation with participation so prevalent in the new South Africa. The notions of participation, empowerment and capacity-building were to overcome the centralized, authoritarian orientations of apartheid. We grew to doubt whether such popularist orientations did in fact represent a rupture from the earlier social engineering dispositions that people claimed they were trying to overturn. Were these not paternalistic, too? The idea that educational projects and processes that involve participation and critique can empower others is very popular in environment and development education, particularly in South Africa. Yet a closer look at the notion of empowerment reveals that:

> When A considers it essential for B to be empowered, A assumes not only that B has no power – or does not have the right kind of power – but also that A has a secret formula of a power to which B has not been initiated. In the current participatory ideology, this formula is in fact, nothing but a revised version of state power, or what could be called fear-power. (Rahnema 1992, p. 123). "Implicit in the notion of empowerment is that power is something to be given by those who have power – a commodity to be bartered"(Popkewitz 1991, p.236).

A further question arises: Who benefits most from popularist education? As Popkewitz (1991-232) pointed out: "The positioning of the popularist, in fact, supports the status quo of the intellectual". Intellectuals, including those of us working in environmental education, can maintain the status quo for ourselves by drawing on the notion of the "disempowered" state of others.

In some instances the new "politically correct" terminology thus appears to sustain prevailing power relationships and social engineering orientations, providing a "new lease on life" to externally driven projects developed on behalf of those others who are required to change, even if it is to become "empowered". At the very least, the use of popularist terms, such as "network", end "empowerment" can inhibit project outcomes, providing a false sense of security and a semblance of progress, what Popkewitz (1984) termed "change as motion" (see also Popkewitz 1995).

The third feature of modernism we explored through research within Share-Net can be termed scientism. Experiences with two sets of Share-Net resources, the Enviro-Facts and the water kits, helped us to clarify the limiting role of scientism and the value of science in environmental education. Scientism refers to an unquestioning belief in the underpinnings of science and the notion that science can solve most of society's problems (Beck 1992). Like Beck, many environmental educators value science but are critical of scientism. Critical reflections on the underpinnings of science are necessary to encourage scientific practices that can truly address the complex, often invisible and usually poorly understood environmental issues of the day – the "risks" of a modern era. By exposing learners to opposing scientific opinions on environmental issues as in the Enviro-Fact sheets, and encouraging them to experience the construction of scientific knowledge for themselves by using equipment such as the water kits, learners develop a more informed understanding of scientific processes and the courage and skills to participate in them. By combining measurement and testing with asking for local knowledge and reading indigenous stories on the topic, learners are also encouraged to set up a dialogue between different ways of knowing. This process Beck refers to as inter-epistemological dialogue, so necessary if society is to collectively address the socio-ecological problems of our time.

Conclusion

On a worldwide scale the developing processes of Share-Net are small but these have had a significant clarifying influence on environmental education in South Africa and beyond. Part of the reason for this shaping influence is the reflexive research-in-action orientation taken in and to the project throughout its evolution (Taylor 1997). This orientation has revealed that many of the conventions of environmental education in this region and other parts of the world are based, somewhat blindly, on limiting modernist assumptions about education and change.

Through Share-Net we came to clarify and value an open-process model of dialogue, encounter and reflection and to see educational materials as resources to support and improve such non-linear processes of learning. Both the water project and the Enviro-Facts emphasized the value of science in environmental education and the problems with scientism. In addition experiences with the water kits taught us that educational materials, just like computers, do not teach on their own. The disposition of the educator who uses the materials, and in fact the social habitue within which they are used, play highly significant roles which should not be underestimated by those who develop and fund such materials. The Enviro-Facts project taught us not to juxtapose "top-down" and "participatory" approaches to resource development as opposites, but to recognize that elements of both occur in many projects, and that the underlying assumptions of both approaches need to be revealed.

We saw that the progressive rhetoric of empowerment, capacity-building, networking and participation sometimes only "empowers" the users of the rhetoric and is not always associated with real changes in project orientations. By comparing Share-Net to the many new initiatives being set up for Southern Africa we learned that networking works best when it happens organically, around tangible endeavours such as resource production. We remained sceptical of top-down, RDDA interventions and came to question technicist assumptions about change and the role of educational materials, projects and project developers in such change.

Of course our growing understanding of the manifestations and the risks of modernist orientations to knowledge, science, education and social chance does not mean that the work we are involved in through Share-Net has moved beyond them. The increased clarity has, nonetheless, enabled us to be more critical of the unfounded conventions we and others often support, and more sensitive to their limitations. As Share-Net is about to support a large-scale, donor-driven programme of environmental education coordination in the Southern African region, we hope to learn how the project can avoid failing victim to, and maintain its challenge to, modernist myths. Hopefully, our capacity to respond, which has been enhanced during this period of study, will enable us to cope with the environmental changes and challenges we must inevitably face together in the future.

Acknowledgments

This chapter tells the story of the collaborative work of many individuals supported by a range of organizations in a variety of ways as has become the pattern of the work within Share-Net. Recent conceptual and editorial comments on the text have been gratefully received from Rob O'Donoghue, Kim le Roux and Heila Lotz. Other support for the research and field activities reflected here has come from the Foundation for Research Development, WWF-SA, Shell SA, Gold Fields, Umgeni Water and the Mazda Wildlife Fund. The collaboration between the authors started formally when Eureta Janse van Rensburg acted as mentor for Jim Taylor's doctoral research, but stretches to many joint courses, committee meetings and clarifying discussions during the many enriching journeys between them.

References

Ashwell, A. (1992). *Project Water: A case study of the development of an environmental education project*. Unpublished M.Ed. Thesis. Rhodes University, Grahamstown, South Africa.

Beck, U. (1992). *Risk Society: Towards a New Modernity*. Sage: London.

Davies, K. (I 997). *Justice, Peace and the Environment: A Year of Special Days*. Share-Net: Howick.

Janse van Rensburg, E. (1995). *Environmental Education and Research in Southern Africa: A Landscape of Shifting Priorities*. Unpublished Ph.D. thesis, Rhodes University, Grahamstown, South Africa.

European Research and Training Centre on Environmental Education (1995). *Environmental Education and Networks in the Commonwealth*. European Research and Training Centre on Environmental Education: Bradford.

Giddens, A. (1982). *Profiles and Critiques in Social Theory*. University of California Press: Berkeley, CA.

Kastenholz, H.G. & K-H. Erdmann (1994). "Education for responsibility within the framework of UNESCO" in *Journal of Environmental Education*, 25(2):15-20.

Lather, P. (1996). "Troubling clarity: The politics of accessible language" in *Harvard Educational Review*, 66 (3):525-545.

Levin, H. M. (1980). "The limits of educational planning" in H. Weiler (ed.), *Educational Planning and Social Change*. UNESCO: Paris.

Lyotard, J. F. (1993). "Answering the question: What is postmodernism?" in T. Docherty (ed.) (1993), *Postmodernism. A Reader*. Harvester Wheatsheaf: Cambridge.

Nel, B.F. (1987). "The problems with technicism: Focus on South Africa". Paper presented at the Early Childhood Education Conference, 1987, Ramat-Gan, Israel.

O'Donoghue, R.B. (1993). *GREEN Water Quality Monitoring in Southern Africa: A Field Guide.* Share-Net, Howick, South Africa.

O'Donoghue, R.B. (1997). *Detached harmonies: A study in/on developing social processes of environmental education in eastern Southern Africa.* Unpublished Doctoral Thesis, Rhodes University, Grahamstown.

O'Donoghue, R.B. and J. Taylor (1988). "Towards participant-centred resource development in environmental education" in *Southern African Journal of Environmental Education*, 7:3-5.

O'Donoghue, R. and E. Janse van Rensburg (1995). *Environments and Methods.* Share-Net, Howick, South Africa.

Papagiannis, G.J., S.J. Klees & R.N. Bickel (1982). "Toward a political economy of educational innovation" in *Review of Educational Research*, 52(2):245-290.

Paxton, L. (1994). *An investigation into the need for environmental information in South Africa: A case study of the Enviro-Facts project.* Unpublished M.Ed. thesis, Department of Education, Rhodes University, Grahamstown, South Africa.

Popkewitz, T.S. (1981). "The social contexts of schooling, change, and educational research" in *Journal of Curriculum Studies*, 13(3):189-206.

Popkewitz, T.S. (1984). *Paradigm and Ideology: The Social Functions of the Intellectual.* Falmer Press: London.

Popkewitz, T.S. (1991). *A political sociology of educational reform.* Teachers College Press: New York.

Popkewitz, T.S. (1995). "Foreword" in P. L. McLaren and J. M. Giarelli (eds.), *Critical theory and educational research.* SUNY Press: Albany, New York. pp. xi-xxi.

Rahnema, M. (1992). "Participation" in W. Sachs (ed.), *The Development Dictionary.* Witwatersrand University Press: Johannesburg.

Robottom, I. (1991). "Technocratic environmental education: A critique and some alternative" in *Journal of Experiential Education*, 14(1):20-26.

Schreuder, D. R. (1994). "The Schools Water Project (SWAP): A Case Study of an Action Research and Community Problem Solving Approach to Curriculum Innovation" in *Australian Journal of Environmental Education*, 10 (September):35-346.

Sparks, A. (1990). *The Mind of South Africa: The Story of the Rise and Fall of Apartheid.* Mandarin: London.

Stout, M. (1992). *Postmodernism, deconstruction and comparative education: The primacy of multiple narratives.* Graduate School of Education, UCLA.

Taylor, J. (1993). "Giving the tools of science away" in *Nature Herald*. Commission on Education and Communication. IUCN Newsletter, 4:11.

Taylor, J. (1997). *Share-Net: A case study of environmental education resource material development in a risk society.* Unpublished Doctoral Thesis, Rhodes University, Grahamstown, South Africa.

Wals, A.F. (1994). "Action research and community problem solving: Environmental education in an inner city" in *Educational Action Research*, 2(2):163-182.

Personal Communications

Masuku, Lynette. Environmental Education Officer, Natal Park Board, researcher on the role of the indigenous story in the 2020 Vision Water Project. 4 May 1997.

Chapter12

Zimbabwe

Education to sustain the Zambezi

Kathy Greaves Stiles

Introduction

Rifa Conservation Camp, Zimbabwe, has been teaching biodiversity and Zambezi River Valley conservation for over 12 years. Located on the Zimbabwe side of the Zambezi River the Education Camp looks across the river to Zambia. Lying within a protected wilderness land use area students can look through binoculars at the agricultural land use on the opposite side of the river.

The education programme at Rifa provides extra-curricular activities directly related to the objectives of some formal education courses, especially Advanced Level Biology and Geography, and teacher college syllabi. These objectives are coupled with the broader environmental education aims of the support organization, the Zimbabwe Hunters Association (ZHA).

Starting with classic field studies, the week long courses have evolved into an indigenous resource management/issue-related learning experience. From an assessment of the present environment of the mid-Zambezi Valley, learners are encouraged to understand the interrelationships within this environment, including human-induced changes. Traditional values and knowledge of the local environment are introduced to advanced level secondary school and teaching college students, who come from education backgrounds that include very little experiential learning in or out of the classroom.

The educational experience is diverse in nature, involving a variety of teaching methods. Issues related to biodiversity and international river management are taught using methods that encourage problem-solving skills, critical thinking and the ability to work and negotiate with others. The overall aim of Rifa is to help develop environmentally literate and responsible citizens in Zimbabwe.

The History and context

Rifa was set up in 1982 as a tented conservation camp on the edge of the Zambezi River upstream of Chirundu. At that time the Zimbabwe Hunters Association, in agreement with National Parks and Wildlife Management (NPWM), decided to use profits from the administration of citizen hunting in Zimbabwe safari areas for the conservation education of youth. It was decided that senior youth and educators would be the target group, especially those from rural and/or disadvantaged schools. The programme was intended to provide field studies and enrichment for the British Advanced Level Biology and Geography which is still used in Zimbabwe.

The Department of National Parks and Wildlife Management was quite happy to have this environmental education camp, which made use of its non-hunting buffer zone on the Zambezi, but does not involve itself directly with environmental education. Since Independence in 1980, NPWM has worked with several NGOs to allow them to use the facilities of the protected areas for education activities that fulfil common aims of NPWM and the NGOs. The base funding for Rifa is provided by the ZHA. There are no fees for schools, with all resource persons being volunteers, including members of the association.

When the camp was set up the education programme of ZHA had two goals. One was to help educate Zimbabwe youth to become citizens who could manage natural resources in a sustainable manner. The second was to build awareness and love of the natural environment, especially the Zambezi Valley, that hopefully would result in a commitment to sustaining its ecosystems.

The conservation ethic of the volunteers was, like others globally, quite protectionist until the early 1990s with the advent of the CAMPFIRE[1] programme (Maveneke 1995; Makombe 1993). The involvement of some ZHA members in the CAMPFIRE programme, combined with increased involvement by educators, brought the issues of community management and sustainable use into the programme.

Relationship of Rifa education to the future of the Zambezi River System

There are 11 shared watercourse systems in the Southern African region. The Zambezi River system is the largest with eight riparian states having legitimate claims on its water resources. The Zambezi Action Plan (ZACPLAN) is one result of an acknowledgement of the need for cooperation among the riparian states in maintaining environmentally sustainable and equitable utilization of the river's resources (Chenje and Johnson 1996). This action plan has acknowledged the importance of education in the sustainable development and management of the Zambezi Basin. It is based on an acknowledgement that:

- The level of understanding of ecological issues (especially ecological effects of development in the basin) is generally weak throughout the Basin, including the population as a whole, politicians, decision-makers/planners, developers and special interest groups.

- The low level of understanding should be mitigated through training. This training should develop ecological/environmental awareness and be provided to groups from school children to high-level decision-makers and developers (Matiza and Dale 1993).

One workshop after another has reiterated the need for education to help sustain the ecosystems of the Zambezi while developing the potential of the area to meet human needs for water, power, and land. A workshop on water and land use in the Zambezi Basin in 1993 (Matiza, Crafter and Dale 1995) followed a workshop on wetland conservation in Zimbabwe in 1992 (Matiza and Crafter 1994). Most recently, a workshop on Wetlands was held in Harare at which time the failure to implement recommendations from other workshops was brought out as a failing of government and NGO sectors. Rifa was one of the few cited examples of wetland and biodiversity education.

As a participant in the 1997 follow-up workshop, I used the Rifa education programme as an example of education on the wetlands of the Zambezi valley. Until recently, there has been very little education in Zimbabwe, especially using local examples and in the context of biodiversity. Biodiversity education has now become a focal point of the Rifa Advanced Level programme, especially for students of biology. The sustainable future of diverse ecosystems, and to some extent species, are issues for which the programme administration has spent much time developing resources and beginning an outreach effort. Rifa has provided the only education programme in Zimbabwe for the A-Level student that involves the Zambezi Valley wetlands and biodiversity issues.

A Week in the Zambezi Valley - the Rifa experience

Imagine thirty 17-19 year old youths in a large school bus arriving at the top of the Zambezi Valley escarpment. Spread before them is a wide rather flat valley filled with trees, including large baobab trees towering above the thick bush. If the valley isn't covered in haze they can see the mountains of the escarpment on the other side and Zambia. The Zambezi River is not visible at this point but the excitement grows as the youth peer into the wilderness. Most of them have never seen the river or any area that is relatively untouched by humans.

The location of Rifa Camp is about four kilometres upstream of the bridge between Zambia and Zimbabwe at Chirundu; adjacent to the Hurungwe Safari Area of Zimbabwe National Parks. Situated on the Zambezi flood plain, it offers students a unique environment that ranges from wetland to riverine to mopane woodland. Impala and waterbuck browse beside elephant while painted hunting dogs and lion stalk their prey. Nearby lie the ruins of villages, which once housed the Kore Kore people before their displacement by the Rhodesian Government in 1956. Students walk up meandering dry riverbeds, hoping to see buffalo, while shaded by riverine trees full of the 100 or so species of birds seen each week.

The camp is on the edge of large tracts of land, which have been set aside by the government as wilderness/protected areas along the Zambezi. This is quite different from the agricultural lands one sees across the river in Zambia (Main 1990).

In addition to its biodiversity, the area is geographically interesting. The valley at this point has both large alluvial deposits as well as outcroppings of other sedimentary rock. Fossil ferns may be found nearby, as well as archaeological remains of villages that go back hundreds of years. There is a series of hot springs next to the camp which is studied as one of the wetland areas. An oxbow lake formed after the building of Kariba dam, several pans or vernal pools, dry tributaries and the Zambezi itself. These water bodies around Rifa provide the diverse study that Rifa has offered over the years. Vegetation varies from colonizers on the new sandbank deposits to mopane woodland to riparian.

The Rifa Centre is built with basic camping facilities, including dormitories for 30 students plus staff to a maximum of 45. Located on the edge of the old river terrace, the camp has views over what once was a channel and island of the Zambezi. Living accommodation is very basic but does include some amenities like flush toilets and electricity. Students are expected to do their own cooking and cleaning up. There are three classrooms, which house a library, laboratory, and museum. These facilities, which are growing with donations from local and international friends, give students an extensive range of resources. It is very tempting for students from disadvantaged

schools to spend long evenings in the library as well as to take advantage of the microscopes to look, for example, at life from pans or impala stomach contents. All this indoor work is of course fitted into the quiet hours of midday when the heat and intense sun send students and staff under the trees.

Over 1,200 students per year, including those from disadvantaged schools, use Rifa as their primary field experience. The students are often from backgrounds that have become distanced or alienated from indigenous knowledge of natural resources and are now following the British education syllabi for A-Level. They often come from schools where there is little if any practical field study. Each school must send 15 students plus two or more of their teachers. They come mainly from the northern and central part of the country.

Teacher education has always been one of the objectives of the programme, mainly by involving classroom teachers in the programme and by offering a few teacher/lecturer weekend camps. Proactive outreach in 1996 brought the first group of students from a teacher-training college during their term time and as a part of their course. Continued outreach with the college and its staff recently brought a second group of student teachers to Rifa.

The background of student teachers is similar to the less advantaged A-level students. The student teachers from the middle level training college are predominately O-Level graduates who will teach only up to O-Level rather than Advanced Level biology. Many have studied general science in rural schools with minimal experiential or hands-on learning (Stiles 1995). As with many other students attending Rifa, the student teachers have little or no experience with learning activities that go beyond "chalk and talk" or "cook-book" experiments.

Teaching practice has changed at Rifa since the camp started in 1982. Global and regional changes in teaching focus and practice have presented a challenge to all educators involved with Rifa. Most educators and environmental specialists involved with Rifa were brought up with traditional didactic field study and lecture methods of education. Thus the teaching at Rifa has been a combination of lectures and field studies with some opportunity for debate during an evening session. The camp is now trying to go beyond "getting the message across" (Taylor 1997) through awareness and ecological knowledge enhancement by involving students in critical thinking about environmental issues – especially local ones.

Examples of Rifa programmes

Each day begins before sunrise as students on cooking duty put kettles of water to boil over deadwood fires. Warm tea and biscuits give a boost to sleepy eyes for the two-, or more, hour hikes into the natural ecosystems of Rifa which are combined with field study and wilderness awareness training.

Rifa has always provided very good field study programmes using the examples of ecosystems and interactions that abound in the vicinity. Students use a variety of ecological field methods, including mark-recapture (bird banding), forest census, tree transects, taxonomic and other studies of the diversity of flora and fauna. Predator-prey relationships are studied side by side with termite communities, and dissections of impala add a special interest in comparing anatomy and physiology of adaptation. Animal behaviour is observed and interpreted, such as vultures at a prepared feast of impala bones. Teachers modify the programme around what is

happening in the local environment. If elephants shake the acacias for seedpods or painted hunting dogs chase and catch an impala in front of the camp, then that occasion becomes part of the study.

Wetland and freshwater studies have always been the examples used for ecosystem and geography field study at Rifa. The type of study has depended on the interest of the schoolteachers and the availability of resources. Detailed work on a series of vernal pools (pans) was initiated through involvement of teachers from several schools interested in chemistry and microscopic study. Donation of a seine net this year from the University of Zimbabwe added a wonderful, at times hilarious, dimension to freshwater study, as students ventured into the crocodile free small pans. Falling into mud, bringing nets full of amphibians, turtles, and other assorted creatures to sort and put back into the murky water, was enjoyed by students and teachers. Students did complex studies of pans and used the less detailed work from the oxbow and Zambezi as comparisons for diversity of species, relating all of this to the a-biotic and biotic aspects of the different ecosystems. Study guides for student research are developed from regional and international freshwater guides such as those from SWAP in South Africa, Caduto (1990), Stapp and Mitchell (1995), and the textbooks used by the schools in Zimbabwe.

The biophysical aspects of the environment are combined with the human related ones as students put their biophysical fieldwork together with a study of the history and potential uses of the mid-Zambezi. Debates and environmental impact assessments are carried out using groups of students and teachers in simulations of the real life potential impacts of tourism, resettlement and river impoundment in the area. This use of role-play has gradually developed from the earlier evening debates and discussion groups. The use of simulations, and role play, though advocated by environmental educators such as Taylor (1985) and Marchinkowski et al (1994) as ways to bring people closer to citizen action, is unfamiliar as a teaching method in Zimbabwe, so it is especially important to use it with teaching college students.

Student-teacher participants are encouraged to think critically when considering how they could use the environment outside the classroom. Each activity is looked at critically after the experience. The field methods used are examples of what they might do, and students are encouraged to think of new, innovative methods that would be fun, while involving pupils as participants in learning and teaching.

The indigenous knowledge systems connection: linking the past to the future

Rifa's education programme is changing. With industrialization and modern development there was a widespread belief that indigenous knowledge was not scientific and did not include a conservation ethic. The importance of indigenous knowledge systems (IKS) to biodiversity and the sustainability of resource use (Biodiversity Support Program 1993) has become one of the focuses of Zimbabwe's response to Agenda 21 and the Convention on Biodiversity. Concepts of ecology and biodiversity conservation are recommended for teaching within the framework of both traditional and modern knowledge. Themes of sustainability now include reference to detailed indigenous knowledge of the environment held by rural people (Matowanyika et al 1995). At Rifa there is now an attempt to balance scientific and indigenous outlooks on the environment which allows the students to sense a continuum of nature by getting reacquainted with the environment of their ancestors.

This year I began to use the resident National Parks scout as a teacher, especially with the student teachers. Sometimes he team-teaches with ethno-botanists from the National Herbarium on loan to us for a week. He teaches in Shona and English, using whatever is most comfortable and/or appropriate. The history of the people who lived in the area before displacement in 1956 is being introduced to students, thanks to story collecting by the scout. Folk tales and medicinal uses of plants are related, while students sit under a baobab making twine as local folk did long ago to use for snares and cloth.

Student teachers' experiences include time to develop some outdoor community focus activities using traditional knowledge of the environment. They are encouraged to use the school community as a resource for IKS, thus helping break down the wall between western style schools and their communities (Stiles 1995). Examples of integration of IKS in teaching are introduced and discussed – those from experience at Rifa and those in some texts from countries such as Namibia and the US (Caduto and Bruchac 1989; du Toit and Squazzin 1995).

The importance of outreach

Rifa's education programme is unique in being designed specifically for conservation of the Zambezi ecosystems and landscape. Until recently the programme has had little outreach beyond the school resource person's interaction before and after the camp. One of the weaknesses of the programme has been its lack of a built in mechanism for evaluation of long-term effects. Short-term effects can be seen through school reports which are full of wonderfully humorous diaries, personal stories, poetry and artwork, as well as the scientific results of assorted fieldwork.

The education programme's strength and weakness lies in its volunteer base. Most educators and field specialists spend one week each year with a student group. The focal persons – the coordinator and resource person – are much more involved and put together groups of people for each school week. This makes each week quite unique, yet at times means an inability to offer the same programme each week. A full-time teaching staff would alleviate some of the problems. However, the ability to use volunteers is a strength in many ways, not least of which is that it involves a large and diverse group of people directly in education for the Zambezi.

The reason for involving an education camp such as Rifa in outreach programmes is that to fulfil the aims and objectives of environmental education it is necessary to go beyond the ecology, environmental science and environmental management education as taught in Zimbabwe schools. Benedict emphasizes the special quality of environmental education as:

> Facilitating the pupil's own inquiring search for understanding of the complex world and the environmental problems we face, and their search for solutions. These two aspects of EE – the need to address the root causes of the problems and the need to teach pupils to actively participate in society – are what give EE its special character.
>
> (Benedict 1991, pp. 14-15)

The programme has never had personnel to follow students back to the school for direct outreach. However, in 1996-97 the programme implementers focused on two outreach projects. First, proactive involvement with the Ministry of Education and WWF Project office has resulted in a project designed to produce Biodiversity

Resource Materials (Stiles 1997). Second, the coordinator and resource officer coordinated youth programmes for Zimbabwe around the CITES and GBF7 conferences in 1997 in Harare (Stiles 1997). Youth have been excluded from active participation in national and international conventions and decision-making processes in this country, as in most others. Youth are discussed, are part of the stakeholder groups, but are not included in the process. Through the outreach of the ZHA programme staff, students were brought directly to the events and participated as stakeholders. The reports from students and other participants at the Global Biodiversity Forum 7 were positive and should lead the way to increased involvement of senior youth in national and global conventions.

The future of Rifa and other EE centre camps in Zimbabwe

With the increased commercialization of national parks in Zimbabwe, the future of NGO backed education within or adjacent to state lands is precarious. Free access to National Protected areas, use of personnel as guides, and siting of camps within NPWM lands is under threat of being changed to a user pay system from a free access system. Although NPWM have verbally agreed to allow student groups to walk through and use the non-hunting buffer areas for field study, there is potential for conflicting interests with commercial use of the same areas by foreign clients.

Finances to run the programmes, and maintain the infrastructure of the EE centres and camps which came indirectly from Parks via ZHA profits from the administration of citizen hunting in NPW lands is disappearing. NPW has no plan for ensuring financial funds or other support to education programmes such as Rifa. Whereas until now the organization did not need to look for outside donors, it will now enter the competition for funds or have to become more user funded. A preliminary study by ZHA indicates no prospect of becoming financially self-sufficient from school fees alone. Loose arrangements between NPWM and organizations in charge of EE programmes, such as ZHA, will have to be formalized.

One hope for the future lies in the forthcoming national biodiversity strategy. The education programme has come to the attention of the consultants facilitating the national strategy workshops, ensuring the inclusion of the Rifa education programme in the workshop. The national strategy team has been very impressed with the education for biodiversity that has been developing at Rifa and the outreach to the Ministry of Education, as well as the involvement with international conventions. If Rifa can be directly included as a centre for biodiversity education, especially as a field centre for student research and learning, the process of finding financial support may be easier, as it will have the backing of two ministries – Environment and Tourism, and Education.

Conclusion

The education programme at Rifa is a flexible, ever-changing response to the needs of both students attending the camp, and national or global trends in environmental education. The focus is on biodiversity and sustainable use, Zambezi wetland and freshwater ecosystems, and the impact of humans on the past, present and future of the Zambezi River Valley.

Teaching methods that give participants an opportunity to develop skills and strategies for dealing with controversial issues are gradually being introduced. Outreach programmes to teacher colleges are giving the colleges needed support and the Rifa volunteer teaching staff a chance to reflect on and make changes to their own practice.

Our hope for the future of the Zambezi Valley lies with the youth that sit with us on the shores of the river. With the cooperation of the government, user groups and support groups, Rifa will continue to provide a unique education for the future of the Zambezi ecosystems and sustainable national natural resources.

Notes

1. Communal Areas Management Program for Indigenous Resources (CAMPFIRE) in Zimbabwe is an innovative and adaptive rural development program. One of its objectives is to change community attitudes toward natural resource management.

References

Biodiversity Support Program, (1993). *African Biodiversity: Foundation for the Future*. Biodiversity Support Program: Washington, D.C.

Caduto, M. (1990). *Pond and brook - a guide to nature in freshwater environments*. University Press of New England: Hanover.

Caduto, M., and J. Bruchac (1989). *Keepers of the earth - native American stories and environmental activities for children*. Fulcrum: Colorado.

Chenje, M. & P. Johnson (eds). *Water in southern Africa*. Print Holdings: Harare.

du Toit, D. and T. Squazzin. (1995). *Tools of the trade - skills and techniques for environmental education in Namibia*. Enviroteach: Namibia.

Kuiper, J. (1994). *Environment education in the formal sector in Zimbabwe*. Unpublished research paper prepared for IDRC. Nairobi.

Main, M. (1990). Zambezi - *journey of a river*. Southern Book Publishers. Halfway House.

Makombe, K. (1995). *Sharing the land - wildlife, people and development in Africa*. IUCN/ROSA: Harare.

Manjengwa, J. (1995). *Environmental education for sustainable development in secondary schools of Zimbabwe. Unpublished thesis for Masters in Environmental Policy and Planning*. University of Zimbabwe.

Marcinkowski, T., T. Volk and H. Hungerford (1994). *An environmental education approach to the training of middle level teachers: a prototype program*. UNESCO-UNEP EE Series No 30.

Matowanyika, J., V. Garibaldi and E. Musimwa, (eds.) (1995). *Indigenous knowledge systems and natural resource management in southern Africa*. IUCN: Harare: Zimbabwe.

Maveneke, T. (1995). "The CAMPFIRE program in Zimbabwe: changes of attitudes and practices of rural communities towards natural resources" in J. Palmer, W. Goldstein, A. Curnow, (eds), *Planning education to care for the earth*. IUCN: Gland.

Stiles, K. (1995). *Inhibitors to change: a case study of teacher change in a rural African context*. Unpublished M.Ed thesis. Rhodes University: Grahamstown, South Africa.

Stiles, K. (1997). *Report to environment liaison forum on CITES COP10 - student projects*. Unpublished report.

Stiles, K. (1997). *Biodiversity resources for formal education in Zimbabwe - project proposal from CDU with ZHA*. Collaborative, unpublished proposal.

Taylor, John. (1985). *Guide on simulation and gaming for environmental education*. UNESCO: Paris.

Taylor, Jim. (1997). *Share-Net: a case study of environmental education resource material development in a risk society*. Unpublished PhD thesis. Rhodes University: Grahamstown, South Africa.

Chapter 13

South Africa

Environmental education as a process of change and reconstruction: The Science and Sustainability Project

Danie Schreuder, Chris Reddy and Lesley Le Grange

Introduction

This chapter describes a local curriculum research and development project in which the concept of sustainability is used reflectively as a unifying theme in a new approach to science education. The project began as the South African chapter of a United States resource materials development programme, Windows on the Wild. This programme of the World Wildlife Fund (WWF) USA focuses on biodiversity and involves the production of environmental education material aimed at supporting teachers in the development of curricula. The resource material comprises activities which are intended to help students understand the concept of biodiversity and factors that threaten biodiversity on a global and local scale.

Interested parties in a number of countries were encouraged to adapt some of the materials for local use and in 1996 a partnership was formed among WWF-USA, a corporate donor (Kodak), WWF-South Africa and the Environmental Education Programme at the University of Stellenbosch where the project is based. At the time, we saw this partnership as an opportunity, using the Windows on the Wild package as a basis, to produce materials that would be responsive to the needs of the local education community and that could be used in South African schools and teacher education institutions.

However, as a result of a process of ongoing dialogue and reflection, the team of authors (biology teachers and environmental educators) appointed to develop the South African material raised a concern that the mere adaptation of US developed materials may be inappropriate for a vastly different South African context. Consequently, a new focus emerged, namely science and sustainability. But before we tell the story of how this new focus developed and the project unfolded, an explanation of the educational context is necessary.

The context

The project is being undertaken in a period of rapid social change in South Africa, associated with a fledgling democracy and the country's re-entry into the global society. This period has witnessed the emergence of a plethora of new policies, including policies on education and environment. For example, the right of every citizen to a healthy environment is embedded in the bill of rights of the new South African constitution. Key policy documents emphasize the importance of using the country's natural resources in a sustainable manner, as well as the need for

sustainable development (Reconstruction and Development Programme 1994, Bill on Environmental Management 1998).

During the early developmental stages of the Windows on the Wild process, national educational policy processes emerged, providing still new challenges. Some significant policy changes included:

- a shift from a content-based to an Outcomes Based Education (OBE) system (National Qualification Framework (NQF) document, 1996; Curriculum 2005 document, 1997);
- a shift from teacher-centered to more learner-centered education (Curriculum Framework document 1996);
- more democratic educational practices and fully participatory processes of curriculum development and training (ANC policy framework, 1995; White Paper on Education and Training 1995); and
- the inclusion of environmental education in the formal school curriculum for the first time (White Paper on Education and Training, 1995; National Qualification Framework Document, 1996; Curriculum 2005 document, 1997).

Another change is the replacement of the 42 school subjects offered to students in South African schools by eight areas of learning. The learning areas idea is to promote a more holistic approach, and essentially involves combinations of the old subjects. Each learning area will have curriculum-linked outcomes (specific outcomes) which learners should attain through learning activities. These learning activities are intended to have a local and contextual focus, and teachers will have to play a much more prominent role in the development of learning programmes (coherent collection of learning activities). In addition, all programmes of learning are to be organized by cross-curricular themes (phase organizers), such as environment, entrepreneurship and personal development.

One of the learning areas is Natural Sciences which includes old subject areas such as Chemistry, Physics, Biology and sections of Geography. Natural Sciences will have four organizing themes, namely Planet Earth and Beyond, Energy and Change, Matter and Materials and Life and Living. In line with these new developments in South African education, it was realized that the Windows in the Wild project could link up with two aspects, namely the theme "life and living", and the cross-curricular theme "environment/sustainability". Using these two organizers for natural science programme development means that natural science processes and learning activities can be directed to more sustainable living practices, thus conflating science education processes and environmental education processes.

The proposed changes challenge the traditional approach to curriculum and resource development, with its strong autocratic character and centralized locus of control, which was used by former apartheid governments to reinforce acute socio-economic and racial differences. The traditional system further contributed to the systematic deskilling of teachers who functioned largely as technicians, merely having to deliver pre-determined and packaged curricula.

This new approach to curriculum development not only challenges the idea of traditional textbooks as primary sources of knowledge, but also the expert-driven notion behind the production of these resources. Engaging teachers who are unfamiliar with developing contextually relevant and appropriate curricula is indeed daunting, but it is important to support the participation of teachers in resource

production and curriculum development. It is here that participatory approaches of reflection in and on action allow for open and emergent processes, focusing on local issues in context.

Although these processes were not unfamiliar to the authors, challenges provided by the demands of new educational policies and developments further inspired us to engage in a collaborative research and development process involving constructive dialogue, reflection and participation. Key to such processes is the generation of resources which are likely to stimulate in learners:

- active exploration of the environment;
- debate on contested issues;
- interaction (group work) in the classroom and the community;
- participation in, and active engagement with issues.

(Lotz, 1986)

In theory, such processes seem to be ideally suited to the demands and context of the present South African education scene. In practice, however, we had to accept very early on that such processes, although rich and very enlightening, are often time consuming and costly. Legitimacy of the process, as well as quality of the resource materials are ensured only by authentic participation, continuous cycles of investigation, dialogue and reflection. This is time-consuming, and not always understood, or in the interest of partners in the process, such as donor-funders.

The emergence of sustainability as a unifying theme

How did sustainability emerge as a focus for science curriculum materials? First, as predominantly life science teachers actively involved in environmental education, we had been concerned with and practised in integrating environmental education processes with life science learning. Before beginning to work with Windows on the Wild, we had pursued the notion of unifying themes, which are those central concepts and ideas around which a curriculum can be developed.

The focus on biodiversity in the existing Windows on the Wild material presented somewhat of a dilemma. As life science teachers, we agreed that the concept of biodiversity conforms to many of the requirements of a unifying theme for the biological sciences, but in the wider Natural Sciences arena of the South African educational context it was less appropriate. Biodiversity is commonly accepted as one – but only one – of the principles of ecological sustainability and therefore is a less encompassing concept than sustainability. Nevertheless, biodiversity is a very important factor in maintaining the capacity of natural systems to sustain life and the sustainability of the earth as a living system.

Second, we became critical of the anthropocentric and instrumental view of sustainability that was evident in most of the materials that we studied. From this anthropocentric perspective, natural resources are to be managed sustainably for the benefit and future of humans and not for the intrinsic worth of nature itself. The contributions of living organisms towards making the earth and its atmosphere livable are regarded as "ecological services" (Lovelock 1994, p. 353) to humans and thus natural resources are treated as commodities for human use and management. Our concern with this position stimulated a search for a new meaning of the concept of sustainability and led us to reflect on natural systems and ecological principles.

Our point of departure lay in a specific interpretation of the concept of sustainability which simply refers to an activity which can endure or persist. As life science educators, we asked ourselves why natural systems seem to persist, and what principles of sustainability are possibly reflected in these systems. We are also fortunate to live and work in a unique plant Kingdom, the Fynbos biome which is world-renowned for natural beauty, and exceptional biodiversity. Many of the examples included in our programmes are related to a variety of Fynbos ecosystems, illustrating these principles. Some of the principles of sustainable living which we observed in these natural systems were:

- living organisms appear not to use more resources than they need to survive;
- living organisms tend not to generate products that cannot be recycled;
- in natural systems species live interdependently;
- all members of natural communities seem to live within the carrying capacity of the environment;
- natural systems seem to have remarkable abilities of self-healing or recovery following natural disasters;
- in natural systems all species, whether they appear to be less or more dominant, play a role in contributing towards stability in the system; and
- biodiversity seems to be characteristic of most communities.

We found that our thoughts were not unique. For example, Chiras (1993) similarly identified five biological principles of sustainability, namely *conservation, recycling, renewable resource use, population control* and *self-healing*. The thinking at the time was not that these biological principles of sustainability should be copied by human beings in order to live more sustainably. We did feel, however, that a more thorough understanding of these principles could help learners develop a better understanding of the constitutive meanings of sustainable living, which we regarded as an achievable and important outcome for this programme.

As an example, natural cycles in which materials are continuously recycled and reused in nature provide ideas for recycling of materials by humans, and give meaning to the importance of the use of renewable resources. This, in turn can serve to encourage the responsible use of energy sources and alternatives such as solar and wind power, and in so doing reduce the stress on fossil fuels and reduce air and other forms of pollution. Lessons from biodiversity in nature include the reality of interdependence and the crucial importance of the niche concept. Applied to human communities, it can serve to demonstrate the value of cultural diversity and tolerance of other cultures and beliefs.

We therefore pursued the possibility of developing materials with sustainability serving as a unifying theme for biology curricula. Our intent was that biological concepts be organized around the theme of sustainability as a means of introducing environmental literacy to biology students (the idea of sustainability as a unifying theme for biology curricula is explored in greater detail by Schreuder, Le Grange and Reddy 1998).

Science and Sustainability Project

The Science and Sustainability Project formally commenced in 1995 when as a small group of university-based researchers we got together to research and develop resource materials that would support a perceived need of middle school science

teachers. The team comprised current and former life science teachers with considerable experience who, for some time, were critical of current inappropriate textbook-driven curricula, undemocratic pedagogical methods, and non-participative approaches to curriculum development. Years of involvement in environmental education made us concerned about general environmental illiteracy and resultant unsustainable living characterized by rampant consumerism and wasteful lifestyles on the one hand, and abject poverty, overpopulation, and unhealthy living conditions on the other. These concerns led to a commitment to a functional approach aimed at integrating environmental education in school curricula. We sought to enrich our experience by sharing our own emerging understanding of sustainability and environmental education with practising teachers through constructive dialogue.

Initially, these ideas served as a basis for a participatory curriculum development process through a collaborative partnership between us, a university-based team, and schools from a historically disadvantaged community in a Cape Town suburb called Grassy Park. After establishing the conceptual basis of the project with a number of selected teacher communities, as well as a number of groups of student teachers, the next phase was to develop suitable resource materials to introduce the concept to a still wider teacher audience. It was decided that the theme and focus of the first phase of curriculum development would be biodiversity, as one of the constitutive principles of sustainability, and also importantly, to retain the conceptual links with the "mother" programme, Windows on the Wild, based in Washington, DC. In subsequent phases as the process develops, the focus will shift to other principles such as recycling, resource use, self-healing and interdependence.

From the outset the process also included students from a variety of courses in the Education Faculty of the University of Stellenbosch. Apart from the fact that their inclusion adds richness to the process, it can also help pre-service teachers become familiar with new ideas in, and approaches to curriculum development in the life sciences. This strategy also has the added advantage that ideas and activities can be tested in practice teaching sessions which are being attended by the authors. In this way, new ideas can be tried, and the activities can be improved and refined.

At the beginning of 1999, other partners were contracted into the process of development of Science and Sustainability, including Rob O'Donoghue, an environmental educator working under the auspices of KwaZulu Natal Conservation Service and Share-Net, a well-established environmental education resource development initiative of the Wildlife and Environmental Education Society of Southern Africa (see Chapter 11). Working in consultation with a wide variety of role players, O'Donoghue produced a full-colour poster, which is serving a dual purpose of introducing the concept of Windows on the Wild: Science and Sustainability, and on the flip side, the concepts of habitat loss in Southern African biomes, endangered species characteristic of the different biomes, and biodiversity loss.

The poster, together with a number of introductory activities focusing on biodiversity, was presented in workshops with two new student teacher groups, a group of local biology teachers, a group of volunteer teachers at Kirstenbosch National Botanic Gardens in Cape Town, and a Conservation Group (KOBIO) at Kleinmond, a coastal community on the Cape coast. The intention of this piloting process was to get feedback on the poster and project as a whole and to elicit different perspectives that could lead to the development of new ideas. The response of all these groups was decidedly positive. Some participants' comments included:

We have had many eminent speakers at KOBIO, but none has elicited the lively and positive response that your presentation had... (Dr. S.W. Walters, Chairman, Kogelberg Biosphere Association.)

I have never learnt as much as I have learnt through the Science and Sustainability sessions. We should have more of this in our programme. (LK, B Prim Ed I student, programme evaluation.)

I must admit, there are a number of ecological concepts that make much more sense to me now. (IS, Senior Biology Teacher participating in pilot WoW workshops at Stellenbosch.)

A great deal of effort and thought has gone into the development of Windows on the Wild – Science and Sustainability, to meet the unique needs and sensibilities of South Africa; I believe the results will set an example for environmental educators around the world. (CB, Volunteer Teacher at Gold Fields Environmental Education Centre, Kirstenbosch NB Gardens after WoW workshop.)

The feedback has been very encouraging to the research team who are continuing with the resource development phase. Presently, a team of experienced teachers is working on a collection of activities designed to introduce the basic concepts of both biodiversity and Curriculum 2005 to participating teachers. These activities will be combined with a project rationale in a Teacher Guide, and together with the poster these will be used in workshops in a number of selected school communities in Southern Africa. After the feedback from participants in these workshops has been processed and integrated into the revisions, a WoW Science and Sustainability file will be produced and disseminated by a local educational publisher. Through this process of sharing and collaboration, resource materials are being produced which can help teachers develop curricula that respond to the demands of Curriculum 2005 and to some of the most serious threats to the unique Southern African environment.

Conclusion

Over the years there have been several attempts by members of the environmental education community to redefine environmental education. Defining and redefining environmental education has not helped us to improve the condition of the environment. On the contrary, the environmental crisis has deepened. When we redefined environmental education we have often tended to uncritically embrace certain key concepts in our pursuit of new formulae. In true modernist tradition, we have often reified these new concepts and ideas, expecting that new icons would succeed where previous ideas have failed. In doing so, we have not only discarded the baby with the bath water, but we have also created false expectations.

Although we have raised concerns around sustainability as a predefined focus for environmental education, we argue that its value should not be discarded but suggest the study, through science, of why natural systems appear to be sustainable as one such process. The principles of sustainability seemingly manifested in natural systems can further be used as images and metaphors for more sustainable human life-styles. This would, however, require us to view science differently, allowing for the integration of fact and value, and for science to help make visible certain ethical principles. In the Science and Sustainability Project this idea is currently being explored through a collaborative resource development process with teachers focusing on threats to biodiversity in a localized environment.

Authors' note:

A paper describing the earlier stages of this project was published in South African Journal of Education, 19(2):127-129. May 1999.

References

Carson, R. (1962). *Silent spring*. Penguin: Harmondsworth.

Chiras, D. (1993). "Eco-logic: teaching the biological principles of sustainability" in *The American Biology Teacher*, 55(2):71-76.

Doll, W. (1993). "Curriculum possibilities in a "post"-future" in *Journal of Curriculum and Supervision*, 8(4):277-292.

Falk, D. (1971). *Biology teaching methods*. Robert Kriegler Publishing Company: Florida.

Fien, J. (1993). *Education for the environment: critical curriculum theorising and environmental education*. Deakin University Press: Geelong.

Jickling, B. (1992). "Why I don't want my children to be educated for sustainable development" in *Journal of Environmental Education*, 23(4):5-8.

Jickling, B. & H. Spork (1998). *Education for the environment: a critique*. Environmental Education Research. In press.

Le Grange, L, C. Reddy & D. R. Schreuder (1997). "Sustainability in curriculum 2005" in *Enviroteach* (3):9-11.

Lovelock, J. (1994). "Gaia" in C. Merchant (ed.), *Key concepts in critical theory*. Humanities Press: New Jersey.

Orr, D. (1992). *Ecological literacy: education and the transition to a postmodern world*. State University of New York Press: Albany.

Republic of South Africa (1995). *White paper on education and training*. Government Printer: Cape Town.

Republic of South Africa (1996a). *Lifelong learning through a national qualifications framework*. Discussion Document.

Republic of South Africa (1996b). *Curriculum Framework Document*.

Republic of South Africa (1997). *Curriculum 2005 Framework Document*.

Republic of South Africa (1998). *Draft national environmental management bill*. Government Printer: Pretoria.

Schreuder, D. R. (1995). "Delusion of progress: a case of reconceptualising environmental education" in *Southern African Journal of Environmental Education*, (15):18-25.

Schreuder, D. R, L. Le Grange & C. Reddy (1998). "Sustainability as a unifying theme in biology curricula" in *Spectrum*, 36(1):4-7.

Sterling, S. (1993). "Environmental education and sustainability: a view from holistic ethics" in J. Fien (ed), *Environmental education: a pathway to sustainability*. Deakin University Press: Geelong.

Tilbury, D. (1995). "Environmental education for sustainability: defining the new focus of environmental education in the 1990s" in *Environmental Education Research*, 1(2):195-212.

Part D

The Americas

Part D

The Americas: The context

Robert B. Stevenson

North and South America is a region of dramatic contrasts in wealth, poverty, literacy, life expectancy, and resource and energy usage. For example, while more than 80% of the population of the United States has some post-secondary education, the average amount of time spent in public education in Latin America is only six years. Although the U.S. has only four percent of the world's population, it uses approximately 20% of the world's oil resources.

Many current policies, such as the North America Free Trade Agreement (NAFTA), are seen as perpetuating, if not exacerbating, the unequal distribution of wealth and resources across the region and the subsequent uneven level of environmental impact. Although NAFTA, for example, is highly contentious because of different views of its impact on the environment and poverty, it is difficult to dispute, however, that in most countries, national rather than global interests determine environmental and resource usage policies. Therefore, it has become increasingly urgent that efforts to establish international cooperation and global agreements on addressing such issues as global warming overcome political and cultural differences and narrow nationalistic interests and move toward policies and practices that will help create a basic and sustainable living standard for everyone in the Americas and of course, on the planet.

Education in all its forms should and can play a significant role in developing the kind of critical and creative thinking that is essential to bring about such a change. The four cases in this section of the book offer significant examples of this important role. The voices represented are from a diverse range of educational settings (e.g. college and university institutions, non-formal adult education, and an NGO that worked with the informal popular media).

Martha Monroe and her colleagues (Chapter 16) illustrate how all these sectors of education should and can work together. Their GreenCOM project in El Salvador provides a comprehensive case of a coordinated national effort that integrates formal education and popular media approaches. It is not surprising, however, given these different educational and cultural settings across this diverse region that these voices do not present an entirely consistent view of sustainable development or what constitutes appropriate educational responses to the challenge of creating more sustainable societies. Bob Jickling in Chapter 14 argues that these very differences should be part of our educational discourse and that teachers should involve students in examining the ethical and language issues concerning the way in which sustainable development is defined and conceived. Yet despite the evident differences there are common concerns and thrusts. One is the use of participatory strategies that attempt to create ownership at the local level. The potential impact and influence of actively engaging students in conducting environmental audits of public buildings is demonstrated by the work of Kohrn and his associates (Chapter 15). This experience not only introduced the students to the technical aspects of energy conservation but also the significant political dimensions that need to be considered. Chapter 17 in this section is a story of an adult education project in an

urban setting. The objectives of this project are to provide an opportunity for people to come together and discuss the important issues in their communities and to help them create alternative "green" livelihoods through localized goods and services.

Chapter 14

Canada

Wolves, environmental thought and the language of sustainability

Bob Jickling

Introduction

I often think my story about wolves begins in the early 1980s. As a schoolteacher in the northern city of Whitehorse, I had to examine my role in the midst of a controversy about wolves. The Yukon Government had initiated a wolf kill programme. I wanted my students to get involved in the issue, to participate in the debate. However passionate my feelings, I was deeply troubled by a lack of philosophical guidance and curricular options; I had received little preparation for such a task. I also knew that every day I faced a class with individuals of different cultural backgrounds and values, some of whom had parents who supported the activities about which I was so sceptical.

However, as important as this experience was, my interest in wolves can probably be traced to a ski trip almost a decade earlier. Crossing a frozen lake one cold winter evening, I encountered a wolf pack. I didn't see them in spite of the full moon in a starry sky. I remember how the night's silence was pierced by the ear splitting cracks as the lake's surface adjusted to the plunging temperature. And then there were the howls of the wolves, howls which sang from all around, then reverberated from the densely forested hillsides. I cannot fully describe, or interpret, the experience, but I remember it like yesterday.

There have been many more lupine experiences in wild places of the Yukon Territory: the mother watching me curiously while her two cubs skipped about playfully unaware of this human presence, the unmistakable odour of wolf as I wriggled into a recently vacated den dug five metres into a sandy bank, or tracks in the sand outside my tent – impressions in the ground that were not there the evening before as I climbed inside for the deep slumber of a weary traveller.

For me, wolves have been there for a long time – really there. They have become part of me through these experiences. Caring about wolves, rooted long ago, remains part of my personal and political activities. Yet, while these activities are motivated by wolves, they are about more. Wolves are both real and metaphoric. They are subjects of care, and they are symbols of a struggle to understand our human place in a more-than-human world.

So far I have given a glimpse of my story. There are other tales. Systematic removal of wolves is not new in the Yukon; it is part of our history. The first biologist hired for the Yukon in the 1950s was given the task of overseeing a widespread wolf-poisoning programme (Gilbert 1994). The scale and methods of this programme would be unthinkable by today's standards. Whereas public norms had relegated wolves to the status of vermin, this is no longer the case. Nevertheless, it is far from

clear that the new science of wildlife management rests on assumptions that are fundamentally different from those of Yukon's pioneer biologists. Marching in accordance to Bacon's dictum, "the secrets of nature reveal themselves more readily under the vexations of art than when they go their own way" (1960, p. 95), wolf controls are now dressed with the "respectability" of science and the "objectivity" of experimental design. Unfortunately, this presumed respectability can mask important philosophical underpinnings.

There are also "frontier" stories such as the one provided by the Yukon Fish and Game Association and its members. This is a Euro-Canadian hunting tale involving, in varying proportions, pursuit of food, pleasure, and trophies. Here the wolf is a competitor.

Last, yet first, there are voices of Yukon First Nations whose people have inhabited this place, now known as "Yukon," for a long time. Theirs is a story of life inextricably linked to the land – their home where wolves and caribou are part of the land.

The stories are interesting in their own right and each of the storytellers has, whether stated or not, an idea about how the complex Yukon ecosystems should be sustained. So the concept of sustainability is important –yet shaped by different ideas, different values. The stories about wolf kills, described further in the next section, give voices to a Yukon case study which grounds an exploration of "sustainability" in place and time.

Through these wolf kill stories, my classes and I are able to examine how the language of "sustainability" allows for an important, yet narrow range of environmental discourse. On the one hand, it enables us to talk about technical requirements – the "what is" questions of what is required to keep ecological processes going. But, on the other hand, I argue that it is less able to guide thinking about other important environmental questions such as: What is good? And, what kind of relationship ought to exist between human societies and nature?

In our classes we consider how the language of sustainability can limit the terms of public debate. Students are encouraged to remain open to possibilities beyond sustainability – to accept sustainability for what it is, but to also explore what it is not. For example, the language of sustainability may be used when trying to optimize "harvest," but it cannot describe the magic of wolves howling on a winter's night, or values lost from a wilderness de-populated of wolves.

Multiple narratives

Any case study about wolf kills will be as controversial as it is complex. Passions run deeply. Just about everyone has opinions. In the Yukon, hunters often want more "game" and some First Nations people claim that hunting caribou and moose is essential to preserving their cultural heritage. Managing wolves – that is controlling wolves – supports these goals. Others claim the wolf is simply a scapegoat. For the latter group the wolf is paying for past indiscretions, for over-hunting and poor management decisions.

As individuals we cannot be value-free and my selection and presentation of these issues to students is filtered by my own predilections. I acknowledge that other stories are possible. However, I am not trying to settle issues about wolf kills.

Instead we examine the adequacy of "sustainability talk". For this we need only present snapshots of various voices. Through the sampling of these voices we can explore limitations of relying on the language of "sustainability" to define our goals.

The case study context

The 1980s and 1990s have seen two large-scale wolf kill programmes in the Yukon. The first was carried out in the 23,000 square kilometre range of the Finlayson caribou herd. In response to increased hunting opportunities and subsequent declines in caribou and moose numbers, this wolf reduction was aimed at increasing the calf survival of the caribou and ultimately the recovery of this herd. Between 1983 and 1989, 454 wolves were killed in what has been described as "one of the most intensive wolf control programmes ever carried out in North America" (Renewable Resources 1995a, p.10). This intervention, combined with reduced hunting, resulted in an immediate increase in moose and caribou numbers. By 1991, two years after the conclusion of the control programme, the Finlayson caribou herd had grown to more than two and a half times its 1983 size. By 1994 the wolf population had recovered to pre-control levels. However, in 1997 the Finlayson caribou herd was again in decline and there were renewed calls for wolf controls.

The second wolf kill began in 1993 and ran until 1997. During this time about 1801 wolves were killed in the 20,000 square kilometre range of the Aishihik caribou herd. Again concern was raised about declining caribou numbers. Because caribou are important to subsistence hunting needs, it was judged that a long-term natural recovery, estimated to be between 20 and 30 years, would not be acceptable to the local people (Renewable Resources 1995b).

First Nations

Wolves have always been powerful symbols for Yukon First Nations people. Both feared and respected, wolves have held a special place in their daily lives. Traditional stories often talk of relationships that can exist between wolves and people; when treated with respect wolves were kind to people and helped them through difficult times. Carrying on with ancient traditions, the wolf remains a clan symbol for First Nations people. As Norma Kassi (1994) says, "I am a wolf by clan system. I am a wolf. In our language we say that we sleep with the wolves. They are my guides and that is what I believe" (p. 214).

However, people who hunt caribou frequently call for action when populations of these species are considered to be too low in an area. Paul Birkel, Chief of the Champagne and Aishihik First Nations said, "This was a very important [Aishihik] herd in the past. When we first found out that the herd was in trouble, we asked our people to cut back hunting voluntarily and we informed the government of the problem" (Buckley 1992). Reminiscing about his experiences as a young child, he remembers how the people living at Aishihik village depended almost entirely on the Aishihik herd for meat. But, the voluntary reduction in caribou consumption, he claims, has resulted in dietary problems for this community (Tobin 1993).

For Chief Birkel, the freedom to hunt caribou is a deeply cultural experience. The ability to live with the land is closely linked to identity and well-being. For him, and his people, the 20 to 30 year wait would mean a lost generation, a generation of

young people with increasingly severed connections to the land of their ancestors. For Birkel, the recovery of the caribou herd is a priority, "If we start a predator [wolf] control programme, right now, then I think there is a chance for the Aishihik herd to bounce back . . . But I think if we wait much longer, we would be in trouble with that herd" (Tobin 1992).

There are hints that this may have been an uneasy decision. A few years later Alex Van Bibber, a Champagne and Aishihik First Nations Elder said while speaking about another nearby caribou recovery programme, "we have abused both the herd and the land. The land is waiting for an apology. Until then, the herd will not be productive and will not give itself to the people" (in Tobin 1995, p. 26). How can we respect the land while enhancing caribou with a helicopter-assisted wolf kill? Is this the best way to sustain caribou populations?

Scientists and managers

Biologists responsible for "wildlife management" have been central to the wolf kills. While their task is to enact public policy, they too hold assumptions that shape policy decisions, as well as policy promotion and implementation. In an insightful comment made during the planning for the Aishihik wolf kill one biologist said, "There are two options: intensively manage or let it follow a natural decline. Both are defendable" (Farnell 1992, p. 8). From a scientific perspective, there were two defensible courses of action: intervene in the ecosystem by removing wolves and monitor the effects, or allow the system to decline and/or recover without human intervention and again monitor the effects. The same biologist went on to say that the "[p]ublic in Yukon prefers intensive management on this herd" (p. 8). A colleague added, "[i]n Aishihik, we need to address public policy . . . and design something scientific, with a set of hypotheses and alternate hypotheses" (Hayes 1992, p. 8).

Yukon residents' preference for intensive management may be debatable, but there was a level of public support for a wolf kill. However, to say that managers simply respond to public will, would be to underestimate the complexity of the relationship. Trained as biologists, it has been easy to see their enthusiasm for science. Steeped in traditions rooted in Bacon's 17th century creed – nature best reveals herself when vexed – there was ready approval of experimental intervention – managers need to manage.

Interestingly, in the later stages of the Aishihik wolf kill, biologists began experimenting with wolf sterilization techniques as an alternative to shooting. In an effective public relations initiative, they invited a newspaper reporter to observe their fieldwork. In a three-page spread the journalist (Tobin 1997) reported that "wildlife managers" propose sterilization of the alpha males and females in wolf packs. The thinking behind this strategy is that the non-breeding dominant pair will defend their territory, but in the absence of a growing pack, will consume less moose and caribou, particularly caribou calves. A healthy pack is referred to as a "tentacled eating machine" (p. 24).

The journalist also reports that Yukon's wolf sterilization represents a "world-wide lead into a new area of wildlife management". These techniques will "replace the more 'intrusive' aerial hunting" and respond to "the public's growing disdain" for this technique. Finally, the article reports a biologist's prediction that the "sterilization will reduce the frequency in which aerial hunting must be carried out.

That will soften public resistance, she feels, and be less of a drain on financial resources" (Tobin 1997, pp. 23-25).

Many opponents of wolf sterilization don't want less intrusive techniques, they want new ethics – new respect for, and relationships with, nature. This management regime projects its technical capabilities, but it tells us little about social and philosophical possibilities. It does not help us consider how we might redefine society/nature relationships. Does, for example, the term "wildlife management" even make sense; is it internally coherent? Can an organism be "wild" while at the same time "managed" by humans? Does "wildlife management" pander to human interests and human usage? If so, should it?

Fish and Game Association

Those aligned with the Yukon Fish and Game Association also seek to influence management decisions. Historian Robert McCandless (1985) provides an interesting background to their role. He argues that completion of the Alaska Highway during World War II brought more than just a road link between Yukon and the southern communities. Increased access meant an infusion of new values, particularly an "Alberta hegemony" which carried with it new attitudes towards wildlife. According to McCandless, a group of these arrivals organized the Yukon Fish and Game Association in 1945 and within two years were literally drafting "game" laws. The results of their outlook reflected a "general antipathy towards Indians and traditional game use" and "a seemingly irrational hatred of wolves" (McCandless 1985, p. 40). Through these efforts, notions of hunting rights began to gain solid footing in the Yukon.

By the 1990s the politics of the Yukon had changed. An agreement on land claims with Yukon First Nations recognized aboriginal rights to hunt and to participate in renewable resource management (Umbrella Final Agreement, 1993). The balance of power is now shifting. However, as hunting opportunities decline, voices from the Yukon Fish and Game Association are heard.

In 1997 the Yukon Government's caribou management team argued that hunting pressure on the Finlayson caribou herd was unsustainable. In spite of a massive wolf kill in the 1980s, the herd was again over-hunted. Reaction by the Yukon Fish and Game Association was to defend its interests. Faced with hunting restrictions, citizens were admonished: Humans are entwined with nature, with wolves and caribou, but that only we humans can manage nature and "manage it we must" (White 1997, p. 7). What might this management look like? After claims that hunters hold conservation ideals and a love of nature, and that they respect the wolf as part of the ecosystem, a compromise is proposed that would entail the trapping of about forty wolves. It appears that wolves, First Nations hunters, and licensed hunters (non-First Nations) all deserve a share of the caribou. But, the wolves take too big a share and must be managed. There is also the lament that the licensed hunters are subjected to legislative controls whereas First Nations hunters are not. "That leaves these people with the feeling of being somewhat less than equal in a country in which they were born" (White 1997, p. 7).

We are again left with intriguing questions. What management assumptions does this Fish and Game Association spokesperson support? How do these assumptions shape a vision of sustainable ecosystems in which humans, wolves and caribou all participate? What is an appropriate relationship between societies – particularly First

Nations and Euro-Canadians – and nature? And, as this balance of power shifts, what privilege is this author defending? Is it reasonable to think about licensed hunting as a right? If not, when is this privilege appropriate? Using the language of sustainability how are we to – or can we – make sense of these contesting beliefs, interests and values?

Opponents of wolf kills

Not everyone supports wolf kills. While some Yukon voices said that it was important to rebuild the Aishihik caribou herd, others were concerned that there was too little known about why the herd was declining. Others claimed that the wolf was made the scapegoat for past excesses, claiming that over-hunting was responsible for the problem. For many, the critical question was whether the wolf kill was a reaction to a biological problem or whether it was just a treatment for symptoms of a much deeper human problem. Many of these voices reflect the sentiments of Aldo Leopold who advocated changing the role of humans "from conqueror of the land-community to plain member and citizen of it" (1966, p. 240). Implementing this outlook would require patience, lengthy periods for recovery of ecosystem health, and proactive measures to prevent human-triggered declines.

For many sceptics, wolf controls are not consistent with care and respect for wildlife. If this kind of practice continues, the intensively managed areas will become less like wilderness and more like farms. Should this happen? Or, should we be more concerned with seeking ways to manage human activity rather than manipulating ecosystems?

Finally, questions were posed about the "rightness" of wolf controls. The words of First Nations Elder Harry Morris have been thought provoking. He said, "we kill wolves, we don't mind killing wolves, but the wolf must not be made a fool of" (pers. comm., 1992). It was his view that helicopter assisted wolf kills do not show sufficient respect for the wolf. This leads to further questions. Are we respectful enough of wolves and other animals in an ecosystem? Is it acceptable to hunt wolves with helicopters? To what ends do we do this? And, can the means employed possibly justify the ends? (Yukon Residents, 1993).

On the language of sustainability

The stories presented here represent complex issues that have not been fully examined; we have just scratched the surface. However, the educational purpose of our study of this issue is not to settle questions of public values. Rather, it is to examine various voices on an environmental issue and see to what extent the language of sustainability is adequate to fully explore it and similar such issues.

To begin, we assume the word "sustain" is relatively straightforward. In *The Concise Oxford Dictionary* (Fowler & Fowler 1964) we find: "Sustain, . . . Keep going continuously. Hence [sustain]able" (p. 1303). In general terms, something is sustainable if it can be kept going continuously. However, before exploring its limits, it is important to acknowledge the importance of "sustainability" and the usefulness of this concept in environmental thinking. Many ecological processes are not sustained – not kept going continuously. Species are going extinct at an alarming rate and whole ecosystems are at risk. So, it is important to talk about sustainability.

However, I believe that the voices presented in this case study show that this alone is not sufficient.

The various voices of Yukon's wolf kill illustrate that environmental issues are about much more than sustainability – all interest groups want sustainable ecosystems. Beyond this, however, there *are* important questions of public value which are often in conflict. First Nations speak of cultural values that grow from a close relationship with the land. Others seek a human role in managing wildlife. Scientists, drawing from the traditions of their craft, seek knowledge through vexatious interventions in nature. Some people who choose to hunt do not want to lose this opportunity – and some of these see hunting as a right rather than a privilege. Then there are opponents who see past practices as unsustainable. For many of them, the only just and respectful way to ensure sustainability of ecosystems lies in challenging societies' most basic assumptions about human-nature relationships.

Questions of public value are often concealed in assumptions about how humans perceive their place in the world. If the ideas, concepts, and language of public discourse do not bring them effectively into public view then they reinforce these assumptions. We all have to ask if making "sustainability" the focus of our educative efforts is really providing students with the tools – the ideas and language – to evaluate and challenge social norms and create new possibilities. All of the voices presented here are interested in sustainable caribou herds, wolf populations, and indeed, ecosystems. The real questions are: Why are we intervening? And, to what ends?

One way of devaluing environmental language, and hence thought, has been through "non-terminology" like that of George Orwell's (1989) "Newspeak". For example, in renewable resource agencies, hunted animals are frequently called "game" and others labelled "non-game;" extractive activities are called "consumptive" while all other activities are lumped together as "non-consumptive". In these examples animals are defined as commodities (game) or in terms of their uselessness as commodities (non-game). The *Yukon Wolf Conservation and Management Plan* (1992) provides a case in point. Two categories of wolf values are identified: consumptive and non-consumptive. Consumptive values are expressions of economic value. All others, including a reference to inherent values, are subsumed under the heading non-consumptive values. Valued activities are defined in economic terms; all others are subsumed by the economic opposite "non-consumptive". This "non-terminology" effectively robs these values of all positive content, casts them in economic language, and effectively inhibits thought (Hargrove 1994).

Perhaps the ultimate Orwellian expression of "reality control" is "doublethink". Doublethink, in the classic satire *Nineteen Eighty-Four*, means "the power of holding two contradictory beliefs in one's mind simultaneously, and accepting both of them (Orwell 1989, p. 223). So effective is the power of universal discourse to reduce meaning that antagonistic concepts can be conjoined in a single phrase resulting, for example, in the familiar "peace is war", and "war is peace" (Orwell 1989). In the real world, philosopher Hebert Marcuse (1964) observes,

> [t]he unification of opposites which characterizes the commercial and political style is one of the many ways in which discourse and communication make themselves immune against expression of protest and refusal. (p. 90)

He adds that it is no less Orwellian when the contradiction is encapsulated in a single word, or cliché. Using the Yukon wolf case study we can now examine the degree to which the language of sustainability serves to conceal, or highlight, contradictions in perspectives.

In spite of vast differences between the perspectives presented in the case study, each is united by a desire for ecologically sustainable ecosystems complete with a full range of fauna, including wolves. What is at stake is not how to bring about sustainability, but why a particular set of actions, predicated on a particular set of values, should be privileged over another. Unfortunately, much of Canadian society has been conditioned to believe that sustainability carries only positive connotations. However, as the different voices show, this view of sustainability does not tend to highlight differences and perspectives. At best, reliance on this language flattens out antagonisms and contradictions. At worst, it leads us down the ("doublethink") path whereby ordinary citizens can increasingly hold, and accept, contradictory meanings for the same term.

Thoughts about teaching

In raising issues like wolf kills I am not interested in educating for sustainability per se. These, and other, issues are about cultural identities, respect, society-nature relationships, and tensions between intrinsic and instrumental values. In order to understand such concepts, we need to get beyond the language of sustainability with its ability to conceal or absorb differences. We need to enable our students to make discriminations and mediate tensions that are not highlighted by sustainability talk. So how as educators can we do this?

We might begin by considering Marcuse's (1964) claim that: "Naming the 'things that are absent' is breaking the spell of the things that are" (p. 68). First, in raising controversial issues, we are fundamentally concerned about philosophy and politics, values and public decisions. In my teaching, I say so. This means helping students to identify the assumptions, implicit and explicit, which ground contesting perspectives. This also means giving them opportunities to weigh the merits of differing views, mediate tensions between contradictory positions, and make judgements. To accomplish these tasks, it is more important to talk about concepts like "respect", "obligations", "responsibilities" and "ethics" than it is to talk about sustainability. And, it is important to speak about cultural, spiritual, aesthetic, and intrinsic values. Participation in public forums, workshops, and consultations have all been used effectively in my community to give student judgements a voice.

Second, we need descriptions of the various perspectives – materials to work with. Throughout the case study presented here, I have used sources from local media. These primary sources have been invaluable. Letters to editors, commentaries, editorials, political cartoons, news reports and feature articles can be woven together over time to develop a profile of an issue. Multi-stakeholder curriculum projects often flatten out, or conceal, tensions. This can make it difficult for students to find out what people really value. On the other hand, citizens are often quite candid when writing a letter or speaking with a journalist. These statements, collected over the life of an issue, reveal much about community perspectives, and the range of existing values. And, they are grist for careful analysis.

Finally, to enable students to reach beyond the status quo, we must be sure they have the linguistic tools needed. I have found that it important to balance images of

wolves as "tentacled eating machines" with language of "respect" and "intrinsic values". It can be effective to substitute terms like "non-human" with creative options such as "more-than-human". Students also respond thoughtfully when more instrumentalist terms such as "resource use" are balanced with terms such as "care for" or "responsibility for" and when "wildlife management" is balanced with terms such as "stewardship" or "management *for* wildlife". Finally, if we are to capture the values and experiences that move so many people, as with my own experiences with wolves, we must make room for talk about "wonder", "magic", and "the sacred".

What I have written will surprise many readers. The slogan "sustainability" has, for so long, seemed unassailable. Becoming a little uncomfortable with the dominant emphasis on this term draws attention to the need for a deep and philosophical discourse within environmental education, a discourse that ranges beyond the possibilities circumscribed by the language of sustainability. If we don't rise to this challenge, we will not know if we are really just reinforcing the status quo or providing students with the tools, the ideas and language, they need to create new possibilities.

Note

1. Some records suggest this number may be low, though the higher figures may include hunting and trapping fatalities separate from government activities.

References

Bacon. F. (1960). "The new organon, Book 1, Aphorism XCVIII" in F. H. Anderson (ed.), *The new organon and related writings*, pp.94-95. The Bobbs Merril Company: Indianapolis. (First published in 1620)

Buckley, A. (1992, February 12). "Government dodges wolf kill issue" in *Yukon News*. pp. 1-2.

Farnell, R. (1992). In "Designing an experiment for large mammal recovery in the Aishihik area, Yukon Territory". Minutes of technical meeting, October 4, 1992, 8. Government of the Yukon: Whitehorse.

Fowler, H. W. & F. G. Fowler (eds.) (1964). *The concise Oxford dictionary of current English*. Clarendon Press: Oxford.

Gilbert, S. (1994). "Science, ethics and ecosystems" in J. Peepre & B. Jickling (eds.), *Northern protected areas and wilderness*. pp. 195-201. Canadian Parks and Wilderness Society and Yukon College: Whitehorse.

Hargrove, E. (1994). "Science, ethics and the care of ecosystems" in J. Peepre & B. Jickling (eds.), *Northern protected areas and wilderness*. pp. 44-61. Canadian Parks and Wilderness Society and Yukon College: Whitehorse.

Hayes, B. (1992). "Designing an experiment for large mammal recovery in the Aishihik area, Yukon Territory". Minutes of technical meeting, October 4, 1992, 8. Government of the Yukon: Whitehorse.

Kassi, N. (1994). "Science, ethics and wildlife management" in J. Peepre & B. Jickling (eds.), *Northern protected areas and wilderness*. pp. 212-216. Canadian Parks and Wilderness Society and Yukon College: Whitehorse.

Leopold, A. (1966). *A Sand County almanac: with essays on conservation from Round River*. Sierra Club/Ballantine: New York. (First published in 1949/1953)

Marcuse, H. (1964). *One-dimensional man*. Beacon Press: Boston.

McCandless, R. G. (1985). *Yukon wildlife: a social history.* University of Alberta Press: Edmonton.

Orwell, G. (1989). *Nineteen eighty-four.* Penguin Books: London. (First published in 1949)

Renewable Resources, Government of the Yukon. (1995a). "The Finlayson program" in C. Olsen (ed.), *Yukon wolves: Ecology & management issues.* Pp. 10-12. Yukon Conservation Society: Whitehorse.

Renewable Resources, Government of the Yukon. (1995b). "The Aishihik program" in C. Olsen (ed.), *Yukon wolves: Ecology & management issues.* Pp. 13-14. Yukon Conservation Society: Whitehorse.

Tobin, C. (1997, February 14). "Lessening the bite ... into nature's meat supply" in *The Whitehorse Star*, pp. 23-25.

Tobin, C. (1995, September 15). "Respect can revive this great herd" in *The Whitehorse Star*, pp. 26-27.

Tobin, C. (1993, January 13). "Chief, CYI hail killing of wolves" in *The Whitehorse Star*, p. 4.

Tobin, C. (1992, January 24). "Webster called fearful of predator controls" in The Whitehorse Star, p. 6.

(1993). *Umbrella final agreement between the Government of Canada, the Council for Yukon Indians and the Government of the Yukon.* Minister of Supply and Services Canada: Ottawa.

White, C. (1997, December 19). "Trap four of five Finlayson wolf packs" in *The Whitehorse Star*, p. 7.

Wolf Management Planning Team. (1992). *The Yukon wolf conservation and management plan.* Yukon Department of Renewable Resources: Whitehorse, Yukon.

Yukon Residents. (1993, December 3). "Wolf kill lacks respect" in *Yukon News*, p. 8.

Chapter 15

El Salvador

Environmental education from the ground up

Martha C. Monroe, Jose Ignacio Mata, Peter Templeton and Carole Douglis

Rarely does the opportunity come along to build a national environmental education system from the ground up. But because of El Salvador's pressing needs and the wisdom of both governmental leaders and the United States Agency for International Development (USAID), El Salvador has been doing so over the last four years.

El Salvador's National Environmental Education Strategy provided the institutional framework for SEMA (Executive Secretariat of the Environment) and GreenCOM (USAID's Environmental Education and Communication Project) to devote staff, engage in projects, and leverage support and commitments from other national agencies and organizations. The Strategy built momentum within the nation to increase awareness and skills among those in education and mass communication to deliver accurate and meaningful environmental concepts to targeted audiences and the general public. The projects undertaken through the Strategy covered all aspects of education and mass media in El Salvador through a synergistic and coordinated plan.

One of the first tasks of the programme was establishing parallel Environmental Education units in each major national agency: SEMA and the Ministry of Education. Staff were hired and over time, projects were launched that emphasized logical extensions of the agency's role: SEMA coordinated non-formal and informal (media) activities; the Ministry of Education dealt with formal education (including primary, secondary and tertiary institutions). Synergism among activities was possible because GreenCOM and other NGOs worked with both agencies and with formal, non-formal, and informal education opportunities.

Environmental education and communication programmes typically either focus on one issue through several channels (e.g., recycling advertisements on radio, school curriculum for 4th graders) or address broad environmental concerns through one channel (environmental education curriculum in public schools). The great benefit of a National Environmental Education Strategy that El Salvador successfully demonstrates is that multiple channels and multiple issues enhance and promote each other. In El Salvador, for example, citizens began to read newspaper articles on solid waste, their students came home with a household garbage survey, teachers were trained in environmental education methods, public parks in urban areas increased the number of litter receptacles, adult literacy programmes covered environmental topics, and extension workers received training in environmental issues. Of course, repetition of any message in multiple media forms is more effective, but the diversity of opportunities also created possibilities for synergism. Increased public awareness of the environment from more news coverage of environmental issues, for example, helped promote the addition of an environmental theme into the formal education curriculum. Media training for environmental

NGO's helped increase the quality of the news coverage in the first place. El Salvador's commitment to create an environmentally literate citizenry enabled such synergistic and sequential planning, all of which increased the momentum and support for environmental education.

This National Strategy culminated in the National Environmental Education Encounter, held in November 1996. Over 1,000 educators from formal education, non-formal education, and the media participated in the process, recounting the experiences and lessons learned in the almost three years of development. For this Encounter, three preparatory meetings were held with the formal education, NGO, and media sectors. During the encounter, 150 people from these sectors worked in small groups to develop a proposal for a National Environmental Education Policy that was later analysed by representatives of these sectors. This policy will be incorporated into the National Environmental Policy, which is currently being developed in El Salvador. The convincing demonstration of interest from the impressive participation of educators indicates that the Strategy achieved its participation goals as well. These professionals contributed to the Encounter because their participation in training and materials development projects over the previous three years was a beneficial and productive process.

The remainder of this case study will explain, in some detail, each element of this plan, how it evolved, and the role it played in building an environmental education emphasis in El Salvador by focusing on the three sectors of education separately.

Formal environmental education

Coincidently, El Salvador began reforming its entire formal education system during the period of GreenCOM activity. Once the new Environmental Education unit was established in the Ministry of Education, a three-pronged approach was used to infuse environmental education throughout the curriculum:

1. make the environment, along with science and health, one of eight central themes for education;
2. prepare environmental education materials to be used to teach major environmental issues through standard subjects like Spanish and math; and
3. train teachers in both environmental content and interdisciplinary teaching methods so they can comfortably use the new materials.

It was relatively easy to introduce environmental subject matter into the formal education system in El Salvador because of the comprehensive educational reform process that was underway. The reform process required revision of the curricular content and the introduction of new values, but vigilance was needed to ensure sufficient treatment of environmental themes in the texts and training materials. In keeping with the plan to make environment, science, and health a major strand in the new curriculum, the Ministry produced a series of beautiful colour textbooks for "Science, Health, and Environment". However, this led to two challenges. First, teachers could not use the texts effectively since they were not aware of environmental issues nor trained to teach with interactive projects. Second, even though the Ministry was aware of the interdisciplinary nature of environmental study, adding "environment" to science and health reduced its potential to be an integrative force in the schools.

The solution to this dilemma addressed the second goal of preparing teaching materials. GreenCOM worked with the Ministry to develop a series of three teacher guides – one each for grades K-2, 3-5 and 6-8 that provide concrete teaching activities, background information, and involve all teachers in environmental exercises. Rather than being adapted from another nation, the guides are completely new and specific to El Salvador. An outside consultant assisted with the first two; the third was developed with in-country expertise. The Ministry of Education paid for printing and an in-service programme was designed to accompany the distribution of the guides with nearly every teacher in the country now having a copy.

Daisy de Campos, environmental education specialist for the Ministry of Education, commented:

> In visits to schools throughout the country, we've observed that interest in environmental issues has increased. Parents and students are demanding more focus on that theme. The guides are the best materials teachers have to respond to this interest.

Additional materials for schoolteachers have been developed by GreenCOM in cooperation with different NGOs. Small, colourful booklets engage children in reading about sea turtles, birds, forests, or air; mathematics exercises and puzzles ask young people to think about consequences of past behaviours and consider alternate solutions. About 10,000 copies of each booklet are printed; 3,000 are submitted to the Ministry of Education to be sent to schools as part of didactic packages; another 3,000 are turned over to the NGO that participated in the development; the remainder are distributed by request to NGOs, teachers, and students, by the Executive Secretariat of the Environment and GreenCOM. Hopefully, private businesses or development organizations will finance new editions of each booklet to allow for wider distribution.

A radio series, "Drop by Drop: the Adventures of Clarita the Water Droplet in her Trip Around the World", offers information, in ten 10-minute radio programmes, related to water and the water cycle. The adventure of Clarita's fall to earth as rain and her travels through rivers until reaching the ocean provide the framework for conveying important information. Two video series with a total of 11 programmes, each approximately 12 minutes, address environmental themes for different educational levels. The five programmes from "Our Home, the Environment", explain about water, soils, forests, biodiversity, and urban environmental problems for secondary students; while six programmes in the series, "The House of Water", address themes related to water for primary students.

The success of environmental education in formal education institutions depends on the quality of preparation that teachers receive about the environment and its problems. Teachers are strongly pressured to cover their curricular themes; making it difficult to address areas outside their specific subjects. For this reason, they often need assistance to see that teaching environmental themes need not add content to their subjects, but rather can help integrate thematic concepts within their subjects.

GreenCOM and the Ministry of Education, therefore, worked to piggyback training in environmental education onto the existing teacher preparation scheme for the reform effort. Model schools were identified where regional programmes were held. Participants were master teachers who then returned to their schools to conduct programmes with their colleagues. Sets of environmental education materials were

made available on loan to the schools clustered around the model schools. In this fashion, master teachers were prepared in the application of environmental concepts, and they prepared approximately 9,000 more teachers. In addition, a corps of Ministry of Education trainers has received additional education, so this aspect of the National Environmental Education Strategy will continue.

Several universities in El Salvador expressed interest in introducing environmental subject matter into their programmes of study as the environmental education effort across the nation grew in prominence. Since universities play a fundamental role in developing the professionals and leaders who will face the challenge of sustainable development and work to craft solutions to environmental problems, their participation in the National Environmental Education Strategy was encouraged.

Each participating university planned an initial seminar on the environmental issues of El Salvador for all faculties. This seminar approached the issues from geographic, geologic, historical, economic, social, political and cultural perspectives. Subsequently, according to the interest expressed, the university chooses the next step from several alternatives. One option is to create this seminar as an elective in all departments. According to the demand, this seminar can later be transformed into a degree programme offered by the university. Another option is to design seminars or workshops about specific environmental topics for relevant degree programmes: for example, a seminar on water quality for biology and chemical engineering departments; or on population dynamics and environmental degradation for the sociology and economics departments. Establishing a seminar in environmental issues as a mandatory course for all students represents a third option. Finally, some universities have begun to design environmental degree programmes, such as the Universidad Centroamericana José Simeon Canas (UCA) which will soon offer a master's degree in environment and natural resources.

Non-formal environmental education

Environmental education in the area of non-formal education encompasses the vast variety of educational opportunities that do not lead to a degree, such as programmes and exhibits at zoos, museums, nature centres, and parks; workforce training and education; civic and religious programmes; extension activities; programmes with civic leaders, decisionmakers, and elected officials; and work with NGOs. To help initiate and support this myriad of activities, a substantial investment was made in professional development for staff members and specialists so they can induct colleagues and others.

At the beginning of its operations in El Salvador, GreenCOM created a multidisciplinary team of professionals from different institutions that related to the growing list of environmental education activities. The Association of Biologists, the National Parks and Wildlife Service, the Salvadoran Institute of Tourism, the National Zoological Park, Fundacion Tazamul, Fundacion Ilopango, the Museum of Natural History, and the National School of Agriculture were involved. A first task of this multidisciplinary team was to prepare themselves in understanding the principal aspects of environmental issues in El Salvador through a series of seminars named "immersion workdays". In each of these seminars, the group analysed environmental issues with the assistance of the best national experts in the subject. Team members later planted the seed for creating environmental education units within their institutions, and proved to be a valuable resource for other people.

The organizers quickly learned that understanding environmental topics was not sufficient. A second component of professional development was offered to help staff develop educational techniques required for their specific areas. For example, park guards learned about environmental interpretation so they could provide education to visitors to the parks; those responsible for mass communication campaigns were offered education in social marketing techniques.

The technical staff of the institutions were expected to design programmes for the different sectors of society such as business and labour associations, unions, cooperatives, churches, etc., thereby multiplying their knowledge of national environmental issues and potential solutions for improving them. For example, agricultural extensionists were helped to transfer environmental technologies related to soil conservation, the rational use of agricultural chemical products, and the promotion of agroforestry to rural farmers. These issues have been integrated into the permanent training programme offered by the main extension institution, thus reaching extension agents in a sustainable fashion. This integration includes revising the programmes and the education of the leaders of these programmes so that they, in turn, educate other extensionists.

GreenCOM developed a different programme for NGO technical staff about the steps to follow for the design, implementation, and evaluation of environmental education projects. This programme was theoretical and practical; after each workshop the participants completed an assignment, the results of which were the basis for the development of the following workshop and the following activity. The first workshop dealt with participatory techniques for executing an environmental assessment of the community. The participants were given a period of two months to carry out their assessment in the field. The results of these assessments were used in a second workshop where they learned to plan an environmental education project. According to the projects that the participants designed, the professional development needs for implementation were evaluated, revealing the need for training in the production of graphic and radio materials. A final workshop at the end of the process provided tools for monitoring and evaluating their projects. As a result of this process, the Initiatives Fund of the Americas for El Salvador received an increase in the number of requests for financing for environmental education from NGOs. Many of these requests were approved and resulted in successful educational projects.

Recognizing their important role in providing environmental education opportunities for citizens through interpretive trails, visitor centres and slide shows, the national parks of El Salvador required another special programme of assistance. The parks are co-managed by different government institutions (e.g., the Salvadoran Institute of Tourism and the Office of National Parks and Wildlife of the Ministry of Agriculture) and NGO's SalvaNatura, AMAR and Cedro. GreenCOM created an inter-institutional team of technical staff from each of these institutions and developed an ambitious training programme to improve environmental education and environmental interpretation techniques, including:

- Design of interpretive instruments (paths, display boards, exhibits, etc.)
- Preparation of low cost educational materials
- Techniques for giving educational talks
- Use of educational props and aids
- Human relations and treatment of visitors
- Management and guiding of groups
- First aid

This group of environmental interpreters developed their own training exercise for more than 120 park guides and guards in the nation's principal national parks. In these parks, the team established different interpretive trails. They later played a fundamental role in the reform of the Museum of Natural History and in the creation of a new educational tool for children called "ecological carts", mobile wagons that carry articles for interactive learning. Currently, the team is assisting the National Secretary of the Family in incorporating an environmental education component in all the recreational parks currently under construction.

Informal environmental education through mass media

The majority of adults in El Salvador depend almost exclusively on the mass media to acquire knowledge that enables them to form opinions and respond to environmental issues. It was therefore very important that the national environmental education strategy include mass media, or informal education, among its principal priorities. An aware and vocal citizenry is likely to create a greater demand for environmental legislation and for environmentally sound decisionmaking. El Salvador's national environmental education strategy included four important features to enhance media coverage of environmental issues: decision-maker priority, a source of reliable information, professional development, and an incentive system.

Winning the cooperation of the communications media to address environmental themes typically depends on the interest shown by the public. The public, on the other hand, displays interest in the environment if it has the opportunity to hear about the topic regularly, a task that only the communications media can do. The media in El Salvador did not leap to the idea of covering environmental topics. Numerous meetings with owners and managers of different media were required to convince them that environmental issues are inescapable and they should anticipate the interests of their readers, listeners, and viewers by providing reputable information. The fact that the environment was a topic of global concern and somewhat "fashionable" helped win their support.

The two most important newspapers in the country assigned journalists to cover the environment. GreenCOM offered to give these reporters all the assistance necessary to do this work well. Since managers, editors, and owners make daily decisions about what gets published or aired, and in what space or time constraints, it was important to continue to cultivate this relationship. Breakfast conferences between media decisionmakers and environmental specialists were one successful strategy that was used for maintaining interest in environmental issues and providing accurate information.

It is not easy for journalists lacking any environmental education to report on environmental issues. Many issues are complex and it is difficult to simplify the concern for the public. The scientific community tends to be a less than helpful provider of environmental information; facts are couched with uncertainties and statistically significant findings are buried in constraining methodology. Individual reporters or media managers may believe environmental issues are merely a tolerable consequence of important economic development; others may equate concern for the environment with a romantic notion of ecological purity. Therefore, in El Salvador, SEMA and GreenCOM took responsibility for feeding environmental information to the media and serving as a link between the media and specialized sources of information. Portions of the agency training (see non-formal education) enabled technical staff to be consulted and interviewed by the media.

Interested journalists looked for information. GreenCOM helped identify these interested professionals and concentrated on them when sending invitations to conferences and when releasing important environmental information. These first interested journalists were exposed to projects developed by NGOs and to concrete aspects of environmental problems (such as heavily polluted rivers, areas of high erosion, etc.) with guided field trips led by technical staff. The opportunity to specialize in environmental topics and techniques for effective media coverage was offered to these journalists in a programme called the National Environmental Journalism Encounter.

The first National Environmental Journalism Encounter attracted 45 journalists from different media. As a result of this programme, some participants prepared commentaries on the management of solid waste, which was viewed by the population of the capital city as a serious problem. These first reports were followed by others that revealed important environmental problems. The reporters seemed to be discovering facts that previously passed unnoticed, such as dangerous levels of pollutants in the river passing through the capital or the growing heaps of trash on the river's edge.

A competition emerged among the different communications media to address topics which they saw affecting the health and well-being of the population. The interest of the population generated a demand for more information, fed by the NGOs, as reliable sources of information about these topics, which began to receive more space for their opinions in the media.

Approximately 150 people attended the Third National Environmental Journalism Encounter. The coverage of environmental topics was rising in the media, reaching 60 to 70 reports per month, with some environmental topics even reaching the editorial pages. This growing interest in reporting about environmental issues is supported by a clever incentive – an awards programme.

Public interest is not the only thing that sustains media coverage of environmental issues. GreenCOM established the National Environmental Journalism Awards in 1996 to stimulate reporters to write about environmental topics and to thank those already covering environmental themes in the media for their efforts. The prizes are awarded annually in three categories: print media, radio, and television, with first, second and third place awards in each category. Three private businesses sponsored the awards. The procedures stipulate that a call for nominations be issued to journalists requesting works published or broadcast in the previous year. A jury was formed of two NGO representatives, one representative of the Communications faculty of the University of El Salvador, one technical staff member from the Executive Secretariat for the Environment and one representative of the Association of Journalists of El Salvador (APES). This jury established evaluation criteria for the awards.

The awards are given each April during the week of Earth Day. The first event in 1996 for works produced during 1995 received a total of 47 entries. In addition to the nine awards, special recognition was given to one of the daily newspapers for its contribution to environmental education. In the second event in 1997, 147 works were submitted. Nine awards were given and nine institutions, media organizations, and journalists received additional recognition for their outstanding contributions in defence of the environment. In only two years, the National Environmental Journalism Awards have achieved enormous credibility and prestige in the union of journalists. This is reflected in the increase in nominations and in the massive attendance at the awards ceremonies, as well as the coverage given by the media.

Synergistic activities

The National Environmental Education Strategy could not have predicted all of the successful tools that became available to promote environmental education, but they evolved as the various education and communication channels were empowered to consider the environment. For example, the media created periodic supplements dedicated to the environment during 1996 and 1997. These supplements were of great use to students and GreenCOM distributed several thousand to schools. To produce these supplements, the newspapers used technical assistance from GreenCOM and through the staff, contacted the best technical specialists and obtained current sources of information.

An existing special section of one newspaper was modified to achieve the goals of the National Environmental Education Strategy with stunning results. El Diario de Hoy publishes a colourful Sunday supplement for children. Because GreenCOM and SEMA staff perceived this supplement as a potentially powerful addition to the set of environmental education tools, they convinced newspaper decision-makers to dedicate one edition each month to environmental themes. "Guanaquin" became an extremely successful example of synergy between mass communication and formal education. By introducing environmental issues directly to children, teachers became more confident of the importance of the topic. The newspaper also printed activities and experiments that teachers could do with students, supplementing the new textbooks and providing needed support for this new curriculum area. GreenCOM offered the technical assistance for the contents and programming, as well as reference materials and specialized sources of information.

Each year, "GuanaquPhin" promotes a contest about the environment for all of the nation's children with prizes donated by the newspaper. In 1994, soon after the birth of the supplement, 2,500 entries were submitted for the first contest titled "Let's Paint El Salvador Green". In 1995, the second instalment of the contest, "Let's Work for our Environment", invited students to submit drawings and proposals for group activities to resolve problems in their neighbourhoods. Ten thousand entries were submitted that year. In 1996, a new contest was announced under the title, "Defenders of the Environment", which received 36,000 entries from across the country. In 1997, the "GuanaquPhin" contest drew more than 101,000 entries, and the latest instalment attracted over 120,000.

In addition to this indisputable indicator of success, GreenCOM evaluated the acceptance and the practical use by teachers and students of the supplement. The results indicated that 85% of the teachers interviewed and a similar percentage of students use the supplement as a reference source for their homework, planning their science, health, and environment classes and conducting the experiments outlined in its pages.

This children's supplement is an example of how mass media can effectively reinforce the work of environmental education in schools. As a product of the evaluation and recommendation of GreenCOM, the contents of the "GuanaquPhin" will follow the guidelines and programming of the Ministry of Education for the science, health and environment subject area. Success is easy to see in this aspect of the National Environmental Education Strategy as the media now cover at least one environmental story a day.

The results of the plan

Since launching the national environmental education strategy in 1994, GreenCOM has led the nation of El Salvador in the organization and education of an environmental community that participated in a process to design a National Environmental Education Policy. That policy was the result of a three-day conference called the National Environmental Education Encounter. Over 1,000 people attended the National Encounter to help the nation move toward a comprehensive environmental education policy. Launched by the president of the country, the event even included the participation of the opposition political party.

In the months leading to the Encounter, three different participatory planning meetings were held to involve representatives from the formal, nonformal, and informal environmental education communities. Participants created a showcase of their achievements and used their successes to fabricate a new plan to continue their work. In small working groups, conference participants exchanged their ideas on the national policy. In the ensuing year, representatives from each group finetuned the policy for presentation to the Ministry of Education and the Executive Secretariat. The synergistic nature of the three areas of environmental education continue to reinforce each other, gather public support, and move environmental awareness farther.

By working closely with the decision-makers in the Executive Secretariat for the Environment and the Ministry of Education, and by involving professionals in the process of designing and extending professional development programmes, GreenCOM has created, enhanced, and breathed life into an entire environmental education community across the country. The capacity to continue this work has been established within organizations and agencies through the development of offices, training systems, procedures, policies, and materials. In just a few years, environmental education has become a transformational force in schools, politics, media and the lives of El Salvadorans.

Chapter 16

United States of America

Conducting environmental audits as a public service

*S. Bruce Kohrn, Walter Simpson, Julie Barrett O'Neill and
Joseph A. Gardella, Jr.*

Introduction

The purpose of this chapter is to describe and examine the evolution of
environmental auditing at the University at Buffalo (UB), State University of New
York, as a public service-learning experience. Students at UB initiated an audit of
campus environmental practices and policies, an effort that later developed into an
internship-style audit of a public building, Buffalo's City Hall.

Student-driven environmental audits have been conducted on campuses across North
America since 1990. The model of the campus environmental audit is based upon a
master's thesis project, *In Our Backyard: Environmental Issues at UCLA, Proposals
for Change and the Institution's Potential as a Model* (Smith 1990), the first
comprehensive examination of the environmental quality of a college campus. This
type of audit serves several important functions. First, when developed as a
component of an environmental education programme, an audit project provides a
hands-on learning experience wherein the campus itself, as a human community and
a set of physical systems, becomes a "learning lab" (Simpson 1996; Eagan and Orr
1992). Second, the product of the exercise serves as an important benchmark for
evaluating the ecological sustainability of a university's operational, educational and
research initiatives. The audit process and its product – an audit report – challenge
an institution to become an environmentally responsible citizen by minimizing its
physical impact on local systems. The report also usually articulates how colleges
and universities may cultivate environmental literacy. Finally, the report
acknowledges the unique obligation educational institutions have to develop
scientific research on ecological phenomena and to develop solutions for living
within ecological constraints.

Environmental audits have commonly featured:

- baseline data outlining current materials and resource procurement and
  use, as well as waste generation and disposal practices for each
  operational area;
- an outline and description of existing operational management systems;
- an analysis of local development and demographic patterns;
- an inventory of ecological and cultural attributes of the institutions,
  surrounding property and local community;
- suggested alternatives to current campus policies and practices; and
- an illustration of the costs and savings (resource and financial),
  anticipated to result from recommended actions.

(Keinry 1995)

In 1995, 20 environmental studies students at UB conducted a comprehensive environmental audit of the university's activities. UB, the largest campus of the largest public university system in the U.S., comprises nearly 100 buildings split between two campuses. The students themselves took the initiative to conduct the audit, and asked Professor Claude Welch and Energy Officer Walter Simpson to serve as advisors. Their 24,000 word report had four focus areas: resource use and infrastructure planning, solid and hazardous waste management, educational and administrative efforts, and an evaluation of the effectiveness of the university's Environmental Task Force. The student report commended the university for the growth of its recycling programme, the hundreds of energy saving projects that had been implemented, its establishment of an Environmental Task Force (ETF) and the university's Building Conservation Contacts Programme.[1] However, it also exposed the absence of a strong commitment to environmental literacy and research and the existence of an automobile-intensive campus planning policy. Among the 160 suggestions for improvement were: the development of an environmental research and teaching institute; adoption of an eco-friendly land use design called UB 2025; the use of unbleached, 100% recycled paper for all university business; and the placement of a moratorium on the construction of new parking lots.[2]

Environmental audits have a demonstrated track record for promoting student understanding of and willingness to work toward policies and practices that are ecologically sustainable. The excellent efforts of the self-organized and self-motivated students at UB served to underscore these educational benefits. In order to continue and reinforce these experiences for subsequent groups of students, we decided that the environmental audit might lend itself well to a public service role that would benefit the students, the university and the community. It seemed fortuitous then when a member of the Buffalo City Council approached Walter Simpson about conducting an environmental audit of Buffalo City Hall after reading an article in the local newspaper about the campus audit.

Development of the Buffalo City audit

The city of Buffalo, New York, with a population that has declined from approximately 500,000 to 300,000 in the last several decades (mainly owing to a demographic shift from the city to the suburbs), is a former centre for heavy industry on the eastern shore of Lake Erie, and has suffered a steady loss of manufacturing jobs for over 30 years. Buffalo City Hall, an imposing 32-story art deco structure built between 1929 and 1931, overlooks the lake and the city. The building was constructed as a testament to industry, commerce and democratic government, and detailed mosaics adorn the interior. Because of its high public visibility, Buffalo City Hall was an appropriate site for this public service pilot project.

In early 1996 Ms. Barbra Kavanaugh, a member of the Buffalo Common Council (the City's elected legislative body), read press reports of the UB Environmental Audit and asked Walter Simpson about the process and its outcomes. Mr. Simpson presented background information on the UB Audit to a meeting of the Common Council. In spring 1996, the Council passed a resolution calling for such an audit of the "city". Coincidentally, Mr. Simpson had previously had several conversations with S. Bruce Kohrn, a local independent environmental consultant and community activist, about the prospect of extending UB's experience with audits into the community as a public service. Also coincidentally, the new chair of the UB

Environmental Task Force (ETF), Professor Joseph Gardella, had formed a new public service subcommittee in part in response to the UB Audit.

In May 1996, Ms. Kavanaugh convened a meeting of Simpson, Gardella, Kohrn and members of the Common Council Staff and the city's Office for the Environment, to sketch out the opportunities for an audit. Working in City Hall presented a unique set of political, practical and physical challenges that played out over the next months. The lessons learned from these aspects of the audit process can be considered nearly as important as the results of the audit itself, and certainly provide an important case study in the development of student internship-based public service in environmental management or sustainable development and planning.

Early on, a team of key leaders was developed between the university and the city to plan the audit. Meetings were also held with the Erie County Office of Pollution Prevention, which provided additional support in developing the programme. Among the key figures for the city, besides Ms. Kavanaugh, were: James Smith, the head of the Office for the Environment (OE); Anthony Lupino, a staff planner in OE and technical liaison for the students; Edwin Marr, Recycling Coordinator for the city's Office of Streets and Sanitation; members of the Buffalo Environmental Management Commission (EMC), a standing advisory body of appointed citizens representing other government, industry and community groups; and Sandra Nasca from the city's Law Office. Besides Gardella, Simpson and Kohrn, other members of the ETF's Public Service and Outreach subcommittee were consulted, including John Sheffer, Interim Vice-President for Public Service and Urban Affairs (a member of the law faculty and former New York State senator).

The first challenge was to define exactly what in City Hall would be "audited". A work plan was developed after a long and substantive meeting with the EMC. Seven areas were defined which would be audited: energy, office practices and recycling, solid waste, pollution prevention, food services, water use and procurement and purchasing policies.

The planning team began to hit politically sensitive roadblocks almost immediately. The City Law Office offered the opinion that liability issues should completely preclude the audit. Essentially, it was felt that problems might be identified that would lead to employee complaints about health and safety (e.g., complaints about peeling lead-based paint and inadequate policies for the handling of common chemicals, such as pesticides and cleaners). The concern was that an increased awareness of these issues would leave the city in a vulnerable position against liability claims. After some editing and changes, including the agreement to leave out of the audit the handling of chemicals of any sort, a finalized work plan was completed (see Figure 1). However, the go-ahead letter of commitment and cooperation from the Mayor's office was not received because of vague concerns raised by the law office. Gardella, Kohrn and Luppino continued to meet with various stakeholders to refine the City Hall work plan and to overcome the law office objections.

Finally, four months later the Mayor issued a letter of approval, and the project moved ahead. Recruitment of a student team for the spring semester 1997 was initiated with UB's Planning, Law, Engineering and Environmental Studies programmes. Nearly 20 students attended a preliminary planning session, and 14 students registered for academic credit for the programme. At the outset, we hoped that the class would draw from each of these programmes. In the end, however, only junior and senior level environmental studies majors took the class.[3]

Figure 1.

**Environmental audit of Buffalo City Hall
areas to be evaluated**

1. **Energy** – This part of the Audit will consist of a survey of all floors and offices for four areas: lighting use, heating, air conditioning, and computer use. Green computer technologies and polices will be evaluated to minimize energy use for computing. Lighting types and wattage will be measured and assessed. Reflective window insulation will also be evaluated. Potential outcomes include recommendations for reducing energy usage through simple changes in practices and potential small capital expenses.

2. **Procurement and Purchasing Policies** – UB currently has an environmental and sustainable product purchasing policy which fits within New York State regulations. This policy encourages the purchase and use of products made from recycled and post-consumer waste materials, and includes paper products, food service products, etc. The current purchasing policies for City Hall will be evaluated with an eye to recommending specific product area policies which have been identified at UB (e.g., paper, computer disks, etc.). This part of the Audit will primarily consist of a comparison of purchasing policies. Potential outcomes will include concrete recommendations for purchasing products made from post-consumer waste.

3. **Solid Waste Management, Recycling and Office Practices** – This part of the Audit will examine the total amount of solid waste generated in City Hall, the amounts of each type of solid waste generated, the percentage of the building's solid waste that is potentially recyclable, and the percentage of the solid waste that is actually being placed in recycling bins. New York State has recommended a recycling goal of 50% of the solid waste stream. The feasibility of meeting such a goal at City Hall will be explored. City Hall offices will be surveyed to measure the percentage of recyclable paper, glass, and other office products (e.g. printer toner cartridges, etc.) that are currently recycled. Potential outcomes include recommendations for additional source separation methods that encourage increased participation in recycling.

4. **Water** – This part of the Audit will consist of an assessment of the current use of plumbing in all restroom and garage facilities to evaluate the possibility of reduced flow or reduction of the number of water sources.

5. **Food Service** – The food service operation will be surveyed to determine the potential use of products which are made from post-consumer waste, including napkins, utensils, cups, etc.

The City Hall audit: what happened?

Most of the students in the class had never been in City Hall and did not know what to expect. The syllabus explained that they would need to work together in teams and be self-starting. Unlike most courses, the syllabus, by design, did not provide weekly assignments for the students to complete. A step-by-step approach to conducting an environmental audit was not provided. The students were required to figure out for themselves what to assess, what data they needed to collect, how to collect and evaluate the data, and how to report their findings. This approach, the syllabus explained, was not unlike the working world. The unstructured nature of the course was a challenge for the students – and the instructors – and, predictably, at the end of the course, the students had mixed reactions. Most were positive about the experience; a few felt that more guidance was necessary and suggested a manual be provided.

The students were not without guidance, however. Kohrn volunteered to "supervise" the students from week to week; Marr and Luppino spent considerable time with

them in class and at City Hall. Marr provided guidance on how to evaluate the solid waste stream, and gave students access to his considerable library of materials. Luppino became a liaison between the students and City Hall staff, and facilitated scheduling and communications. Frank, a local energy consultant, provided expert guidance on energy-related issues.

The organization of the course was open, determined by the students as they worked through the problem of designing, conducting and then writing about the audit. The semester divided itself into three phases: preparation, implementation and reporting. During the initial preparatory phase, the audit was introduced and discussed. Based on negotiations and discussions with City Hall, the availability of professional support, and the number of students, the class was divided into two teams: energy, and office practices and recycling/solid waste. The goals and objectives of the audit and the differences between teams were discussed; for example, energy was more technically oriented, recycling less so. Students made their own choices with five selecting energy and nine recycling.

The class got down to work right away, with the exception of one class meeting in which an organizational psychologist spoke on what the students might reasonably expect to encounter from City Hall staff, particularly given the resistance from City Hall during negotiations. She raised good points about people skills, survey questions and organizational culture, in general, and led a valuable discussion on how to dress, how to act, how to approach City Hall personnel, and what to say. She also did some role-playing exercises with the students on interview techniques. The students appreciated this background, and said they felt comfortable in the initial stages of approaching employees in City Hall.

During their preparations, the students worked with Frank, Kohrn, Luppino and Marr to develop work plans, a schedule and a mechanism for informing City Hall employees of their activities. The teams were asked to sketch out their weekly activities, including their planning efforts for the semester, and were encouraged to revise their work plans several times during the semester.

As part of their preparations, the students designed data sheets and surveys, and made plans with City Hall staff to facilitate data collection, including plans to coordinate janitorial service, garbage pickup, interviews with employees, etc. The instructors emphasized that the project was always to be considered a work in progress involving an iterative process of design, implementation, and evaluation, and that changes to the work plan were to be expected based on their experiences. For example, after several weeks of research and preparation, the recycling team had developed surveys for City Hall offices, with questions to ask, data sheets to fill out, and responsibilities delegated. On the first day of the implementation phase, the team walked into the first office on their list armed with theses surveys. After spending a few minutes talking to the staff, they immediately recognized the shortcomings of their survey. They then spent the next hour huddled in the hallway rethinking their approach to presenting themselves, to asking questions, and to conducting the survey. They said they learned more in five minutes about these issues than in three prior weeks of research.

Although City Hall employees were informed that the students would be working in the building, few people seemed initially to know what was going on and the first encounters were awkward. However, word quickly spread around the building. Once the students talked to people in several offices and became more comfortable with their routine and presentation, few City Hall staff were surprised by the students'

requests when they walked into a new office. The staff then began to ask questions and make suggestions.

The students quickly assessed the recycling behaviour of employees through their surveys and by their quantitative analysis of the solid waste. After the kinks in scheduling were worked out with custodial staff, students went through the garbage and recycling bins in the basement, and analysed the waste stream floor by floor.[4] This created an impressive "visual" and became the focus of a media event where television crews filmed and interviewed the students, faculty and City Hall representatives.

The experiences of the energy team were very different from those of the recycling team. Although the recycling team had good guidance and access to resources, they needed to design their own study. The energy team, however, was able to utilize the methods for engineering analysis and design developed by Mr. Frank for his own work. Their purpose was to investigate the heating, ventilation and air conditioning systems (HVAC); to evaluate the use of energy-consuming office machinery such as computers, monitors, printers, copiers, heaters, fans, window-mounted air conditioners, coffee pots, hot plates and refrigerators; to evaluate the efficiency of the elevator system; to assess employee behaviour and attitudes regarding energy usage and conservation; and to assess natural gas and electricity procurement. The students also reviewed an earlier engineering study that had resulted in retrofitted lighting throughout the building.

While the energy team had access to a "boilerplate" methodology for evaluating energy procurement, consumption and efficiency, they were stymied by an inexplicable lack of cooperation from some corners of City Hall and the public utilities. For reasons never fully explained, the energy team was unable to obtain information they needed for their work. First, they never received the promised list of mechanical equipment in City Hall nor permission to investigate on their own in restricted areas of the building. Second, the students never received the promised utility billing histories that would have provided information on how much the city was spending for the purchase of natural gas and electricity and how much City Hall consumed. This was a significant setback for the students, because they were then unable to evaluate the environmental impacts of existing operations and provide quantitative measures of potential costs savings for the implementation of their recommendations.

The audit report and recommendations

Each team was required to write a weekly progress report. Different leaders came forward at different points in the project, and eventually the responsibility for writing, compiling, and editing became the responsibility of just two or three students. This final reporting stage of the audit process was more involved, and took longer than the students predicted, so that only a draft report was produced by the end of the semester. The same students that had taken the lead throughout most of the project then volunteered to complete the editing during the summer. Drafts of the report were submitted to several faculty and City Hall staff for comments and critical evaluation. The final report was submitted to the Mayor in his office, in front of television cameras and reporters. He was interested, asked many questions, and made a commitment to implementing many of the students' recommendations. The students were clearly pleased, and the meeting provided a good conclusion to their work.

In the report, the students made several recommendations, such as:

- Given the high percentage (67%) of recyclable materials found in the trash, the emphasis of solid waste collection should be geared towards recycling rather than garbage disposal, by providing more recycling bins and improving employee education.
- Office products made of recycled materials should be purchased (at estimated savings of nearly US$12,000 annually).
- An educational programme for employees about energy efficient office practices should be introduced.
- A professional engineering study should be conducted to examine capital improvements to the HVAC system.

In addition to these recommendations, the students also commended the city for its efforts to improve lighting efficiency. The retrofits of 4,972 lighting fixtures in City Hall save over US$130,000 annually, and provide environmental benefits by reducing air pollution related to the generation of electricity.

Problems and issues in conducting environmental audits

There are many issues to be considered when students conduct an environmental audit. We discuss several of these below.

Multiple tasks. An environmental audit project involves many tasks, including: identifying a client organization and negotiating the ground rules for the audit, recruiting students and arranging appropriate academic credit, planning the audit, providing technical training, gathering information and conducting the audit, analysing data and drawing conclusions, writing and editing the report, presenting the report, and following through to ensure implementation of recommendations. Some of these tasks are preparatory to the actual audit, and may be best accomplished by faculty or advisors who are supervising the audit. Other tasks (e.g., planning, information gathering, analysing data, writing and presenting) belong to the students. Of course, it is beneficial if students are also involved in other facets, especially follow through and implementation of their recommendations.

Time requirements. As a rule of thumb, assume the entire audit process will take at least twice as long as anticipated. In our experience, this means the audit is a project that will take two 16-week semesters, yet most students do not have two semesters to commit to the project. As suggested above, an alternative approach would be for each team of students to limit their tasks so that they can complete a portion of the audit in one semester. However, recruiting a second group of students to complete the audit may result in a loss of continuity for the project, a lack of closure for the first group of students, and a lack of ownership in the project for the second group. Thus far, one or two students have been willing to continue work the next semester or during the summer. One solution is to conduct the audit on a smaller facility or to take on fewer tasks. The latter strategy requires careful monitoring and guidance by the supervisor or instructor because the students tend to take on too many issues.

To save time, the identification of a client organization and the negotiation of the terms of the audit should be completed prior to recruiting students. In the case of the Buffalo City Hall environmental audit, an entire semester was spent arranging for the audit and overcoming various organizational barriers.

The student portion of the audit cannot be rushed if the goal is to produce a positive learning experience for the students and a professional, helpful audit for the "client". If the facility to be audited is large, such as a college campus or a very large building like Buffalo's City Hall, then one semester is required to train students, gather and analyse data, make recommendations and draft the report. A second semester will be needed to edit and finalize the report, present it and seek to implement its recommendations.

Another time saving alternative would be to allow each audit team to prepare and submit its own report, without coordinating with the other teams to produce a single comprehensive document. The separate reports can then be compiled with a cover letter from the instructor to submit to the client. This approach would lose the cohesiveness of a single final report, and the students would lose the experience of working together to coordinate, edit and compile the final document. However, this approach would save time at the end of the semester, and avoid the problem of coordinating too many incompatible student schedules without sacrificing the substantive content of the audit report.

Overcoming barriers by kicking it off right. In our experience, an environmental audit of a college or university campus can be initiated without much fanfare or official approval. Campus communities tend to be decentralized, open, permissive forums where student projects are tolerated if not embraced. Community institutions or political entities, like Buffalo City Hall, are different. They generally are closed organizations. Conducting an effective audit of an off-campus entity requires an invitation, as well as top-level approval and support. In the case of City Hall, we were invited in by a member of the City Council, negotiated mayoral support, and had the full cooperation of the Office for the Environment.

Obtaining support from the client organization's leadership is one thing but communicating it to members of the organization is another. To maximize the likelihood that the organization's staff will cooperate with student auditors, it is essential that top-level support be communicated right from the start – personally and via written documents. A "kick-off" meeting involving all parties is an ideal way of introducing everyone to the project, allaying fears and assuring the major players within the client organization that the project has the organization's blessing. Even so, students must be prepared to encounter roadblocks and resistance. Overcoming them is part of the learning experience.

Audit scope. As a practical matter, the scope of the environmental audit must be limited. In most cases, students will not have enough time to investigate all environmental impacts associated with a client organization, nor will they possess or have access to the technical skills necessary to tackle some issues. Taking on too much may lead to frustration and sloppy work, thus undermining the whole project.

With the Buffalo City Hall audit, it was clear that the city was more interested and open to having students delve into some areas than others. Thus, the scope of an audit should be subject to negotiation so that the project is in the client's "comfort zone". To maintain project integrity, students and faculty involved in environmental audit projects must decide which limitations and restrictions they will accept. We felt that we could live with the City Hall-imposed limitations, at least as a first step in working with them.

Another scope issue pertains to how the audit defines "environmental". Does it include human environmental health and safety issues (e.g., indoor air quality,

ventilation rates, employee exposure to chemicals, etc.) or is the focus entirely on the client facility's impact on the natural environment? We have thus far chosen the latter focus for the audits, because health and safety issues are generally already addressed by a health and safety officer at each facility. Also, as previously explained, the City Law Office raised certain concerns regarding liability, and would not approve the project if these issues were to be addressed in the audit.

Supervision and budget. One might hope that an environmental audit could be conducted without a budget and funding. But as a practical matter, good will and good intentions may only go so far! If the project is to be sustainable, replicated and expanded over a course of years, as we hope to do in Buffalo, a funding source is needed. Primary costs include travel and reimbursable expenses for students and project supervision costs.

A self-sustaining, long-term project is unlikely if all supervision is by volunteer faculty and staff who must find time above and beyond their normal responsibilities to participate in the audit process and to work with the students. The Buffalo City Hall project needed assistance from adjunct faculty and local environmental professionals who should be reimbursed for their efforts. Thus, to continue this project, we realize that securing funding is essential. It remains to be seen in our case whether funding will come from the university, an outside grant or from future audit clients (perhaps as a percentage of savings generated by audit recommendations).

Product vs. process. There is a tension between turning out a highly polished professional document (most likely to produce the desired environmental changes in the client's facility), and letting the students do it themselves. It is important to strike the right balance. Most students are not experienced enough to conduct the technical aspects of the audit or to direct and manage the project by themselves. In addition, writing and editing may not be student strong points. In our experience, students need outside help and guidance from faculty advisors or from other technical resource persons. But ultimately the students must have a sense of ownership of and responsibility for the project. This may somewhat compromise the quality of the final document but, as an educational activity, the first priority should be the learning experience.

It is important to keep in mind that the students' learning experiences are about more than acquiring procedural knowledge of an audit or about how various human practices impact the environment. Participation in an audit also teaches students about themselves, about working together and about working in their communities to undertake real projects. It is an exercise in personal empowerment.

Faculty supervisors must be careful not to rob the students of all these intangible outcomes by being too intrusive. On the other hand, the experience can be negative if student leadership does not emerge and the students are allowed to flounder too long. As instructors, we are striving for the right balance between teacher guidance and student initiative.

Concluding thoughts on the student learning experience

What do students learn by doing an environmental audit? An environmental audit is, by its nature, a hands-on experience that involves getting out into the community and working cooperatively with others. Students learn how to plan, execute and

"public awareness" (for they are aware!) into a realm of active, critical and creative engagement.

This chapter briefly examines one community's move to action. In the Quinte bio-region of Eastern Ontario, a number of people are attempting to create a greener, more self-reliant and sustainable community through a project titled *Growing Jobs for Living Through Environmental Adult Education*. The project is premised on the idea that environmental adult education and participatory research, linked to struggles to democratize structures and processes, is key to developing a healthier and more sustainable community. It involves a process of reflection and action which builds awareness, knowledge, cohesiveness, and skills in order to create a stronger foundation for community transformation.

The role of education

In 1997, as one possible remedy to socio-environmental problems, the report *Our Common Future* by the World Commission on Environment and Development emphasized formal and non-formal education. It suggested that education could be used as a critical tool to help people make changes in their own behaviours and attitudes and address their own needs and concerns. Five years later, *Agenda 21* (1992:36.3) re-emphasized this idea and called for an expansion in environmental education activities and programmes. But in spite of this belief in the importance of education and a proliferation of educational activities, environmental problems not only persist but grow. I believe this situation is due to three major problems: two well known, the other less so.

The first problem is the focus on "individual behaviour" change as the goal of education. This is painfully similar to Nancy Reagan's "Just Say No" campaign against drugs in the United States. A sole focus on "individual behaviour" ignores the fact that environmental problems are political and economic. It ignores the fact that the capitalist system is maintained through the exploitation of people and abuse of natural resources and has the power, money and means to continually manipulate society through the medium of advertising. As Michael Welton (1996:55) argues, the [deepest] educative process at work in the twentieth century has been "learning to consume".

The second is that in order for education to play a critical role and truly help people to challenge existing socio-ecological problems and bring about concrete change, new frameworks will need to be developed since modern education was primarily

> designed to further the conquest of nature and the industrialization of the planet...[it has] tended to produce unbalanced, under-dimensional people tailored to fit the modern economy (Orr quoted in Hicks and Holden 1995:186).

A third problem has been the dismissal of the importance of non-formal or public education and/or its limited framing in terms of "public awareness". There is a strong and extremely important focus on environmental education for school children and a marked exclusion of adults. In her article, ironically titled *Approaches to Environmental Education: Towards a Transformative Perspective*, Constance Russell (1997, p.38) argues that the reason environmental education focuses on children is because for the most part, adults "are considered beyond repair". At this critical moment in the planet's history this preconception is grievous for it is the adults of this world who are the voters, consumers, workers, employers, parents,

media personalities, land and business owners, activists, civil servants, poets, musicians, and educators to name but a few crucial societal roles. It is the adults who "are the force of social and political change, in both the domestic and global arenas" (Lipschutz 1996, p.2). As adult educator Michael Welton (1997, p.21) argues,

> [r]esistance to and transformation of societal structures emerges from the adult population, and is premised upon men and women's ability to learn new ways of seeing the world and acting within it.

Right now is an excellent time to reach out to these adults who play such critical roles because, according to Livingstone et al in their most recent OISE Survey, adult education is the largest sphere of learning in Canadian society today. More adults, probably reflective of contemporary demographics and economics, are engaging in formal and non-formal learning activities than ever before.

The notion of sustainability

> Achieving greater levels of sustainability would require that individuals, organizations, and societies change many of the things they do. (Slocombe 1995, p.10)

Before beginning any discussion about educational activities geared towards creating increased community "sustainability", it is important to look at the term itself and the debate which surrounds it.

In her paper titled, *Considering Sustainability from a Canadian Sociological Feminist Perspective* (1996), Margrit Eichler notes that sustainability has been left as an illustrative and fluid term. She contends that although "we all know that our current way of organizing ourselves is unsustainable... ideas of how to re-organize ourselves are diverse and often co-incide with particular interests" (p. 6).

Herman Daly (1996, p.1) agrees that sustainability "is a term that everyone likes but nobody is sure of what it means". He observes that following the publication of *Our Common Future* (1987) "the term rose to the prominence of a mantra – or a shibboleth" and began to form an important part of the vocabulary of economists, environmentalists and eventually, educators. The report defined "sustainability", or better said "sustainable development", as the ability to meet the needs of the present generation without sacrificing the ability of the future to meet its needs. Daly (1996, p.2) suggests that while

> not vacuous by any means, [the] definition [and purpose] were sufficiently vague to allow for a broad consensus. Probably that was a good political strategy at the time – a consensus on a vague concept was better than a disagreement over a sharply defined one.

But by the 1990s this vagueness was no longer a basis for consensus. It became instead the breeding ground for disagreement which "set the stage for a situation where whoever [could] pin his or her definition to the term [would] automatically win a larger political battle for influence over our future" (Daly 1996, p.2). But could there realistically be an all encompassing definition of sustainability that would suit all peoples in all places of the world? I think not. And therefore this begs the question: should developing this definition be the role of education/educators? Although this does not often happen, I would agree with Daly when he argues that

> ... most important concepts are not subject to analytically precise definitions –
> think of democracy, justice, welfare, for example. Important concepts are more
> dialectical than analytic, in the sense that they have evolving penumbras which
> partially overlap with their "other".... If all concepts were analytic we could not
> deal with change and evolution. Analytically defined species could never evolve if
> they at no time and in no way overlapped with their other. All important concepts
> are dialectically vague at the margins (p. 2).

My own personal experience as an adult educator has shown that, in fact, it is not an all encompassing definition people require, but rather the way or means to attempt to create a collective "home-grown" framework for sustainability. Each community is different; the needs and concerns are simply not the same. The most beneficial role education can play is to provide the opportunity for women, who have played and will continue to play the most critical role in the struggle to save the planet as advocates for social justice and environmental preservation (Clover 1995), and men to debate and determine for themselves what it is they wish to sustain and the most effective ways of reaching that goal within their own unique context. This must, however, be done by keeping in mind fundamental questions of power and social reproduction in the formation of individual identity and personal decision-making. Education cannot afford to ignore imbalances such as gender, race, class and human/Earth relations in its analysis and understanding of power distribution. Power is often shared unequally and therefore, it is important to recognize and re-organize this imbalance in order to realize collective energy and ability.

Sustainability will only be achieved through communities attaining control over their resources, consumption, production and knowledge base. Community control means that the decision-making processes and organizational structures are designed to give all members of a community the power and means to better manage their own affairs. What is required is a transformation from "hierarchical to non-hierarchical structures so as to allow for the maximum participation by community members in the decision-making and development process" (Nozick 1992, p.99). This does not mean that communities must become economically self-reliant in total isolation but that they recognize their own potential and knowledge and make better use of them.

The Growing Jobs for Living project

> I believe this community can solve its problems...The days of government
> providing these things are long gone. It's time to go back to the days when we did
> these things ourselves.(McDougall, *The Intelligencer*, Belleville: Ontario.)

The Quinte bio-region, located on Lake Ontario approximately 200 kilometres east of Toronto, provides a classic example of the socio-economic and environmental problems facing the Canadian people. As an area of relatively established industrial production dating back to the earliest European settlement of Ontario, the Quinte region has seen a sharp rise in unemployment as a result of plant and factory closures related to the North American Free Trade Agreement (NAFTA) and other globally related shifts. From 1991-1995, over 2,500 jobs were lost in the Quinte region and many more people are "underemployed". This sharp rise in unemployment has been accompanied by a rise in violence and crime. There are also a number of serious environmental problems related to past and continued industrial and agricultural production. The Bay of Quinte was identified by the International Joint Commission for the Great Lakes as one of 43 areas of concern owing to severe environmental and water quality problems (throughout the Great Lakes). Rising instances of ill-health in the region may be linked to these factors. In

addition, and equally, if not more, frightening is the fact that numerous small local businesses in the centres of cities or towns have fallen victim to the homogenization or "Americanization" process of superstores such as Walmart, Toys R US and McDonalds. This process erodes culture and collective memory, without which people lose the creative and imaginary ability to envision change.

There are numerous examples of community economic initiatives across Canada (see Nozick 1992; Roberts 1995). They most often revolve around individual "ecopreneurs" who create their own solutions but with little widespread support. "They are bright squares of new material in an old threadbare quilt. Some of the cloth is different, but the basic weave is still the same" (Clover et al 1998). All too often these projects end up being little more than the hobby for a minority and make little contribution to educating the community about sustainable alternatives (Fien 1993). The Quinte region reflects this limitation in its many attempts to develop "green" jobs which have been isolated and ultimately difficult to implement and unsustainable due to lack of broad government and community support.

The primary goal of the *Growing Jobs for Living* projects is to use environmental adult education theory and practice and participatory research as tools to help people to create a healthier and more sustainable community. Its objectives are: to provide an opportunity for people to come together and discuss important issues in their communities; to help them create alternative and more diversified "green" livelihoods and localized goods and services, thereby reducing dependency on large businesses and governments; and to repair environmental damage.

Through a variety of teaching and learning methods, the project will create an inventory of the social and environmental work that needs to be done, the kinds of diverse work in which people would like to engage in the community, and the available resources to support this work. An implementation plan then will be developed to bring needs, dreams and resources together.

Environmental adult education

> Education is how we live our lives and how you live with everything around you. Everything in existence teaches us something about life... everything around us educates, how we interact with the land, minerals, trees, sky, animals everything, even our thoughts. Our thoughts too can become a force, for we are in charge of them. (Profeit-Le Blanc 1996, p. 14)

The concept of environmental adult education (EAE) in the *Growing Jobs for Living* project is concerned with people and their futures as well as the rest of nature. The environment does not just provide physical support to humans, but psychological, emotional, cultural and spiritual sustenance as well. For as D. H. Lawrence noted in *The Alexandria Quarter* in 1958, "[we] are the children of our landscape; it dictates behaviour and through it, the measure to which we are responsive to it. I can think of no better identification".

Environmental adult education is a process of teaching and learning which begins with the daily lived experiences of women and men living in communities and is linked to confronting and challenging the root causes of socio-environmental damage. It relates personal and structural perspectives and seeks to understand relationships of power and knowledge. EAE is also concerned with knowing ourselves as mammalian species trying to live more lightly on the land,

cooperatively and creatively in this biosphere. The learning process is a dynamic, life-long process of discovering and re-discovering what we know about the rest of nature, and how we teach and learn from one another (Hall and Sullivan 1995).

Since not all people learn in the same way, environmental adult education can use a diversity of methods and processes such as storytelling, art, popular theatre, poetry, music, and small group discussion to tap into the knowledge and potential of all adults. In particular, nature and community are called upon to play the important roles of teacher and site of learning. EAE is a process which attempts to promote the development of concrete personal and, most importantly, collective action.

Educational components of the project

Study Circles
Study circles, a concept originating in Sweden, typically involve a group of 5-15 people who meet to discuss social and political issues of concern and to develop the skills necessary for taking effective action. They help people, within their own community spaces,

> to explore important topics, consider a range of viewpoints, challenge commonly held assumptions, and achieve learning that enables people to take constructive action. The essence of the study circle is free discussion and exploration with all views being valid.
>
> (Gibson & Bishop, 1998)

Gibson and Bishop suggest that the following basic principles underlie study circles:

* acting in accord with and contributing to wider equality and democracy;
* promoting the liberation of individuals and communities from economic and social oppression;
* working to enhance cooperation and companionship;
* exercising a group's freedom and the right to set objectives to suit its needs;
* organizing for continuity and planning;
* facilitating active participation; and
* taking action.

Although there are a variety of approaches to study circles, in the Quinte region a thematic approach generally has been adopted. This involves focusing on a single theme or topic of concern in the community. To date, some of the topics or themes that have been the focus of discussion have been: the meaning of democracy; the life of a single mother on welfare; workfare and working in menial jobs for welfare benefits; the work of the Women's Learning Centre; the creation of consumer unions; the Remedial Action Plan for cleaning up the Great Lakes; the demise of Green Check, a green business; and breast cancer and the environment. Since the inception of the *Growing Jobs for Living* project in May 1997, approximately 10-15 people from various sectors (such as education, health, small business, farming) and community organizations (such as women's anti-poverty) have been coming together to discuss these community problems and share their work. Each week, a different person has acted as a facilitator of the meeting while someone else keeps a record of the discussions.

A community survey

A community-wide survey was designed and undertaken with three objectives in mind. The first objective was to identify past environmental and job-creation initiatives that had taken place in the community over the past 10 years. Specifically, the survey sought to address the following questions: If the initiatives were still active, what had been their successes and what assistance would they need to make their success more visible to the wider community? If the initiatives had not succeeded, what were the primary reasons? A second objective was to identify what various community members felt were the most important environmental, social and economic issues and to use the wide range of responses as a basis for discussion in future study circles. The final objective of the survey was to identify key environmental, social and business groups in the region, and to solicit support for and/or participation in study circles, interviews, workshops, the steering committee and so on.

What the survey revealed was that almost all the environmental programmes started in the Quinte area had been cancelled, primarily due to government cutbacks or lack of community support. It also showed that there are very few initiatives taking place in the community to create alternative employment. In fact, none of the people interviewed could identify any organization engaged in this type of activity. Although unemployment continues to rise, there is no space or opportunity for people to collectively engage in developing alternatives. Finding work in an ever more "workless" environment must take place in isolation. A final important piece of information garnered from the survey was that all the members of the organizations or groups interviewed felt that there was a need for an umbrella group to act as a coordinating body, playing a networking role for the many small but active community groups who often work in isolation.

Participatory research workshops

Although nearly everyone carries out research in their everyday life, research is usually regarded as something only conducted by experts in universities or government agencies. Participatory research involves ordinary people in systematically investigating, analysing and acting on their own situations. They become both the researchers and the researched, both the knowledge generators and the knowledge users. Their needs provide the research agenda, their experiences constitute part of the data and the applications they have in mind guide the kinds of knowledge or outcomes that are created. As Maguire (1987) argues, it is a "process of knowledge creation [which] is more than a new set of research techniques... it is a systemic approach to personal and social transformation" (p. 3) through helping "ordinary people understand the connections between their individual experiences and broader social, economic, and political struggle" (p. 101). In other words, rather than merely recording observable facts, participatory research "has the explicit intention of collectively investigating reality in order to transform it" (Harris 1992, p. 38).

A goal of the project is to organize a series of participatory research workshops in which people can use their imaginations, creativity and problem solving skills. The workshops are more structured than the study circles and use skilled adult education facilitators (both from within and outside the community). A variety of different types of workshops are planned to take place over the next two years.

For example, one type of workshop, which will be the most frequent, will focus on developing ideas for a variety of sustainable or "green" jobs which are needed in the communities, identifying the resources available to support these jobs and

eventually, developing an implementation plan for initiating and sustaining such jobs. Participants will come from environmental groups, social justice organizations, Native groups, local businesses, and the unemployed and underemployed, etc. Special attention will be paid to addressing and working creatively but critically with the imbalance of power that occurs when different groups of people are brought together. Alongside the workshops, participatory researchers will conduct individual interviews with women and men in the community who are unwilling or unable to participate in the workshops or study circles processes in order to obtain their input. The first of these workshops took place in March 1998.

Another type of workshop will be organized to provide interested community members with the educational skills and methods to enable them to work in the community. Other workshops will focus on examining connections between socio-political and economic forces and the environment, and use storytelling and nature as a site of learning to help people connect with their ecological self. The first workshop which took place in October 1997 was a combination of all of these. The purposes were to:

- introduce the Growing Jobs for Living project;
- identify some key principles of a sustainable community;
- provide participants with facilitation skills;
- strengthen partnerships and share resources;
- create energy and motivation and discuss ways to motivate others;
- identify socio-environmental problems and break them down into smaller bites so that realistic concrete solutions could be devised and initiated; and
- have fun.

For two and one-half days the facilitators introduced participants to a variety of educational methods (such as poetry and music creation, popular theatre, small group discussion and mural creation) to explore, debate, laugh about and work through complex community problems. The participation and contribution by participants confirmed the power and creative potential of participatory research. Some of the comments on the final evaluation were:

- Informative, interesting, an incredible learning experience;
- I learned things that I'm anxious to utilize;
- I would like to continue to participate in the educational process of not only this community but myself as well; and
- It was a good interchange of ideas, but I'm not sure of the outcomes.

The last comment is reflective of the feelings of many adults. Most adults, primarily due to lives full of commitments but also to a lack of alternatives, are accustomed to short-term, goal-oriented learning activities. Although they want to be involved, they are often unclear and even sceptical about engaging in long-term learning activities. It is one of the biggest challenges of working in communities with adults.

A final aspect of the project is to use the local media and presentations at local schools and organizations to interest more and more people in the project. To date, two articles have been carried in local newspapers and presentations have been made to such groups as: First Nations Technical Institute, Mohawks of the Bay of Quinte, Environmental Studies programme at Loyalist College, Local Training Adjustment Board, Catholic Teachers' Union, and Community Development Council. Information is also being shared regionally and globally through the Learning for

Environmental Action Programme (LEAP), a Toronto-based international non-governmental organization with members in over 109 countries.

Conclusion

Given that socio-environmental problems are increasing, that neither scientists nor technology can solve these problems, that cultural identity is being eroded, that crime and violence are escalating, and that both the federal and provincial governments have abdicated much of their social responsibility, a number of people in Quinte have engaged in a journey. A long-term process in which they will need to learn to think, act and work creatively and collectively together if they are to have a healthier and more sustainable place in which to live and work. For "a journey is not a round tour; it does not return home, and it does not even necessarily end" (Kaptchuk 1983, p. 164). There will be a number of successes, but there are also a number of challenges and the major one is to get local politicians and the business sector to invest more money/resources/time in this project.

Through study circles, workshops, surveys and interviews the project will combine local generated environmental research findings with job needs through a process of community revitalization. Building public awareness and support by including people from all sectors of society into the educational process is essential before any significant change is possible. Sharing information regarding *Growing Jobs for Living* beyond the community has not only confirmed the potential and validity of the project, but has generated considerable interest in future outcomes.

The study circles have proven to be an excellent space to network and exchange information and ideas. The participatory research workshop has provided a training opportunity and stimulated a variety of progressive ideas and suggestions for green jobs and potential resources. The survey has provided useful information on the variety of initiatives that have provided people with hope and energy. The main reason that education and participatory research are critical tools for change is because at the heart of life is every person's longing for connection, meaning, mystery, knowledge, and delight.

References

Clover, Darlene, Shirly Follen and Budd Hall (1998). *Learning our way out:environmental adult and popular education.*

Daly, Herman E. and John Cobb (1989). *For the common good.* Beacon Press: Boston.

Dobson, Ross (1993). *Bringing the economy home from the market.* Black Rose Books: Montreal.

Eichler, Margrit, *Considering Sustainability from a Canadian Sociological Feminist Perspective*, paper prepared for the UNESCO MOST project on Sustainable Development as a concept for the Social Sciences, Institut fuer sozial-oekologische Forschung, Frankfurt, Germany, November 1996.

Fien, John (ed.) (1993). *Environmental education: a pathway to sustainability.* Deakin University Press: Geelong, Victoria.

Hall, Budd (1981). "Participatory research, popular knowledge and power: A personal reflection" in *Convergence* 14(3):6-17.

Hall, Budd and Edmund Sullivan (1994). "Transformative Learning: Contexts and Practices" in *Awakening Sleepy Knowledge.* Transformative Learning Centre, OISE: Toronto.

Harris, Elayne (1992). *Dreaming Reality: Small Media in Community Development as Critical Educational Practices*. Unpublished doctoral thesis, University of Toronto, Toronto.

Hart, Mechthild U. (1992). *Working and educating for life: feminist and international perspectives on adult education*. Routledge: London.

Hicks, David and Cathie Holden (1995). "Exploring the Future: A Missing Dimension in Environmental Education" in *Environmental Education Research*, 1(2):185-193.

Kaptchuk, Ted (1983). *The web that has no weaver*. Congdon & Weed: New York.

Lipschutz, Ronnie D. (1996). *Global Civil Society and Global Environmental Governance*. State University of New York Press: Albany, New York.

Maguire, Patricia (1987). *Doing Participatory Research: A Feminist Approach*. The Center for International Education, School of Education, University of Massachusetts: Amherst, MA.

Nozick, Marcia (1992). *No Place Like Home: Building Sustainable Communities*. Canadian Council on Social Development: Ottawa.

Orr, David (1992). *Ecological Literacy: Education and the Transition to a Postmodern World*. State University of New York Press: Albany, New York.

Profeit-LeBlanc, Louise (1995). "Transferring Wisdom through Storytelling" in R. Jickling (ed.) *A Colloquium on Environment, Ethics and Education*. Whitehorse: Yukon.

Rich, Adrienne (1993). "Notes Towards a Politics of Location" in Greta Gaard (ed.) *EcoFeminism: Women, Animals, Nature*. Temple University Press: Philadelphia.

Roberts, Wayne and Susan Brandum (1995). *Get a Life!* Get a Life Publishing House: Toronto.

Rowe, Stan (1990). *Home Place*. New West Publishers Ltd: Edmonton.

Russell, Constance L., "Approaches to Environmental Education, Towards a Transformative Perspective" in *Holistic Education Review*, 10(1), March 1997:34-38.

Slocombe, D. S. (1993). "Getting to the Heart of Sustainable Development: A Further Appraisal" in *Canadian Journal of Environmental Education*, 1:7-34.

Tilbury, D. (1994). "The International Development of Environmental Education" in *Environmental Education and Information*, 13(1):1-20.

Tilbury, D. (1995). "Environmental Education for Sustainability: Defining the New Focus of Environmental Education in the 1990s" in *Environmental Education Research*, 1(2):195-212.

United Nations, *Agenda 21*, UNCED, Rio de Janeiro, Brazil, June 1992.

Welton, Michael (1986). V*ivisecting the nightingale:reflections on adult education as an object of study*. OISE Press: Toronto.

Welton, Michael (1987). *Knowledge for the people*. OISE Press: Toronto.

World Commission on Environment and Development (1987). *Our common future*. Oxford University Press: Oxford.

Conclusion

Chapter 18

Conclusion

Education and sustainable development: perspectives and possibilities

Robert B. Stevenson

The previous chapters have presented stories from educators describing their educational efforts to address the challenges of building sustainable communities and societies. The authors have told their stories of their experiences in carrying out this educational work. Historically, story telling has been a means of passing on the accumulated knowledge and traditions of a culture. Story telling, however, also can serve as a form of narrative inquiry for both authors and readers. By reflecting on and learning from their experiences in writing these stories, the authors have constructed new understandings and knowledge of their educational practice. At the same time, in narrating their stories – including their trials and tribulations, their successes and failures – they have provided a source of ideas and insights that offer opportunities for readers to reflect on their own educational situations and activities. Readers who are able to make connections to their own setting can deliberate on and construct new understandings about their own educational endeavours in stimulating children and adults to think about and take actions toward creating more sustainable forms of living.

This kind of knowledge and process of knowledge generation can be contrasted with the forms of knowledge and knowledge production that dominate Western educational systems. Since the period of the Enlightenment and the advent of modernity and scientific thought, knowledge has been viewed as something to be discovered, categorized and distributed. The industrial and scientific revolution and the emergence of the scientific method resulted in a worldview that attained – and retains to this day – a hegemonic status in Western society. This dominant worldview casts the discovery of truth as demanding a detached posture of objectively observing the external natural and material environment, commodifies knowledge and culture, delineates education and schooling as serving primarily an economic function, and assumes human control over nature and elite groups having power and control over other people. The contributors to this book have portrayed a very different worldview, one that emphasizes: the integration of different knowledge systems (indigenous and modern, local and global, cross-disciplinary); education and schooling that serves cultural, civic and liberating, as well as economic, purposes; human connectedness with nature and with each other; and distributed power through participatory democracy.

Stories and worldviews embody the assumptions we make about our societies and ourselves, about our public and private interests. They reveal not only how we experience and understand the world, but how we view the human condition and our relationships to each other and to nature, as well as what we see as progress or development. In other words, these stories and their accompanying worldviews can serve both as mirrors that reflexively can tell us much about our own values, priorities and commitments in relation to education and the environment, and as windows on the educational possibilities for helping people develop the capacity to build a better and more equitable quality of life for everyone.

Education and sustainable development as public interests

Historically, formal education has been viewed as an institutional response to a common social need and the manifestation of a shared public interest (Connell 1996). That interest is the cultivation and perpetuation of a civil society. Of course, the question of what constitutes a civil society is widely contested. Irrespective of how it is defined, however, schools serve the public purpose of educating students for the responsibilities of citizenship by preparing them to understand the need for and the working of a civil society (Sizer 1997) and by developing their literacy, without which people cannot fulfil their civic duties. Although this education also serves the individual's interests, societies have a collective interest in the young learning these responsibilities well as the survival of cultural and civic traditions, including democracy, is dependent on such learning. In other words, this civic function is not the only function that schools perform but it is central to the institution of mass schooling in all societies.

In democratic societies, the ideal of education is viewed as not only liberating (in developing individual potential) but essential for liberty (Schlecty 1990). There are dual assumptions underlying this view, however, that must be questioned. The first assumption is that schooling offers all individuals equal educational opportunity and only the ability and effort of the individual determines his or her liberation. The second is that society has attained its democratic potential and the role of education is simply to develop the skills and inculcate the values to maintain existing social arrangements and structures. These assumptions were widely questioned in the 1960s and 70s when the inequalities and social ills created by urban factories led so-called progressives in Europe, North America and Australia to argue for another, very different purpose of schools – of transforming the existing social order, essentially to a more equal, humanistic and democratic society. Schools, as well as other social institutions, in this view, are not seen as reflecting democratic ideals but instead as contributing to the maintenance of social and economic inequalities. A goal of education, it is argued, should be to critique dominant cultural patterns and identify alternatives that provide greater social justice and enhance the human potential of the disadvantaged. This function, while a marked contrast to the cultivation and perpetuation of existing cultural and civic norms, also represents a view of education as serving the common good or the public interest of all citizens.

The call for a sustainable development agenda reflects the identification of a similar common need, in this case for the conservation or sustainable utilization of natural resources. Around the beginning of the last century, the conservation movement in Europe and North America highlighted the importance of natural resources to their societies and introduced a public concern for preserving, first, single species and later, areas of natural significance through sound management. That concern has been extended both in scope and reach so that it is now widely recognized that our global society has a collective or shared interest in the preservation of complex ecosystems and genetic diversity for the present and future inhabitants of planet earth. Fien and Tilbury (Chapter 1) describe how the World Conservation Strategy, in first giving currency to the term "sustainable development", drew attention to "the dilemmas facing rural people in developing countries who are sometimes compelled to over-utilize natural resources in order to free themselves from starvation and poverty" and how, at the Earth Summit, the Third World or the South pointed to the undermining of global sustainability "by the mass consumption lifestyles of many people in the North". Both these situations, and the relationship between them, are illustrated in Chapter 3 where Passingham describes how the over-exploitation of the coconut crab and sea-cucumbers to satisfy the restaurants serving the tourists

visiting Vanuatu in the South Pacific threatens the future life of coral reefs and the livelihood of the local people who depend on gathering food from the reef. Further examples of the direct relationship between economic survival and ecologically sustainable management of natural resources can be found in Uttarakhand in India (Chapter 7) where the emergence of a market economy and a centralized system of forest management fragmented families and undermined sustainable community development, and in Annapurna in Nepal (Chapter 6) where initial efforts at tourist management and resource conservation negatively affected the livelihood of local communities. These realizations, Fien and Tilbury explain, linked poverty, development and environment and led to a call for "a new world ethic of sustainability" with two key sets of principles – a responsibility to care for nature and a responsibility to care for each other. The role of education in addressing this global public interest emerges from the recognition that a sustainable society, no matter how defined, can only be shaped by the beliefs and actions of its citizens.

Educational reform and economic development as private interests

The original purpose of public formal education in Western civilizations in the pre-industrial era was confined to the development of the basic skills of literacy and numeracy and the transmission of a common culture among the masses. The advent of industrialized society added a credentialing and sorting function in which schools were expected to help select those youngsters with the ability to meet the needs of industry for skilled workers. This introduced an economic, as well as a cultural and civic, purpose of schooling (Schlechty 1990) that served private as well as public interests.

The post-industrial era has witnessed government policies throughout the industrialized world that have further emphasized the economic ends of education, virtually to the exclusion of other purposes. For example, in the United States, an influential report commissioned by the Reagan administration, A Nation at Risk (1983), invoked images of global economic warfare in admonishing American schools for failing to provide a highly trained workforce to compete in the emerging world economy and to provide students with the high level of academic skills needed to obtain good jobs and promote the country's economic growth and well-being. The relationship between the nation's economy and the purposes of schooling was made clear:

> knowledge, learning, information, and skilled intelligence are the new raw materials of international commerce and are today spreading throughout the world as vigorously as miracle drugs, synthetic fertilizers, and blue jeans earlier... Learning is the indispensable investment required for success in the "information age" we are now entering.
> (National Commission for Excellence in Education, 1983, p. 7)

This agenda, which has been aggressively pursued by governments from both major political parties during the last two decades, emphasized that the ability of the United States to regain its economic superiority in a global economy was dependent on a more direct link between a reformed educational system, highlighted by increased academic standards, and a productive workforce. Nearly 20 years later, the recently released final report of the National Commission on Mathematics and Science Teaching for the 21st Century, chaired by Senator John Glenn, advocated a similar but even more narrow focus for educational institutions, arguing that the

future wellbeing of the United States and its people depends not just on how well its children are educated generally, but on how well they are educated in mathematics and science specifically. From mathematics and the sciences, the Commission argued, will come the products, services, standard of living, and economic and military security that will sustain the country at home and around the world – reflecting the worldview that all problems are amenable to technical solutions and that one country must maintain an economic and military superiority over other countries.

This reform rhetoric, in appealing to national interests, may at first suggest another view of education as essentially serving a broad public interest. However, an examination of the underlying assumptions and the means of implementing this agenda reveals a different orientation. Although arguing that "a high level of shared education is essential to a free, democratic society and to the fostering of a common culture" (p. 7), the proponents of this view are concerned that perceived educational failures threaten a core part of American culture, namely the opportunity "to raise one's state in life and shape one's own future" (p. 15). Education is viewed as offering the promise

> that all children by virtue of their own efforts, competently guided, can hope to attain the mature and informed judgment needed to secure gainful employment and to manage their own lives, thereby serving not only their own interests but also the progress of society itself.
> (National Commission for Excellence in Education, p. 8)

Thus, the central purpose of education is viewed as enabling individuals to pursue their own economic self-interests which it is assumed in turn will produce the most economically productive society. In other words, the primary function is one of advancing private interests, although the argument is framed in terms of reinforcing a common cultural value, a commitment to enhancing individual success or achievement – defined essentially in economic terms. This view of education as a private good also is evident in the recent restructuring and refinancing of post-secondary education where individual "consumers" are required to pay a much greater proportion of educational costs and educational institutions are expected to compete with each other in the marketplace.

The current approach to educational reform in much of the Western world focuses on upgrading students' cognitive skills by narrowing and intensifying the school curriculum (e.g., teaching more science and math, eliminating "soft" electives, establishing core curriculum, raising academic standards), introducing standardized testing, instituting tougher discipline policies, lengthening the time students spend in school, and creating a free market system that emphasizes competition among schools. These initiatives are advocated for their academic payoffs for students, rather than the economic motives that underlie them, but the result is that the educational enterprise is redefined "as largely a pre-occupational training centre whose functions is to produce the kind of applied skills immediately needed by the emerging model of world capitalism" (Shea 1989, p. 30). They also represent a means of selecting and allocating to the labour force those students with the cognitive skills for meeting the needs of the high technology industries, and leaving those unable to demonstrate advanced educational achievement, as defined by their acquisition of high status (particularly scientific and technological) knowledge, a destiny in dead-end, low paying jobs, mainly in the service sector.

This educational reform agenda is not confined to the United States, but has become widespread throughout the G7 or industrialized countries. In fact, the history of

formal schooling and educational reform in Western society is characterized by an increasing emphasis on the economic purposes or role of schools within an increasingly dominant economic view of the world.

Globalization, markets and social and environmental injustices

Globalization, or more specifically global economics, which represents not a de-industrialization, but a global re-organization of industry, finance and trade (Connell 1996), has significantly contributed to the hegemony of a capitalist economic development model. The OECD countries have been transferring labour-intensive, low-skilled industries – and their associated environmental problems – to developing countries with low wages and few environmental regulations, while they maintain control of the new information technologies and the multinational world economy. Future progress is claimed by governments and the media to be dependent on more investment in and better use of high technology, an integrated and free market world economy, and the education of a more skilled and productive workforce; a strategy which has "produced short-term profits, but at the expense of pollution, hazardous wastes, dangerous workplaces and human exploitation" (Shea 1989, p. 27). At the same time, in order to compete in a global economy, these countries have pursued a free market ideology of moving from a welfare to a competitive state. Across most of the advanced capitalist world there has been an historic shift from the state to the market as the major social decision-maker through governments downsizing the state apparatus, privatizing public functions, deregulating controls, and promoting a corporate management culture (Connell 1996).

The questions that have been left out of the rhetoric associated with this shift to a global market economy are: Whose interests does this particular economic development agenda serve? Who benefits and who does not? The impact of these economic and educational policies on the working class poor in the OECD countries and on Third World minority populations are repressive and signs are already evident that they are exacerbating existing inequalities and injustices. Social reforms conducted under this economic worldview have intensified the effects of colonial relations of economic and political domination through the Third World's debt to the rich nations and the World Bank's imposition of economic growth and debt reduction policies as the solution to the problem of poverty in the poor nations. It was 30 years ago that Lappe (1971, p. 16) argued that the world could not sustain an agricultural system that is "geared to the production of steaks for profit rather than of cheap food for us all". Yet today we are even further removed from such a change as agricultural lands and workers are being displaced in many developing countries by factories and sweatshops producing non-essential luxury items for export to the wealthy classes in the rich nations.

An alternative perspective on education and development

Not only must the dominant global economic model be questioned on the basis of exacerbating inequalities and social and environmental problems, but any economic model for education must be viewed as limited, "simply because it fails to embrace the whole of what it means to be human" (Goodlad 1997, p. 11). Preparation for life must involve more than preparation for work given that one's quality of life involves more than economic factors. Education must help people to think critically, to

develop a sense of personal identity (of becoming someone), to learn to live together and to care for one another. Schools traditionally have focused on a narrow range of human endeavours (e.g., cognitive mastery in the conceptual-verbal-quantitative terms associated with scientific rationality), but that range has become even narrower in recent decades as instrumental purposes of education have been stressed. The purpose of schooling must go beyond not only vocational education, but also liberal education. To base the school curriculum on the traditional disciplines of knowledge alone, "is quite simply to teach our young about life; to turn out observers *of* it, not participants *in* it" (Martin 1997, p. 22). We need more than spectators, we need people who can act upon the world, who can integrate thought and action.

If education is to play a significant role in "motivating and empowering people to participate in local changes towards more sustainable lifestyles and living conditions" (Fien & Tilbury, Chapter 1), then we need to combat the power of private interests and reorient the focus back to the public rather than private good in both education and development. That means a public good that is not defined in narrow national and economic interests, but one that emphasizes the quality of life of all citizens and inhabitants of the planet. In other words, education must project a larger point of view of a world of nations and of planet Earth.

In contrasting interpretations of sustainability that prioritize sustainable economic growth with those that emphasize sustainable human development, Fien and Tilbury (Chapter 1) argue that the latter "focuses upon issues of social equity and ecological limits, and thereby, questions worldviews and development models that are predicated on assumptions of unlimited economic growth". The challenge is to find a more equitable, just, economically and environmentally sustainable worldview. This task demands changes in the ways of thinking, working and living that currently dominate most Western societies, particularly as they relate to the global economy and the relationships with Third World nations (Shea 1989).

Although, as Fien and Tilbury point out, sustainable development is still an "evolving concept", a framework of sustainable development requires educators who have a vision "in which social development, ecological well-being, and economic prosperity" are addressed, and which is "founded on an ethic in which the common good or social justice underpins a respect for all learners" (Vargas 1998). Of course, as Jickling (Chapter 14) illustrates in his case study of different groups' views of wolves, the task of establishing the common good can be fraught with value conflicts, such as between intrinsic and instrumental values of wildlife. Jickling also cautions that the language of sustainability may conceal such important conflicts or contradictions in perspectives (resulting, for example, from different cultural identities) if it narrows the debate about ways of thinking about the environment to technical questions of what constitutes a sustainable ecosystem.

Helping youth and adults identify the values and cultural assumptions underlying different perspectives is particularly important in challenging the dominant technological worldview and in developing an environmental ethic and social consciousness. For example, Fuhke (Chapter 5) incisively portrays the "gradual shift" that has taken place in Indonesia from a traditional belief in the importance of people being in harmony with nature (because the natural elements were seen as imbued with spiritual values), to a modernist viewpoint that humans should have dominance over nature and exploit natural resources. The author describes how urbanization has led to an estrangement from the natural environment and an attitude that nature needs "no extra care or attention ... except to cut it back", while

images of economic prosperity and material consumption have created new priorities and devalued and undermined the conservation of natural resources. Such stories emphasize the need to consider "the cultural context without simply accepting values and practices because they are traditional" (Passingham, Chapter 3).

Educational approaches and possibilities

The stories told in the 15 case studies in this book suggest a number of important features of educational programmes and activities that reflect the alternative perspective on education and development and respond to the global challenge of developing sustainable ways of living. They reveal a focus on developing environmental thoughtfulness, a commitment to the ethic of human interdependence with nature and each other, and a sense of collective responsibility for community development. While the storytellers indicate that a global perspective is critical, they recognize that learning and action must be taken at the local level and emphasize the need for authentic participation in the study of local issues. They describe approaches that attempt to address the social, economic and environmental dimensions of development and "the complex interactions of socio-economic, cultural and political factors" (Galang, Chapter 4) by critically inquiring into local issues and integrating modern and indigenous ways of knowing, local and global perspectives, the authentic participation of all stakeholders, and the work of all education sectors (formal, non-formal, informal).

A common problem in school curriculum, especially in centrally issued documents, related to environmental education is a tendency to focus on abstract knowledge of general global environmental problems (such as pollution and the extinction of wildlife). The result is that many teachers include such broad environmental topics or problems by covering discrete elements of knowledge about these topics without connecting them to local situations and the lived experiences of students and glossing over the complexities, nuances and controversial aspects as they are played out in local contexts (Stevenson 1997). In contrast, Jickling (Chapter 14) embraces the complexities and different perspectives on a local issue, wolf management, to help his students explore the importance of values in addressing and resolving environmental issues. Hopkins and McKeown (Chapter 2) emphasize that the curriculum also cannot include all sustainability issues, and advocate the selection of a few locally relevant issues. Pande (Chapter 7) offers one such possibility in describing a school programme in India that reorients the curriculum to focus on studying the local village as an ecosystem, connecting the concept of sustainability to the carrying capacity of this ecosystem and empowering "young people to work for a sustainable future for themselves, their families and their communities" (Fien). An important component of the exploration of a local environmental issue should be "an attempt to balance scientific and indigenous outlooks on the environment" which also enable students, such as those attending the Rifa Conservation Camp in Zimbabwe, to become acquainted with their ancestors' views of nature. (Stiles, Chapter 12)

At the university level, Kohrn and his colleagues (Chapter 16) detail a programme in which students conduct energy and waste management audits of local public buildings, providing not only a practical learning vehicle for students but a valuable community service. The lessons students learn from participation in environmental audits are strengthened, however, when the university subjects itself to an audit and supports both educational and management actions to address concerns revealed by

the audit and to promote more environmentally oriented curriculum and more sustainable forms of campus management (Calvo et al, Chapter 9).

If these kind of local school initiatives are to become commonplace and to be sustained, then systemic policies are needed to provide teacher support, especially when teachers are working in difficult circumstances. Csobod's story (Chapter 10) of a systemic reform effort in Hungary to incorporate education for sustainability in a national curriculum, in an Eastern European context undergoing major political transformation, is an example of promoting a curriculum and pedagogical vision but allowing teachers the autonomy to determine a significant proportion of the curriculum content and encouraging and supporting them "to develop democratic approaches to teaching by fostering participatory, problem-solving, community-oriented, cross-curricular learning". This story reminds us of the dangers of centralized or top-down policies that attempt to mandate or control change rather than promote democratic and authentic participation of teachers in order to develop their ownership of and a commitment to educational initiatives. Other approaches to teacher development and support can be found in two intriguing stories from Southern Africa (Chapters 11 & 13). Taylor and Van Rensburg describe the Share-Net approach of "a network of collaborating resource developers and users", in contrast to the traditional centre-to-periphery RD&D (research, develop and disseminate) approach to teacher and curriculum materials development. This network has produced field guides, practical environmental action and technical information pamphlets, booklets on environmental issues, and water quality testing kits using a combination of experts and collaborative teacher groups, but without shirking from "the contentious nature of much scientific information" or treating knowledge as given.

> Thus the resources produced through Share-Net are seen as tools to support encounters (with environment and environmental issues, for example the field guides to support field work or the water kits to assess water quality), dialogue (to discuss what is being learned, for example, the Issues for Debate section in Enviro-Facts) and reflection (a critical review of learning, stimulated, for example, by the ACTION acronym which encourages the development of catchment conservation plans).
>
> (Chapter 11)

The authors emphasize that this kind of network works best when allowed to evolve organically around tangible endeavours such as the development of resource materials. However, engaging teachers, especially those, "unfamiliar with developing contextually relevant and appropriate curriculum", in collaborative resource and curriculum development can be a "daunting" and time consuming task (Schreuder et al, Chapter 13). Nevertheless, the processes of active exploration, constructive dialogue and debate, and critical reflection in relation to specific environmental issues provide a substantive and meaningful form of professional development that is difficult to match through any other approaches.

Agenda 21 (see Chapter 2) identified the need for a broader participatory approach which considers local needs and values. Many of the case studies highlight strategies for enabling such participation, both in terms of the students or learners and the range of people engaged in educational work, either with schools or community groups. For example, in Wales (Chapter 8) future participation in environmental decision-making is promoted by non-formal educators in the form of National Park rangers using a participatory educational strategy, an environmental forum in which students are actively involved in decision-making about an actual development situation in their community or park. The authors cite Hart's (1993)

argument that "[o]nly through direct participation can children develop a genuine appreciation of democracy and a sense of their own competence and responsibility to participate". This argument could be extended to adults and approaches to informal or community education. A unique approach is taken in Vanuatu (Passingham, Chapter 3) where community theatre – using song, dance and humour (which require little in the way of equipment) – draws on the tradition of story telling to enable the exploration of environmental issues through audience participation. This theatre group is able to reach out to audiences that are not served by any traditional educational services. In the Philippines (Chapter 4), teachers at Miriam College are engaged in educating parents and in other community outreach through their own NGOs and offer workshops organized around an identified set of key environmental principles and concepts, using a diverse range of teaching strategies.

One sector of the community that is often neglected, especially in many developing countries, is women, despite their important role as "primary managers of natural resources" in such countries as Nepal and India (Chapters 6 & 7). This role, as well as their common role as gatekeepers of cultural values and social justice, suggests that women are a critical target group for community environmental education (Clover, Chapter 17). Community or adult education, however, must go "beyond the simple notion of public awareness into a realm of active, critical and creative engagement" (Clover, Chapter 17). Such engagement is illustrated by Gurung (Chapter 6) who describes the role that informal education can play and reinforces the importance of creating local ownership in the context of building the capacity of local communities to manage their own natural resources in a sustainable manner. As Clover argues, in the Growing Jobs for Living project, "sustainability will only be achieved through communities attaining control over their resources, consumption, production and knowledge base" such that "all members of the community [have] the power and means to better manage their own affairs" (Chapter 17). In large industrialized cities such as Toronto, this means educating people about the possibilities of alternative "green" jobs and goods and services that they can "work creatively and collectively" to create.

Finally the benefits of coordinating and integrating the formal, non-formal and informal education sectors are evident in El Salvador (Chapter 15) which provides a comprehensive case of an impressive national effort that uses school and popular media approaches and encourages the examination of various environmental issues through a variety of participatory strategies. GreenCOM staff in El Salvador recognized the importance of addressing initial teacher preparation, in-service teacher education and curriculum reform if environmental themes and concepts are to be integrated within formal education, and the need to invest in the professional development of staff and specialists involved in non-formal "programmes and exhibits at zoos, museums, nature centres, and parks; workforce training and education, civic and religious programmes; extension activities; programmes with civic leaders, decision-makers, and elected officials; and work with NGOs". They also astutely recognized that public awareness and understanding is dependent to a large extent on educating journalists who report on environmental issues. Providing the media with appropriate information was supported by establishing incentives for good environmental reporting through the creation of national environmental journalism awards. The periodic newspaper supplements that were produced by journalists were of such quality that they then could be used by teachers, as well as by parents, thereby creating a "successful example of synergy between mass communication and formal education". A synergy across educational sectors is particularly important given the need to share with other educational agents "the

educational work that presently is culturally assigned to the school"
(Martin 1997, p. 25).

These stories are mere snapshots of some of the innovative approaches to education and sustainable development that are taking place around the world. The editors of this volume hope that they inspire readers to respond to the global challenge in their own local settings and create their own educational journey to help the children and adults in their community to build more sustainable ways of thinking, acting and living. After all, there are many more stories of educational endeavours with such aims that are yet to be told or yet to be written.

References

Connell, R. (1996). "Education in a fractured world". Inaugural lecture, Sydney University.

Goodlad, J. (1997). *In praise of education*. Teachers College Press: New York.

Lappe, F. (1971). *Diet for a small planet*. Ballantine Books: New York.

National Commission for Excellence in Education (1983). *A Nation at Risk*. Washington, DC.

National Commission on Mathematics and Science Teaching for the 21st Century (2000). *Before it's too late*. A Report to the Nation. Washington, DC.

Schlecty, P. (1990). *Schools for the 21st century: Leadership imperatives for educational reform*. Jossey-Bass: San Francisco.

Shea, C. (1989). "Pentagon vs. multinational capitalism: the political economy of the 1980s school reform movement" in C. Shea, E. Kahane & P. Sola (eds.), *The new servants of power: A critique of the 1980s school reform movement*. Praeger: New York.

Sizer, T. (1997). "The meanings of 'public education'.", in J. Goodlad & T. McMannon (eds.), *The public purpose of education and schooling*. Jossey-Bass: San Francisco.

Stevenson, R. B. (1997). "Developing habits of environmental thoughtfulness through the in-depth study of select environmental issues" in *Canadian Journal of Environmental Education*, 2:183-201.

Vargas, (1998). "Sustainable development education: Precluding cultural collision". Paper presented at the Comparative and International Education Society Conference, Buffalo, New York.

Biographical summaries

Julie Barrett O'Neill is an Urban & Regional Planner with Peter J. Smith & Company, Inc., a Buffalo-based urban planning firm. After graduating from University at Buffalo, the State University of New York in 1995 with an Environmental Studies degree, Julie went on to obtain a joint Masters of Science in the Urban Planning and Law degree programme from the University of Iowa. She recently passed the New York State Bar Examination and is currently applying for admission to the New York State Bar.

Javier Benayas del Alamo is Senior Lecturer in ecology in the Faculty of Science at the Autonomous University of Madrid, Spain where he leads the Ecocampus Department. He teaches environmental education and interpretation within the environmental sciences curriculum. He is also the coordinator of the environmental management programmes at the University. His main line of research focuses on the definition of quality indicators for environmental education and interpretation programmes and the preparation of a model for sustainable management in university campuses. One of his most recent books, *Viviendo El Paisaje* (Living the landscape), has been awarded a prize by the Spanish Ministry of Education.

David Brinn has worked for the Brecon Beacons National Park since 1983. He was appointed to his present post of Education Officer in 1992. Having recently completed his MSc at the International Centre for Protected Landscapes, Aberystwyth, David is currently researching methods to assist with the evaluation of educational programmes in the UK's National Parks.

Susana Calvo Roy has a degree in Political Sciences and Sociology. She works for the Ministry of the Environment, Spain, where she is a member of the Technical Office of the Secretary General for the Environment, which includes the Environmental Education unit. She is the coordinator of the Spanish Strategy for Environmental Education and Deputy Chair of the IUCN Commission on Education and Communication.

Darlene E. Clover is Assistant Professor, Department of Educational Psychology and Leadership Studies, University of Victoria, British Colombia. She previously worked at the Ontario Institute for Studies in Education at the University of Toronto where she conducted research in the areas of feminist environmental action, social movement learning, non-formal learning in the labour movement, and environmental adult education. She has taught and facilitated workshops in environmental adult education around the world and co-organized the four-day International Journey for Environmental Education at the 1992 United Nations Conference on Environment and Development in Rio de Janiero.

Eva Csobold is Head of the Department of Open Learning of the Coordination Office for Higher Education in the Professors House in Budapest, in Hungary. She is a member of the IUCN European Committee on the Environmental Education and Communication and the Secretary of the Hungarian National Environmental Education Committee. She has worked on MSc courses in environmental and development education in Hungarian, UK and Danish Universities. Her main research areas are the development of action competence through education and successful methodologies in education for sustainability. She is a reporter and editor of *Greenwaves*, an environmental protection and nature conservation programme of Hungarian Television.

Carole Douglis is the Communications and Marketing Officer for the African Wildlife Foundation, based in Nairobi Kenya. AWF is working to help people manage wildlife sustainably and profitably. Her editing skills were used on this chapter while she served as the GreenCOM Resource Centre Director in Washington DC.

John Fien is Director of the Griffith University EcoCentre in Brisbane, Australia. He was the Co-Director of the UNESCO Asia-Pacific regional project on *Learning for a Sustainable Environment: Innovations in Teacher Education* and the designer of the UNESCO multimedia professional development programme, *Teaching and Learning for a Sustainable Future*. He has published widely in the fields of environment, development and geography education, including *Education for the Environment: Critical Curriculum Theory in Environmental Education* and *Teaching for a Sustainable World*.

Ulli Fuhrke is currently the head of Pusat Pendidikan Lingkungan Hidup, in Indonesia. At university he read social anthropology, economy and architecture and worked in urban planning in Berlin for some years. He studied environmental science in the Faculty of Architecture at Petra University, Surabaya, Java and has lectured on environmental education at Berlin's Technical University. Between 1987 and 1992 he established and managed the Environmental Education Centre in Seloliman, East Java, Indonesia. As the founder-member of the firm ACT (Appropriate Communication and Development) he has held many consultancy jobs in ecological planning, environmental education and communication, architectural landscape (permaculture) and town-planning projects.

Angelina Galang is a professor at Miriam College where she has been teaching for over 30 years. She has held various administrative posts from Academic to College Dean to Vice-president of Academic Affairs. Concurrent with these positions, she headed the Environmental Planning Department at the undergraduate level for a decade and the graduate Environmental Studies programme since 1993. She conceptualized Miriam-PEACE and led it in a volunteer capacity until 1998 when she was officially appointed Executive Director of the Environmental Education Centre which houses Miriam-PEACE. Active in the NGO scene, she was at one time Vice-president of Haribon, a leading Philippine NGO and is President of the Environmental Network of the Philippines.

Joseph Gardella, Jnr. is presently Professor of Chemistry and Associate Dean for External Affairs for the College of Arts and Sciences at the University at Buffalo, State University of New York. Dr. Gardella's background is in analytical chemistry. He served as Chair of the UB Environmental Task Force for four years, when programmes such as the UB Audit were extended into the community, and worked on the development of relationships between government and the university as a key part of the ETF work. In Buffalo, Joe also collaborates with Bruce Kohrn on community-based environmental chemical analysis programmes as a public service learning programme.

Hum Bahadur Gurung has been associated with the Annapurna Conservation Area Project (ACAP) of the King Mahendra Trust for Nature Conservation, Nepal since 1986 as Conservation Officer, Officer-in-Charge, Conservation Education and Extension Officer. He now works for the United Nations Development Programme as Programme Manager of the Sustainable Community Development Programme, known as *Nepal Capacity 21*. His research interests include participatory action research and community-based approaches for environmental education, sustainable development and ecotourism management in protected areas.

José Gutiérrez Pérez is Senior Lecturer in educational research methods in the Faculty of Education at the University of Granada, Spain where he teaches programme evaluation and research methodologies in environmental education. His research focuses upon the evaluation of environmental education centres and the assessment of their educational programmes. He played a key role in the development of the National Strategy for Environmental Education, Spain. He has published a number of books and is a member of several editorial boards for international environmental education journals.

Chuck Hopkins is senior advisor to UNESCO Transdisciplinary Project, *Educating for a Sustainable Future*. He is currently serving as the UNESCO Chair of an international project focusing on reorienting teacher education to address the concepts of sustainable development. He is also advisor to the Deans of the Faculties of Education and Environmental Studies at York University, Canada. In addition, he is Executive Director of the John Dearness Environmental Society, a Canadian environmental NGO, and is Chair of the Education for Sustainable Development Working Group of the UNESCO – Canada Man and the Biosphere Committee (MAB). He has also been Superintendent of Curriculum with the Toronto Board of Education and was the Chair of the World Congress for Education and Communication on Environment and Development (ECO-ED). He was a member of the Canadian team that helped prepare the *Tbilisi Declaration* and was also one of the drafters of Chapter 36 of *Agenda 21: Education, Public Awareness and Training*.

Jose Ignacio Mata, a native of Spain, was the Resident Advisor in El Salvador and architect of the Environmental Education Project. He was employed for five years by GreenCOM/El Salvador to coordinate this USAID-funded project. He is currently working the same magic with another GreenCOM project in Panama.

Eureta Janse van Rensburg was a senior lecturer appointed to the Murray & Roberts Chair of Environmental Education based at Rhodes University at the time of writing. Her research interests include new research methodologies in environmental education. She teaches post-graduate and non-graduate environmental education courses. She was president of the Environmental Education Association of Southern Africa and is the editor of its journal, *The Southern African Journal of Environmental Education*.

Bob Jickling teaches environmental philosophy and environmental education at Yukon College in northern Canada. He has been active in the field of environmental education for many years. A long-time steering committee member of EECOM, the Canadian Network for Environmental Education and Communication, Bob is also the founding editor of the *Canadian Journal of Environmental Education*. His research interests include relationships between environmental philosophy, education, and teaching. A long-time Yukon resident, much of his passion is derived from travel through this magnificent northern landscape by foot, ski, and canoe.

Bruce Kohrn is an adjunct lecturer in Environmental Studies at the University at Buffalo, State University of New York and has taught the Environmental Audit course since its inception. He has worked in the environmental sciences since 1981, and is founder and President of SBK Environmental Research, Inc., an independent environmental consulting firm based in Buffalo specializing in community-based research. He conducts collaborative and participatory research projects involving scientists and the non-technical public, and has also been involved in the development of environmental education materials for secondary school students

and undergraduates. He also provides sustainability training workshops for businesses, students and community groups.

Lesley Le Grange teaches biology education, environmental education and research methodology in the Faculty of Education, University of Stellenbosch. His current research interests include curriculum development, teacher professional development and how post-modern science can enhance thinking and practice in science education, environmental education and educational research.

Martha C. Monroe is an Assistant Professor and Extension Specialist at the School of Forest Resources and Conservation at the University of Florida where she works on environmental education and communication projects. From 1996-97 she worked with GreenCOM as the Resource Centre Director, helping to share their successes with others in the field of environmental education and communication.

Rosalyn McKeown directs the Centre for Geography and Environmental Education at the University of Tennessee, Knoxville (UTK). She has taught in teacher education programmes at UTK and the State University of New York at Stony Brook for six years. She co-directs the River-to-River Project (a Russian-American teacher exchange programme) and the Tennessee Solid Waste Education Programme for K-12 teachers and students. Her research interests include assessing environmental literacy. She is the president of the Tennessee Environmental Education Association and sits on the board of the North American Association for Environmental Education.

Lalit Pande is the Director of the Uttarakhand Environment Education Centre, a voluntary organization based in Almora, India. He holds masters and doctoral degrees in environmental acoustics and mechanical engineering, but abandoned this career to work for social and ecological sustainability in his own community in the lower Himalayas.

Steve Passingham worked as an Education Advisor in the Ministry of Education in Vanuatu from 1989 to 1993 and then as the United Kingdom's Department for International Development (DFID) Regional Education Advisor in the Pacific between 1995 and 1998. He presently holds the similar position for South-East Asia. He has been actively involved in the work of Wan Smolbag Theatre for several years, most particularly during the preparation and implementation of the third phase of DFID support.

Chris Reddy is a lecturer at the Faculty of Education, the University of Stellenbosch where he teaches in environmental and science education to undergraduate and post-graduate students. His research interests include investigating the links between teacher professional development and curriculum/materials development, school-based curriculum development, and reflective teaching practice for pre-service courses.

Danie Schreuder is head of the Environmental Education Programme in the Faculty of Education at the University of Stellenbosch. He has extensive experience in the development of school-community links, and has initiated a number of resource development projects including *We Care*, the *Schools Water Programme* and the South African development of the *Windows on the Wild* project. He was a founder member of the Environmental Education Policy Initiative which has been instrumental in the development of recent new education policy in South Africa.

Walter Simpson is Energy Officer at the University at Buffalo, State University of New York, where he coordinates the University's nationally recognized energy conservation programme. He promotes campus environmental stewardship through the University Green office and teaches in the University's environmental studies programme.

Bob Stevenson is an Associate Professor in (and former chair of) the Department of Educational Leadership and Policy at the University at Buffalo, State University of New York, where he also co-directs the Graduate School of Education's Collaborative Research Network. His research interests focus on environmental education, teacher professional development, participatory and action research, and school reform and change. Bob's work has been published in four co-edited books and a variety of international journals. He has served on the editorial boards of the *Australian Journal of Environmental Education*, the *Canadian Journal of Environmental Education*, and the *Southern Africa Journal of Environmental Education*.

Kathy Stiles is an education and training consultant who has lived in Zimbabwe since 1987. She is a volunteer resource person and coordinator of education at Rifa Camp and has been involved in working with environmental NGOs for a number of years. She has helped set up the network of environmental education in Zimbabwe and its connection to the network of environmental education in South Africa. Her current research focuses on policy and strategy for environmental and development education in Zimbabwe and southern Africa.

Jim Taylor is the Director of environmental education for the Wildlife and Environment Society of South Africa (WESSA). Founded in 1926, WESSA is the oldest and largest non-governmental, membership-based, environmental organization in South Africa with a major commitment to environmental education. He is also responsible for coordinating the Southern African Development Community's (SADC) Regional Environmental Education Programme. This programme includes all fourteen Southern African member countries and aims to promote wider networking, training and resource material development. In 1997 he was given a human rights award for contributions to environmental education.

Peter Templeton is a Programme Officer with the Academy for Educational Development, working with the Latin American projects of GreenCOM, the USAID Project on Environmental Education and Communication. Peter provided headquarters' support for the El Salvador Project, and translated this chapter from Spanish.

Daniella Tilbury is a Senior Lecturer in environmental education and sustainable development at the Graduate School of the Environment, Macquarie University, Sydney. She is currently the Chair of the "Education for Sustainable Development Product Group" of the IUCN Commission in Education and Communication (CEC). Over the years, Daniella has acted as an environmental education consultant to a number of government and non-governmental organizations. Recently, she worked with John Fien and Bill Scott assessing the strategic role of education within conservation policy and programmes of the World Wide Fund for Nature (WWF) International at the global level. As part of this evaluation, she visited projects in Colombia, Venezuela, Brazil, Spain as well as Italy, Madagascar, South Africa, Tanzania, Malaysia, Hong Kong and China.

Jane Wright has a background in environmental sciences and is a chartered town planner. She has ten years experience of working with community groups in urban and rural areas and has helped to develop a number of environmental education projects for schools. She has worked in two national parks, and as Local Plans Officer for Brecon Beacons National Park.